CONTROVERSIES IN PHILOSOPHY

General Editor: A. G. N. Flew

Each volume in this series deals with a topic that has been, and still is, the subject of lively debate among philosophers. The sort of issues that they embrace are only partially covered, if covered at all, by the usual collections of reprinted work.

The series consists largely but not entirely of material already published elsewhere in scattered sources. It is a series distinguished by two guiding ideas. First, the individual editors of the various constituent volumes select and collect contributions to some important controversy which in recent years has been, and which still remains, alive. The emphasis is thus upon controversy, and upon the presentation of philosophers in controversial action. Second, the individual editors are encouraged to edit extensively and strongly. The idea is that they should act as firm, fair and constructive chairmen. Such a chairman gives shape to a discussion and ensures that the several contributors are not merely heard, but heard at the moment when their contributions can be most relevant and most effective. With this in mind the contributions as they appear in these volumes are arranged neither in the chronological order of their first publication nor in any other possibly arbitrary sequence, but in such a way as to provide and to reveal some structure and development in the whole argument. Again, and for similar reasons, the editorial introductions are both substantial and forthcoming.

Although most of the contributions in each volume have been published before as articles in journals, the editors are asked not to confine themselves to this source. There will be a fair element of previously unpublished material and, even more frequently, extracts will be taken from books.

Weakness of Will

EDITED BY

Geoffrey Mortimore

CONTRIBUTORS
Aristotle, John Benson, Neil Cooper, P. L. Gardiner,
W. F. R. Hardie, R. M. Hare, H. J. N. Horsburgh,
Steven Lukes, Gwynneth Matthews, A. Phillips Griffiths,
Plato, Gerasimos Santas, Irving Thalberg

MACMILLAN
ST MARTIN'S PRESS

First published *1971* by
MACMILLAN AND CO LTD
London and Basingstoke
Associated companies in New York Toronto
Dublin Melbourne Johannesburg and Madras

Library of Congress catalog card no. 70–124950

SBN 333 10512 5 (hard cover)
333 10528 1 (paper cover)

Printed in Great Britain by
WESTERN PRINTING SERVICES LTD
Bristol

Foreword by the General Editor

The classical philosophical problem of the possibility and the nature of weakness of will arose from considering a contention which seems to have been characteristic of the historical Socrates. This contention is the paradox, represented with especial force in Plato's *Protagoras*, that 'No one willingly does wrong'. (Since the Greek word thus and usually translated by 'does wrong' is also at least equally commonly employed in non-moral contexts, the Socratic thesis might perhaps be alternatively and more persuasively rendered as 'No one is willingly mistaken'.) What makes this thesis at least plausible even in a moral context is – to put the supporting argument in an inevitably inaccurate nutshell – the idea that what ought to be done is to pursue what is good, and hence that to do what one ought to do must be to achieve what is good (for you). The notion of weakness of will was introduced into the discussion by Aristotle as a means of bridging at least part of the gap between the paradox and the familiar facts that we are often, very understandably, reluctant to do what we ourselves recognise that we ought to do.

In recent years a very similar problem has been raised in a fresh context by the exploration of the idea that to make a primary moral judgement necessarily involves a personal commitment. In so far as this is correct it would seem that to act in accordance with this commitment must be a criterion of the sincerity and authenticity of the commitment itself. This is a thesis which in this particular context Professor R. M. Hare has made very much his own. But more generally applied it may seem a matter only of shrewd common sense. For who would not agree with Descartes's observation in Part III of his *Discourse on the Method* that 'in order to know what their opinions really were I should attend rather to what they did than to what they said'?

Mr Mortimore entitles this collection *Weakness of Will* rather than *Moral Weakness* or *Can a Man Willingly do Wrong?* because he wants, and properly, to present both the classical and the modern discussions as concerned with special cases within a wider, and not specifically moral, investigation of the connections between sincerely believing that there are reasons for acting in some way and actually so acting.

ANTONY FLEW

University of Keele,
Staffordshire,
England

Contents

Acknowledgements

The following have been reprinted with permission of the authors (or translators), the editors of the journals concerned and the publishers:

Chapter I Plato, *Protagoras*, 351b–358d, translated by W. K. C. Guthrie in Plato, *Protagoras and Meno* (Penguin Books: Harmondsworth, 1956).

Chapter II Gerasimos Santas, 'Plato's *Protagoras* and Explanations of Weakness', *Philosophical Review*, LXXV (1966) pp. 3–33.

Chapter III Aristotle, *The Nicomachean Ethics*, book vii, chapters 1–3, translated by W. D. Ross in *The Oxford Translation of Aristotle*, ed. W. D. Ross (1925) vol. IX.

Chapter IV W. F. R. Hardie, *Aristotle's Ethical Theory* (The Clarendon Press, Oxford, 1968) chapter xiii, pp. 258–92.

Chapter V R. M. Hare, *The Language of Morals* (Oxford University Press, 1961 imp.) pp. 19–20, 168–70.

Chapter VI P. L. Gardiner, 'On Assenting to a Moral Principle', *Proceedings of the Aristotelian Society*, LV (1954–5) pp. 23–44. Copyright © 1955 The Aristotelian Society.

Chapter VII H. J. N. Horsburgh, 'The Criteria of Assent to a Moral Rule', *Mind*, LXIII (1954) pp. 345–58.

Chapter VIII R. M. Hare, *Freedom and Reason* (The Clarendon Press, Oxford, 1963) ch. 5, pp. 67–85.

Chapter IX Steven Lukes, 'Moral Weakness', *Philosophical Quarterly*, XV (1965) pp. 104–14.

Chapter X Gwynneth Matthews, 'Weakness of Will', *Mind*, LXXV (1966) pp. 405–19.

Chapter XI A. Phillips Griffiths, 'Acting with Reason', *Philosophical Quarterly*, VIII (1958) pp. 289–99. The author has added a supplementary note to the original article, and this appears at the end of Chapter XI as note 4.

Chapter XII Neil Cooper, 'Oughts and Wants', *Aristotelian Society*, supp. vol. XLII (1968) pp. 143–54. Copyright © 1968 The Aristotelian Society.

Chapter XIII   John Benson, 'Oughts and Wants', *Aristotelian
    Society*, supp. vol. XLII (1968) pp. 155–72. Copyright © 1968
    The Aristotelian Society. Reprinted in this collection under the
    title 'Wants, Desires and Deliberation'.
Chapter XIV   Neil Cooper, 'Second Thoughts on Oughts and
    Wants': written for this collection.
Chapter XV   John Benson, 'Further Thoughts on Oughts and
    Wants': written for this collection.
Chapter XVI   Irving Thalberg, 'The Socratic Paradox and Rea-
    sons for Action', *Theoria*, XXI (1965) pp. 242–54. This has been
    revised by the author and is reprinted here under the title
    'Acting Against One's Better Judgement'.

Editor's Introduction
Geoffrey Mortimore

I

The controversy in this volume arises from a philosophical doctrine which has been widely regarded as running directly counter to common sense, and which has therefore been called paradoxical. In one of its various formulations, the doctrine holds that no one omits to do an action when he thinks he ought to do that action rather than the other alternatives open to him, and when it is physically and psychologically possible for him to do it. A failure to act in such circumstances is commonly taken to be a typical case of weakness of will, and those who have advanced the paradox have either wanted to deny that there is such a thing as weakness of will, or – more frequently – to insist that cases of weakness of will are not correctly or completely characterised in this way as failures to act on one's convictions about what one ought to do, when it is possible to act on them.

What kind of doctrine is it? There are grounds for thinking that Socrates' paradox (Chapter I) is an *empirical* doctrine, about what it is in human nature to do. R. M. Hare's thesis (Chapters V and VIII), on the other hand, is that it is *logically impossible* for a man to fail to do what he believes he ought to do, under these conditions. There are obvious problems with both sorts of paradox. Of the first, we might ask how philosophical argument could possibly be relevant to a contention about human nature. To the second, we might reply that if the doctrine were true it would be very puzzling that we have gone on so long finding ordinary cases of weakness of will describable and unproblematic. Are there not, we might ask, only two ways of interpreting the second kind of paradox, on both of which it turns out to be, in different ways, defective? *Either* the key term, 'believes he ought', is used in its ordinary sense, in which case the describability of ordinary cases of weakness of will makes the doctrine plainly false; *or* the term is being redefined, in which case the paradox will indeed be true by definition, but can hardly be regarded any more as paradoxical.

Before considering whether these questions can be answered, something further needs to be said about the general character of the case which is represented as in some way impossible. The paradox does not specifically concern *moral* beliefs, though these have frequently been the centre of attention in discussions of it. The central question can be formulated in another way to indicate its general scope: Can a man wittingly and under no compulsion omit to do an action, A, when he believes there are better reasons for doing that action than for doing any of the other actions open to him? For the sake of brevity I will henceforth use 'believes that he ought to do A' as an elliptical way of talking about such a belief. Clearly, if a man thinks that moral reasons are overriding, then the paradox holds that his moral beliefs will always issue in action when action is possible. But it concerns no less the possibility of a man failing to act for the best, when the reasons in question are purely prudential ones.

II

In Plato and Aristotle (Chapters I and III) the question always concerns the possibility of a discrepancy between action, and the agent's belief about the consequences of the action for *himself*, for it is an unquestioned assumption that this is *the* basic kind of assessment appropriate to actions and human qualities. Thus, in Socrates' discussion of the nature and unity of what he regards as the most important human excellences or virtues (e.g. courage, justice, etc.), it is assumed that if these qualities are valuable it is because of their consequences for the man who possesses them. Socrates' version of the paradox is that no man knowingly and non-compulsively does an action when the resultant evils for him outweigh the resultant good. His conclusion, that 'to make for what one believes to be evil . . . is not, it seems, in human nature . . .', gives some reason to believe that the paradox is advanced as an empirical truth.

What Gerasimos Santas brings out very clearly (Chapter II) is that instead of arguing directly for a contention about human nature, Socrates embarks on a programme of showing that what are commonly advanced as explanations are 'absurd'. Socrates' strategy, as it is brought to bear on the one explanation he considers ('overcome by pleasure'), is to argue that the explanation turns out to be logically inconsistent with the very feature of the situation which generated the demand for an explanation, viz. that the man believes that the evil which will result from his action outweighs the good.

The argument is not a seductive one. It appears to demand the assumption which Socrates introduces (but may not accept) that 'good' and 'pleasant' are interchangeable; and it depends on a serious equivocation. The central contention that the good/pleasure could only overcome the evil/pain if it were a match for it looks like a truism if it is taken as a statement about the relative influential power of the good or evil, or – strictly speaking – of the agent's beliefs about them. But to arrive at the conclusion that the explanation is absurd, Socrates needs to slide from this interpretation of 'is a match for' to another, so that 'pleasure is a match for the pain' can be taken as a statement about what the agent believes to be *the comparative amounts* of pleasure and pain resulting from his action.

Despite the poverty of the argument, Socrates' case for the paradox raises questions of considerable importance. The first, of course, concerns the types of explanation that can be offered for a man's pursuing evil, and Santas explores one which Socrates neglects – in terms of the intensity of the agent's desire for the immediate pleasure. Secondly, we might ask what Socrates would have shown if he had produced an exhaustive list of the kinds of explanation which might be offered, and *if* he had 'dissolved' them all. To argue from this to the conclusion that it is not in human nature to pursue evil requires, it seems, the assumption that in the absence of countervailing influences, beliefs about the comparative extent of resultant goods and evils always issue in evil-minimising actions. Is this really an assumption about human nature, or could it be regarded as a logical truth? We shall see that even some opponents of the paradox (in either its empirical or logical form) are disposed to allow the logical necessity of a man's doing what he believes he ought to, if there are no countervailing influences whatsoever.

Aristotle's reply to Socrates (Chapter III) is very fully treated by W. F. R. Hardie in Chapter IV, and I will say comparatively little about it here. Aristotle is in sympathy with Socrates' doctrine. But his view appears to be that it is a *logically* absurd supposition that we could act against our better judgement. What we have in Chapter III are not arguments for this position, but an account of how ostensible counter-examples can be reconciled with it. This involves Aristotle in an enterprise very like that of R. M. Hare in Chapter VIII: the attempt to distinguish various states of mind, and – correspondng to them – senses of 'knowledge'. Aristotle considers the agent's state of consciousness at the time of deliberation, distinguishing various defective forms of awareness or attention in order (1) to give an account of what people could mean when they say that a man knows that what he is doing is not for the best, and (2) to show that in saying this they are not talking about a central case of full knowledge.

III

In Hare's revival of the paradox in recent years the dominant idea is that it is possible to mark out a central sense of 'believe that one ought', and a corresponding state of mind, such that the paradox is a logically necessary truth. But the motivation and assumptions behind Hare's paradox are strikingly different. The paradox now no longer arises from the idea that there is something empirically impossible or logically inconceivable in the idea of a man wittingly pursuing pain or evil for himself. Hare's preoccupation is with *value-judgements* (one species of which are evaluations of an action in terms of its effects on the agent) and with what he regards as a mistaken view of value judgements – descriptivism. The corrective to any attempt to treat value-judgements as descriptive of matters of fact is to see that their central function is to guide choice and action. It is from this latter contention that his paradox flows.

Hare's brief discussion of the paradox in *The Language of Morals* (Chapter V) is a sequel to an earlier statement that if there are judgements which have a distinctive action-guiding function, then there must be a logical connection between accepting them ('assenting to them', in Hare's terminology), and action. What Hare does is (1) to define 'value-judgement' so that a person does not count as accepting one unless he acts on it, given opportunity and possibility; and (2) to assert that there are judgements which satisfy the definition. Here, then, is a technical definition, designed to mark out an important class of judgements with a distinctive function. What are we to take it to imply for the logical possibility of a person failing to do what he believes he ought to do, when 'believes he ought' is used in its ordinary and non-technical sense?

Replies to Hare have frequently taken him to task for the discrepancy between his account of what is involved in accepting a value-judgement and the way we actually use the expression 'believes that he ought' in ordinary discourse. Thus, Gardiner (Chapter IV) – concentrating on *moral* judgements and principles – argues that the criteria for ascribing the acceptance of a principle are not 'precise and simple' and are certainly not confined to what a man does.

The term 'criteria' appears a good deal in the controversy, and never with any explanation of its sense. This is not because there is an agreed clear definition of this technical term. On the contrary the notion is itself the subject of considerable controversy among philosophers. So there is no non-problematic way of giving an account of what criteria are. The briefest sort of account would be that criteria or criterial conditions are those conditions whose satisfaction provides grounds for an assertion which are logical, rather than scientific or inductive. So that if a set of criteria, x, y, z, are sufficient for the truth of the statement that Jones believes he ought to do A, then the conjunction of the assertion that x, y and z hold, with the denial that Jones believes he ought to do A, will involve some kind of logical blunder: self-contradiction, logical oddness (supposedly something short of self-contradiction but closely related to it), a misuse of language, or ... The characterisation of the blunder is itself controversial.

So Gardiner's view is that even if a person fails to act when he avows 'I ought to do A', we may still have logically adequate grounds for saying that he believed he ought, such as, for example, his later reactions of guilt or remorse. But this reply fails to meet Hare head-on. Towards the end of Chapter V Hare admits that the criteria for the ordinary use of 'thinks that he ought' include what a man feels after he acts. So these points about ordinary usage evidently do not disturb Hare; indeed, there is an approving comment on Gardiner's reply in Hare's later discussion in Chapter VIII.

But how are these points about ordinary language to be dealt with? Hare's closing remarks about the elasticity of the criteria for 'thinks he ought' suggest that he thinks that a central sense or use of 'thinks he ought' can be distinguished, which does have a strict logical connection with action. In Chapter VII, H. J. N. Horsburgh attempts to develop just such a position: that 'accept' and 'assent' can be used in an 'attenuated sense', but that when not so used there is a strict logical connection between 'assenting to a moral principle prescribing A' and 'doing A'. Further, taking up one of Hare's closing remarks in Chapter V, he argues that there are degrees of assent, and that corresponding to the non-attenuated sense of 'assent' there is the locution 'fully assent', which is such that it is again logically necessary that a man who fully accepts a moral principle acts on it.

In arguing for his view he does not follow Hare in emphasising the distinctive action-guiding function of moral judgements. In part his position is supported by statements about what we ordinarily mean by certain key expressions: 'it seems to be generally admitted that A cannot be said to accept a moral rule unreservedly if he sometimes transgresses it'. Yet this is something a great many people *would* strenuously deny. How can Horsburgh defend himself against the charge that instead of separating out the central case of full acceptance, from which the 'weaker criteria (guilt, remorse, and so on) are derived . . . by a process of stretching or dilution of meaning', he is setting up his own definition of 'fully accept' which is a radical tightening-up of ordinary criteria?

But Horsburgh has a second and more interesting kind of argument: that in order to give an adequate account of the logic of terms like 'accept', we have to recognise that the central case of acceptance is that from which it follows logically that a man will act. The kernel of the argument is that our recognition of the various degrees of assent is necessary to avoid drawing the unacceptable conclusion that the predicate 'believes he ought to do A' is 'radically ambiguous'. We would otherwise be tempted to draw this conclusion, thinks Horsburgh, because of the multiplicity of kinds of criteria for statements about a man's 'ought'-beliefs, and because, while a man's actions can be sufficient to ascribe acceptance of a principle, so could his reactions if he failed to act.

But while the strategy is interesting, some serious difficulties should be briefly mentioned. Firstly, is it obvious that one kind of criterial condition could provide logically adequate grounds for the statement that a man believes he ought to do A? Could continued feelings of discomfort after failing to do A be adequate grounds if a man did not offer advice and recommendation to others to do A, react in certain ways to others' failure to do A, and so on? Could we even identify a man's reaction as remorse without being satisfied that he makes genuine efforts to make amends and mend his ways? But secondly, even if a man's reactions could provide logically adequate grounds, would it follow that the expression 'believes he ought' was radically ambiguous? We would need to be a good deal clearer about the notions of criteria and of ambiguity in order to draw this conclusion, or to be worried by it if we drew it. And finally, does Horsburgh succeed in extricating himself from the difficulty, if there is one? For even on his account we have one use of 'assent' for which guilt and other reactions provide logically adequate grounds, and another use for which consistent action is both a necessary and sufficient condition. So that if we were tempted at the beginning to draw conclusions about radical ambiguity, we should still in the end be tempted to say there are two distinct senses of 'assent'.

IV

What we still need, then, is some case for discriminating different senses of 'believes he ought', and for asserting that one of them is central. This Hare undertakes to provide in Chapter VIII (taken from his later work, *Freedom and Reason* (1963)). Hare begins with the contention that the action-guiding function of moral terms is central enough 'for us to call it part of the meaning of those terms'. Therefore the central case of believing that I ought to do A must be a case of accepting the judgement, 'I ought to do A', as a guide to conduct. But even if we accept this argument, why should we think it logically impossible for someone to accept a judgement as a guide to conduct and then not act on it?

The question Hare is particularly concerned with (and this becomes clear in section 5 of Chapter VIII) is whether a man can think, at a particular time, that he ought to be doing a particular action, and then not do it. He wants to consider the possible states of mind of someone who consciously avows, 'I ought to be doing A'. The key to the interpretation of his argument lies in his remark that 'the inquiry . . . will be, as are most philosophical inquiries, at one and the same time about language and about what happens; for to ask about different senses of "ought" and "think that one ought", in the way that the philosopher asks this, is at the same time to ask about different possible states of mind; the two inquiries are inseparable'. What Hare wants to do, then, is give an account of a state of mind, and of the sense of 'thinks he ought' corresponding to it, such that: (1) it follows from the basic action-guiding function of a word like 'ought' that they are, in a very good sense, central; and (2) it is a logical truth that the man who thinks he ought (in this sense) to do A, does A.

Hare's crucial distinction is between the man who says 'I ought to do A', prescribing to himself, and the man who says it, albeit sincerely, and does not prescribe. For only in the former case can the man really be accepting the judgement as a guide to action. If we say that the second man thinks that he ought to do A, then we must recognise that this is a different and non-central sense of 'thinks he ought'; Hare wishes to say that his judgement and his belief are not fully prescriptive. To this is added the further doctrine that it is logically necessary that if a man really does prescribe to himself, then he will act, if it is physically and psychologically possible.

The question of the status of Hare's account is taken up by

Lukes in Chapter IX. Lukes remarks that 'Hare's doctrine is curiously self-protecting' and that all the counter-examples Lukes puts up 'could be described in Hare's terms'. This would be true if Hare were only prepared to give an independent account of one of the key terms 'prescribe' and 'psychologically impossible', defining the other in terms of it. Thus, one might take him to be using 'psychologically impossible' in the ordinary sense, and to be so defining 'prescribe' that if it is psychologically possible for a man to act, and he does not act, it follows that he is not prescribing to himself. But Hare wants to say something about different states of mind, and the notion of prescribing is meant to have some independent informative value. Prescribing seems, at the very least, to be some kind of activity – making a judgement or addressing an imperative to oneself, with the intention of guiding choice and action. The difficulty is that as soon as such an independent account is given, it begins to look exceedingly dubious that it follows from a man's prescribing, that he acts if it is physically and psychologically possible. Unless, that is, 'psychological impossibility' is not given any independent account, and is defined solely in terms of its being entailed by a man's prescribing to himself and yet failing to act.

In *The Language of Morals*, as we saw, Hare offered a technical definition of 'value-judgement'. At the end of Chapter VIII Hare says that what he has been doing is defining the technical term 'prescriptive' so that prescriptive uses of words can be located (and also, presumably, fully prescriptive beliefs). His substantive thesis is that such uses exist. But what is this latter thesis? If it is simply that we do use sentences like 'I ought to do A' to guide our conduct, then we are still left with the need for an argument showing that since these uses are central (and this contention itself requires close examination), the central, 'full-blooded' use of 'thinks he ought to do A' is one from which it follows logically that he does A. But, as we have seen, what independent account Hare gives of this 'central sense', and of the corresponding state of mind, only casts doubt on the doctrine that there is a tight logical connection with action.

However, his 'substantive thesis' may also be the contention that we do think that some of the judgements made using words like 'ought' are such that their acceptance entails action. Hare's definition of 'value-judgement' in Chapter V is in terms of what a man recognises he must assent to if he assents to a judgement; so that it appears that in order to identify a judgement as a value-judgement we have to find a man who already thinks that certain judgements are such that their acceptance entails action. Hare's last example in Chapter VIII seems designed to make the same point, that if we reflect about it, we will see that we already think of certain judgements in this way. But if this is Hare's position, it is odd that he does not present more evidence from ordinary discourse to support it.

V

Replies to Hare (see Chapters IX and X) have followed Gardiner in emphasising the variety of ways in which we ordinarily allow that there may be some kind of 'breakdown' between a man's acceptance of a principle and his acting on it:

(i) A man may fail to apply the principle to the relevant particular cases. This kind of breakdown is not, of course, immediately relevant to either weakness of will or the paradox as it arises in Plato or Hare.

(ii) Then there are claimed to be various possibilities of breakdown between a man's believing he ought to do a particular act, A, and his deciding not to do A:

(a) Lukes (Chapter IX) emphasises the possibility of a man believing he ought to do A and yet failing seriously and attentively to *think* that he ought to do A at the time of decision. It may just slip his mind, or there may be a failure of attention, as in some of Sartre's cases of *mauvaise foi*. In Lukes's view, such failures do not always force us to revise our opinion that the agent believes he ought to do A.

(b) It is also argued that we ordinarily allow the possibility of a breakdown between thinking that one ought to do A and deciding to do it. This may take the form, at one end of a continuum of cases, of failing to take any decision at all, or – at the other end – of calmly deciding not to do A.

(iii) Finally, there is the possibility of deciding to do A, and failing to do it.

How does the concept of weakness of will relate to these categories? Gwynneth Matthews (Chapter X) and Irving Thalberg (Chapter XVI) tend to associate the concept with the breakdown between decision and action. But the fact is, surely, that cases in both categories (ii) and (iii) can equally well be called cases of weakness of will. The range of application of the concept is a topic that deserves further attention; thus far, only Matthews has attempted any sort of account. However, it is a question which does not bear directly on the paradox.

Where, then, do the 'ordinary-language' replies to Hare leave the controversy? What clearly demands further exploration at this stage is the character of the relation between 'believing one ought to do A' and 'doing A'. For critics of the paradox generally allow that statements about what a man believes he ought to do have *some* logical implications for what he will do under certain conditions; but the connection is said to be much looser than the paradox allows. This loose logical connection is supposed by Cooper (Chapter XII) to account for the features of 'ought'-judgements which philosophers like Hare want to emphasise – their 'providing reasons for action, being used to commend, recommend, enjoin and so on' (p. 193 below).

But why allow that there is any connection at all? For cannot the amoral egoist believe that certain sorts of actions are wrong, and not care a jot whether he does them or not? The standard prescriptivist answer to this is that such cases only make sense if we suppose the amoralist to be using terms like 'wrong' purely descriptively, to mean 'condemned by conventional morality', for example. What is not questionable, the reply continues, is that there is a logical connection between statements about what they believe they ought to do in a non-descriptive sense of 'ought' and, at the very least, the statement that they *care* about doing A.

This reply might be reinforced with the contention that when, in the central sense of 'ought', a man believes he ought to do A, he believes there is a reason to do A; and the notion of believing that some consideration is a reason for acting in a certain way *cannot* be logically detached from the notion of caring about acting on that consideration. For surely, the reply runs, a man could not be said to believe that a consideration, R, was a reason for action unless he was disposed to notice whether R is the case, to give consideration to R in answering the practical question, 'What shall I do', and to offer it to others when they are answering this question? And could we make sense of the notion 'giving attentive and serious consideration to R, as a factor supporting A, in deciding what to do' without allowing at least a loose logical connection between this notion and 'doing A'?

But how is this loose logical connection between 'believing one ought to do A' and 'doing A' to be represented? What we are looking for, it seems, is a statement of the form 'If a man thinks that he ought to do A, and if . . ., then he will do A', such that its denial would be self-contradictory or logically odd. One possibility, considered by A. Phillips Griffiths in Chapter XI, is that the statement is logically necessary if the gap is filled by the claim that 'there are no countervailing factors', where a countervailing factor would be any want or inclination which ran counter to the belief. If such a statement *were* logically necessary, it follows that, at least in the limiting case described in Chapter XI, other facts about a man could not be logically adequate grounds for ascribing the belief to him. There is, however, a doubt about whether Phillips Griffiths is prepared to go this far. For in constructing his test case of a man who avows that he ought to do A but never does A, he finds it necessary to stipulate that the man does not feel 'derelictions of remorse'.

In any case, there is usually some inclination conflicting with a man's belief about what he ought to do, and we need to ask whether there is some logically guaranteed 'if . . ., then . . .' statement connecting belief and action in this kind of case. But now we face the contention of several of the writers in this collection that other kinds of criterial conditions can be logically adequate grounds for the ascription of the belief that I ought to do A. If this were so, it might seem that we could only construct a logically necessary 'if . . ., then . . .' statement of the above type by adding the further condition that no logically adequate set of non-action criteria has been or will be satisfied.

What needs closer examination is whether other criterial conditions could be logically sufficient. Could we ascribe the belief that one ought to do actions of a certain type to a man who never acted in this way, even when there was no particularly strong counter-inclination and he was in a normal mental state (not hypnotised, not grief-stricken, and so on)? This is the question which arose in discussing Horsburgh's arguments in Chapter VII. Is it not necessary, in order to identify feelings of discomfort as remorse, that a man do something to make amends, make some effort at reform? Considerations of this kind might lead us to entertain the idea that it is at least logically necessary that if a man thinks he ought to do actions of a certain type he will do actions of that type on at least 'a fair number' of the occasions when he is in no abnormal mental state and when there is no unusually strong counter-inclination; and – as a corollary – that it is logically necessary that if a man thinks he ought to do a *particular* action, A, then under these conditions he will be more likely to do it than not.

But the latter looks more like an expression of the empirical view that <u>men are on the whole rational</u>, than like a logical truth.

The question of the character of the logical connection between 'believing one ought to A' and 'doing A' is one of the main points of difference in the exchange between Neil Cooper and John Benson in Chapters XII–XV. Cooper's thesis that 'believing one ought to A' implies 'wanting to A', rather than 'deciding to A', is meant to drive home the familiar point that the criteria for ascribing moral beliefs embrace more than a man's actions. Benson follows Cooper in using 'want' in a very broad sense to embrace what is involved in believing one ought to do something. But he asserts that if a man decides to do B rather than A, then it follows logically that at the moment of decision he wanted to do B in preference to A.

Benson, it should be noted, concentrates on the logical connection between '*thinking* one ought to A' and '*deciding* to A'. This leaves the further question – which only Gardiner considers in this volume – of the character of the logical connection between 'deciding to A' and 'doing A'. Benson's view is advanced as a view about an (obvious?) logical feature of 'wanting' (in the broad sense in which he uses the term). But it appears that his position also derives from his view of the account it is proper to give of a man's deliberation, of what can enter into it and determine its outcome. This introduces the second closely related range of issues which arise out of the controversy – issues concerning explanation.

VI

As Matthews points out at the end of Chapter X, one of our puzzles about weakness of will concerns explanation. Reference to a man's belief that he ought to do A can explain his doing A, so that at the very least it seems legitimate to demand an explanation of a man's failure to do what he sincerely avowed he ought to do. As we saw, the assumption that an explanation is required, lies at the root of Socrates' argument for the paradox.

It is thus highly relevant to the controversy to ask for an account of the explanatory force of a reference to a man's 'ought'-beliefs, what kind of explanatory requirement there is in cases of a man ostensibly acting against his 'ought'-belief, and what kinds of explanation can satisfy it. Now one of the most popular kinds of explanation of a man's acting against his better judgement is that in terms of the comparative intensity of his desires. Santas cites it as an important type of explanation which Socrates neglects, and Cooper takes up the topic in Chapter XII at the beginning of his exchange with Benson. Cooper considers this kind of explanation because, in his view, the paradox arises from the mistaken assumption that if a man believes he ought to do A in preference to B, then he desires to do A more intensely than he desires to do B. However, there is no indication of this assumption in Hare's account of the paradox, though Santas finds traces of it in Socrates' argument (pp. 59 ff. below).

Cooper's view is that in one central kind of weakness of will a man believes he ought to do A rather than B, but desires to do B more than he desires to do A. Two ranges of issues are prominent in his dispute with Benson. The first concerns the distinction between desires and wants (where 'want' is used in a wide sense to embrace what is involved in thinking one ought to do A, or that there is a better reason for doing A than B). Benson doubts whether – with the exception of a rather narrow class of physical inclinations – the distinction can be made in cases of weakness of will, and whether the comparative intensity of a man's desires is logically independent of the evaluations he is making at the moment. The second range of issues concerns the possibility of explaining decisions and actions by reference to a man's desires. Benson's central doubt about Cooper's position derives from his view of the role desires can play in decision. It appears that, on Benson's view, desires can impede deliberation, or prevent a man acting on his decision; and they can enter deliberation as factors the deliberator takes into account. But he shows some reluctance to allow that desires can conflict with wants as determinants of decision; and he wants to say that if desires do determine a man's decision, then he cannot be acting as the result of deliberation. This view of the logical character of deliberation and decision is clearly very closely linked with Benson's view (mentioned in the last section) that it is logically necessary that if a man wants to do A in preference to B, he does A; but it is not clear whether it is offered as a ground for the latter view, or as a corollary.

The dispute between Cooper and Benson thus raises some important questions about our conceptions of deliberation and of the determinants of its outcome. The answers one gives to them plainly affect the account one gives of the informative and explanatory force of the concept of weakness of will. In Benson's view a central kind of weakness of will is the case of a man who has not formulated his wants (in the broad sense) clearly, and references to his 'weakness' would presumably convey no more than this. Cooper's conception of weakness, on the other hand, is the traditional one of a failure to make an effort and struggle hard enough against one's desires.

Filling out the concept of weakness or strength of will in terms of inner activities or goings-on has proved a persistent temptation for philosophers and psychologists, but it poses obvious problems. What account can be given of the activities? Is struggling just trying to keep one's attention focused on the 'really important' considerations, or addressing exhortations to oneself? Some philosophers have not been satisfied with such an account and have insisted on a special sort of activity – an effort of will – which is said not to be susceptible to further analysis. The examination of these different ways of filling out the explanatory force of a reference to weakness of will is an important philosophical task. One line of attack for those who still hold some form of the paradox might be to attempt to show that the traditional 'fillings' are in various ways defective – incoherent, empty, or based on metaphors and myths – so that radical revision of our conception of cases of weakness of will is required. Such a programme would bear some resemblance to Socrates' programme of 'dissolving' the common explanations of the pursuit of evil.

The attempts to fill out the notion of weakness of will in terms of inner activities are attempts to make the explanation of a man's backsliding complete. One response is to reject the attempt as not appropriate to the kinds of explanations we offer for human behaviour. For our explanations of a man's decisions in terms of his 'ought'-beliefs may be of such a logical type that it always makes sense to allow that everything could have been exactly the same and yet the man have decided differently. (Many, of course, would regard this as the central tenet of the doctrine of the freedom of the will.) Thus in Chapter XVI Irving Thalberg builds up a case in which one after another of the candidate explanations of a decision against one's better judgement are ruled out, so that the decision can only be explained in a very partial way indeed. But the question is whether the possibility of such a case is merely the result of our inadequate psychological understanding, or a consequence of the logical type of explanation which we have to employ in accounting for human behaviour.

VII

What emerge from the controversy are a number of alternative ways of characterising cases that we would ordinarily call cases of weakness of will. If we leave to one side the contention that they are cases where a man believes he ought to act but it is psychologically impossible for him to do so, we have two main alternatives. The first is to admit that the man really thought that he ought to do A, and that he could have done it. The second is to insist that what he believes was not a full-blooded 'ought'-judgement (Hare), or that he did not fully accept 'I ought to do A' (Horsburgh), or that, at the moment of decision, he did not believe that he ought to do A in preference to the alternatives (Benson).

There are two questions about these alternatives which need to be considered. Firstly, how are they to be assessed? We can complain that the key terms just are not used like this in ordinary discourse. But if we take the view that the terms are being used in special senses, can we also claim (as Lukes does in Chapter IX) that these contentions are 'manifestly at variance with the facts'? For on that view we seem to be faced with an alternative conceptual scheme for describing human agents, and are there now any neutral facts with which these contentions are manifestly at variance? Could we, for example, criticise the second alternative on the grounds that it makes no room for the indisputable phenomenon of the inner struggle, or is this phenomenon itself a reflection of the conceptual scheme with which we operate?

Secondly, what changes in our view of ourselves and others would be involved if we started to operate with the second alternative? What conception could we have of decision-taking if we took Benson's view that if I eventually decide to do A, this entails that I thought there was a better reason for doing A than the alternatives? Could a man weigh considerations as reasons in his deliberation with the reservation that only his decision will tell him whether he really thought they were reasons at all? Does the conceptual scheme imply a more passive view of ourselves: not setting out to decide on the basis of considerations we are antecedently convinced are reasons, but reflecting on various considerations and waiting to see whether one really thought they were reasons or not?

Further, how would our critical reactions to others be affected? On Horsburgh's view any critical reaction will have as its object a failure fully to accept a principle. This looks markedly different from the traditional view of the backslider as the man who fails to struggle hard enough. Finally, how would such ways of conceiving of cases of weakness of will affect our ways of teaching morality? Are our current ways of teaching strength of will misguided, or do they just need to be redescribed?

The striking feature of the controversy over the various versions of the paradox is that there is no really seductive argument for any of them. But it would be wrong to dismiss the controversy as the fruitless process of one philosopher setting up an oversimplified view of the relation between belief and action, and others reminding him of commonsense facts and ways of talking about possible discrepancies between belief and action. The paradox raises, in a provocative way, a whole range of important issues concerning the concepts we use to describe and explain human beings as deliberators, choosers, and agents.

The reply might be that, once raised, these issues are best approached without paying particular attention to the paradox. But they certainly cannot be approached without paying particular attention to the cases that proponents of the paradox find problematic. For the cases of ostensible breakdown between belief and decision, or decision and action, are precisely those which sharpen our understanding of the logical relations between concepts, of the different kinds of explanatory force, and so on.

Obviously, if the controversy is to go on, some philosophers must be ready to stand up and defend the paradox. From those who do, we can demand greater clarity about the status of the doctrine being defended, and about the kinds of arguments they think would settle the issue one way or another. We can also expect some account of how the standard 'ordinary-language' reply to the paradox is to be met. And the scope of the controversy will be appreciably widened if more attention is paid to the relations between conceptual theses and alternative ways of looking at the human agent – the different ways in which we might conceive of deliberation and decision, and the different kinds of attitude we might have to ourselves and others as successful or unsuccessful agents.

PART ONE

The Socratic Paradox

I Can a man knowingly pursue evil?

Plato

EDITOR'S NOTE

In Plato's dialogue, the Protagoras *(from which the following extract is taken), Socrates relates a discussion he has recently had with Protagoras, a wealthy and successful Sophist who is visiting Athens. The discussion is conducted in the presence of two other Sophists, Hippias and Prodicus. As a Sophist, Protagoras offers instruction to young men (usually for a fee) in the conduct of their private and public affairs. The discussion begins with Protagoras explaining his calling and claiming to be able to make his pupils good citizens. Socrates says that he doubts whether good citizenship and virtue can be taught, to which Protagoras replies that virtue can be taught by all to all, though some men are better at teaching it than others.*

Socrates then raises the question of how the various virtues (courage, justice, temperance, etc.) are related: whether they are parts of a single whole, virtue; or whether they are all really one and the same thing. The discussion eventually turns to the relation of courage to 'the other parts of virtue', and at the beginning of the following extract, Socrates broaches two new topics which he claims will help them with their inquiry into the nature of courage.

The first is Socrates' suggestion that the terms 'good' and 'evil' (as used of the consequences for a man of his own actions) are interchangeable with 'pleasant' and 'painful', respectively. The second is the question of whether a man's knowledge of goods and evils (identified in the discussion with pleasures and pains) necessarily governs his actions. The conclusion that the pursuit of evil is always the result of ignorance is seen to establish the central importance in a man's practical life of his capacity to assess accurately the goods and evils resulting from the various courses of action open to him. The way is thus open for Socrates, later in the dialogue, to argue that courage consists in knowledge, knowledge of what is and is not to be feared, and to suggest that the other virtues as well are to be assimilated to knowledge. As Socrates

*himself points out, he seems by this stage to have got himself into
the position of arguing that virtue is teachable after all.*

Well, said I, you speak of some men living well, and others badly?

He agreed.

Do you think then that a man would be living well who passed
his life in pain and vexation?

No.

But if he lived it out to the end with enjoyment, you would count
him as having lived well?

Yes.

Then to live pleasurably is good, to live painfully bad?

Yes, if one's pleasure is in what is honourable.

What's this, Protagoras? Surely you don't follow the common
opinion that some pleasures are bad and some pains good? I mean
to say, in so far as they are pleasant, are they not also good, leaving
aside any consequence that they may entail? And in the same way
pains, in so far as they are painful, are bad?

I'm not sure, Socrates, he said, whether I ought to give an
answer as unqualified as your question suggests, and say that
everything pleasant is good, and everything painful evil. But with
a view not only to my present answer but to the whole of the rest
of my life, I believe it is safest to reply that there are some pleasures
which are not good, and some pains which are not evil, others on
the other hand which are, and a third class which are neither evil
nor good.

Meaning by pleasures, said I, what partakes of pleasure or gives
it?

Certainly.

My question then is, whether they are not, *qua* pleasant, good.
I am asking in fact whether pleasure itself is not a good thing.

Let us, he replied, as you are so fond of saying yourself, investigate the question; then if the proposition we are examining seems
reasonable, and pleasant and good appear identical, we shall agree
on it. If not, that will be the time to differ.

Good, said I. Will you lead the inquiry or should I?

It is for you to take the lead, since you introduced the subject.

I wonder then, said I, if we can make it clear to ourselves like
this. If a man were trying to judge, by external appearance, of
another's health or some particular physical function, he might

look at his face and hands and then say, 'Let me see your chest and back too, so that I may make a more satisfactory examination.' Something like this is what I want for our present inquiry. Observing that your attitude to the good and the pleasant is what you say, I want to go on something like this. Now uncover another part of your mind, Protagoras. What is your attitude to knowledge? Do you share the common view about that also? Most people think, in general terms, that it is nothing strong, no leading or ruling element. They don't see it like that. They hold that it is not the knowledge that a man possesses which governs him, but something else – now passion, now pleasure, now pain, sometimes love, and frequently fear. They just think of knowledge as a slave, pushed around by all the other affections. Is this your view too, or would you rather say that knowledge is a fine thing quite capable of ruling a man, and that if he can distinguish good from evil, nothing will force him to act otherwise than as knowledge dictates, since wisdom is all the reinforcement he needs?

Not only is this my view, replied Protagoras, but I above all men should think it shame to speak of wisdom and knowledge as anything but the most powerful elements in human life.

Well and truly answered, said I. But I expect you know that most men don't believe us. They maintain that there are many who recognise the best but are unwilling to act on it. It may be open to them, but they do otherwise. Whenever I ask what can be the reason for this, they answer that those who act in this way are overcome by pleasure or pain or some other of the things I mentioned just now.

Well, Socrates, it's by no means uncommon for people to say what is not correct.

Then come with me and try to convince them, and show what really happens when they speak of being overcome by pleasure and therefore, though recognising what is best, failing to do it. If we simply declare, 'You are wrong, and what you say is false', they will ask us, 'If it is not being overcome by pleasure, what can it be? What do you two say it is? Tell us.'

But why must we look into the opinions of the common man, who says whatever comes into his head?

I believe, I replied, that it will help us to find out how courage is related to the other parts of virtue. So if you are content to keep our decision, that I should lead the way in whatever direction I think we shall best see the light, then follow me. Otherwise, if you wish, I shall give it up.

No, you are right, he said. Carry on as you have begun.

To return then. If they should ask us, 'What is your name for what we called being worsted by pleasure?' I should reply, 'Listen. Protagoras and I will try to explain it to you. We take it that you say this happens to you when, for example, you are overcome by the desire of food or drink or sex – which are pleasant things – and though you recognise them as evil, nevertheless indulge in them.' They would agree. Then we should ask them, 'In what respect do you call them evil? Is it because for the moment each of them provides its pleasure and is pleasant, or because they lay up for the future disease or poverty or suchlike? If they led to none of these things, but produced pure enjoyment, would they nevertheless be evils – no matter why or how they give enjoyment?' Can we expect any other answer than this, that they are not evil on account of the actual momentary pleasure which they produce, but on account of their consequences, disease and the rest?

I believe that would be their answer, said Protagoras.

'Well, to cause disease and poverty is to cause pain.' They would agree, I think?

He nodded.

'So the only reason why these pleasures seem to you to be evil is, we suggest, that they result in pains and deprive us of future pleasures.' Would they agree?

We both thought they would.

Now suppose we ask them the converse question. 'You say also that pains may be good. You mean, I take it, such things as physical training, military campaigns, doctors' treatment involving cautery or the knife or drugs or starvation diet? These, you say, are good but painful?' Would they agree?

They would.

'Do you then call them good in virtue of the fact that at the time they cause extreme pain and agony, or because in the future there result from them health, bodily well-being, the safety of one's country, dominion over others, wealth?' The latter, I think they would agree.

Protagoras thought so too.

'And are they good for any other reason than that their outcome is pleasure and the cessation or prevention of pain? Can you say that you have any other end in mind, when you call them good, than pleasures or pain?' I think they would say no.

I too, said he.

'So you pursue pleasure as being good, and shun pain as evil?'

He agreed.

'Then your idea of evil is pain, and of good is pleasure. Even enjoying yourself you call evil whenever it leads to the loss of a pleasure greater than its own, or lays up pains that outweigh its pleasures. If it is in any other sense, or without anything else in mind, that you call enjoyment evil, no doubt you could tell us what it is, but you cannot.'

I agree that they cannot, said Protagoras.

'Isn't it the same when we turn to pain? To suffer pain you call good when it either rids us of greater pains than its own or leads to pleasures that outweigh them. If you have anything else in mind when you call the actual suffering of pain a good thing, you could tell us what it is, but you cannot.'

True, said Protagoras.

'Now, my good people,' I went on, 'if you ask me what is the point of all this rigmarole, I beg your indulgence. It isn't easy to explain the real meaning of what you call being overcome by pleasure, and any explanation is bound up with this point. You may still change your minds, if you can say that the good is any-thing other than pleasure, or evil other than pain. Is it sufficient for you to live life through with pleasure and without pain? If so, and you can mention no good or evil which cannot in the last resort be reduced to these, then listen to my next point.

'This position makes your argument ridiculous. You say that a man often recognises evil actions as evil, yet commits them, under no compulsion, because he is led on and distracted by pleasure, and on the other hand that, recognising the good, he refrains from following it because he is overcome by the pleasures of the moment. The absurdity of this will become evident if we stop using all these names together – pleasant, painful, good, and evil – and since they have turned out to be only two, call them by only two names – first of all good and evil, and only at a different stage pleasure and pain. Having agreed on this, suppose we now say that a man does evil though he recognises it as evil. Why? Because he is overcome. By what? We can no longer say by pleasure, because it has changed its name to good. Overcome, we say. By what, we are asked. By the good, I suppose we shall say. I fear that if our questioner is ill-mannered, he will laugh and retort, What ridiculous nonsense, for a man to do evil, knowing it is evil and that he ought not to do it, because he is overcome by good. Am I to suppose that the good in you is or is not a match for the evil? Clearly we shall reply that the good is not a match; otherwise the man whom we speak of as being overcome by pleasure would not have done wrong. And in what way, he may say, does good fail to be a match for evil, or evil for good? It is not by being greater or smaller, more or less than the other? We shall have to agree. Then by being overcome you must mean taking greater evil in exchange for lesser good.

'Having noted this result, suppose we reinstate the names pleasant and painful for the same phenomena, thus: A man does – *evil* we said before, but now we shall say *painful* actions, knowing them to be painful, because overcome by pleasures – pleasures, obviously, which were not a match for the pains. And what meaning can we attach to the phrase *not a match for*, when used of pleasure in relation to pain, except the excess or deficiency of one as compared with the other? It depends on whether one is greater or smaller, more or less intense than the other. If anyone objects that there is a great difference between present pleasure and pleasure or pain in the future, I shall reply that the difference cannot be one of anything else but pleasure and pain. So like an expert in weighing, put the pleasures and the pains together, set both the near and distant in the balance, and say which is the greater quantity. In weighing pleasures against pleasures, one must always choose the greater and the more; in weighing pains against pains, the smaller and the less; whereas in weighing pleasures against pains, if the pleasures exceed the pains, whether the distant, the near, or vice versa, one must take the course which brings those pleasures; but if the pains outweigh the pleasures, avoid it. Is this not so, good people?' I should say, and I am sure they could not deny it.

Protagoras agreed.

'That being so then, answer me this', I shall go on. 'The same magnitudes seem greater to the eye from near at hand than they do from a distance. This is true of thickness and also of number, and sounds of equal loudness seem greater near at hand than at a distance. If now our happiness consisted in doing, I mean in choosing, greater lengths and avoiding smaller, where would lie salvation? In the art of measurement or in the impression made by appearances? Haven't we seen that the appearance leads us astray and throws us into confusion so that in our actions and our choices between great and small we are constantly accepting and rejecting the same things, whereas the metric art would have cancelled the effect of the impression, and by revealing the true state of affairs would have caused the soul to live in peace and quiet and abide in the truth, thus saving our life?' Faced with these considerations, would people agree that our salvation would lie in the art of measurement?

He agreed that they would.

'Again, what if our welfare lay in the choice of odd and even numbers, in knowing when the greater number must rightly be chosen and when the less, whether each sort in relation to itself or one in relation to the other, and whether they were near or distant? What would assure us a good life then? Surely knowledge, and specifically a science of measurement, since the required skill lies in the estimation of excess and defect – or, to be more precise, arithmetic, since it deals with odd and even numbers.' Would people agree with us?

Protagoras thought they would.

'Well then,' I shall say, 'since our salvation in life has turned out to lie in the correct choice of pleasure and pain – more or less, greater or smaller, nearer or more distant – it is not in the first place a question of measurement, consisting as it does in a consideration of relative excess, defect, or equality?'

It must be.

'And if so, it must be a special skill or branch of knowledge.'

Yes, they will agree.

'What skill, or what branch of knowledge it is, we shall leave till later; the fact itself is enough for the purposes of the explanation which you have asked for from Protagoras and me. To remind you of your question, it arose because we two agreed that there was nothing more powerful than knowledge, but that wherever it is found it always has the mastery over pleasure and everything else. You on the other hand, who maintain that pleasure often masters even the man who knows, asked us to say what this experience really is, if it is not being mastered by pleasure. If we had answered you straight off that it is ignorance, you would have laughed at us, but if you laugh at us now, you will be laughing at yourselves as well, for you have agreed that when people make a wrong choice of pleasures and pains – that is, of good and evil – the cause of their mistake is lack of knowledge. We can go further, and call it, as you have already agreed, a science of measurement, and you know yourselves that a wrong action which is done without knowledge is done in ignorance. So that is what being mastered by pleasure really is – ignorance, and most serious ignorance, the fault which Protagoras, Prodicus, and Hippias profess to cure. You on the other hand, because you believe it to be something else, neither go nor send your children to these Sophists, who are the

experts in such matters. Holding that it is nothing that can be
taught, you are careful with your money and withhold it from
them – a bad policy both for yourselves and for the community.'

That then is the answer we should make to the ordinary run of
people, and I ask you – Hippias and Prodicus as well as Protagoras,
for I want you to share our discussion – whether you think what I
say is true.

They all agreed emphatically that it was true.

You agree then, said I, that the pleasant is good and the painful
bad. I ask exemption from Prodicus' precise verbal distinctions.
Whether you call it pleasant, agreeable, or enjoyable, my dear
Prodicus, or whatever name you like to apply to it, please answer in
the sense of my request.

Prodicus laughed and assented, and so did the others.

Well, here is another point, I continued. All actions aimed at this
end, namely a pleasant and painless life, must be fine actions, that is,
good and beneficial.

They agreed.

Then if the pleasant is the good, no one who either knows or
believes that there is another possible course of action, better than
the one he is following, will ever continue on his present course
when he might choose the better. To 'act beneath yourself' is the
result of pure ignorance; to 'be your own master' is wisdom.

All agreed.

And may we define ignorance as having a false opinion and being
mistaken on matters of great moment?

They approved this too.

Then it must follow that no one willingly goes to meet evil or
what he thinks to be evil. To make for what one believes to be evil,
instead of making for the good, is not, it seems, in human nature,
and when faced with the choice of two evils no one will choose the
greater when he might choose the less.

II Plato's *Protagoras* and explanations of weakness

Gerasimos Santas

Understanding the sorts of explanations that can be offered in cases of weakness (weakness of will, weakness of character, and moral weakness) is an important aspect of the philosophical problem of *akrasia*.[1] In a case of weakness a man does something that he knows or believes he should (ought) not do, or fails to do something that he knows or believes he should do, when the occasion and the opportunity for acting or refraining is present, and when it is in his power, in some significant sense, to act in accordance with his knowledge or belief.

(The first and last of these characteristics are explicitly stated by Plato and Aristotle (Chapter I above; and *Nicomachean Ethics*, 1152a). Occasion and opportunity may be associated with circumstances that give rise to temptation and circumstances that make the object of the temptation available, respectively: one may be tempted by the sight or smell of food but the food may not be available, or it may be available but one has no desire for it. Both must be present to have a case of weakness (or strength), and both conditions are usually implicit in Plato's and Aristotle's discussions.)

Because of the first of these characteristics, which are the *given* characteristics of cases of weakness, it always makes sense to raise the question why the man acted in this way – that is, contrary to his knowledge or belief. But, aside from this, it is necessary to find a correct answer to it if we wish to understand the man's behaviour and to reach a reasonable evaluative attitude towards the man. Finally, if we discover the sorts of explanations that are (and the sorts that are not) available in cases of weakness, we should be in a better position to understand the relation of knowledge of value (or value beliefs) to conduct.

In this paper I want to examine in some detail a long and elaborate argument that Plato offers in the *Protagoras*, 352–356c[2] (pp. 30–4 above), to the effect that certain explanations commonly offered in cases of weakness are untenable or absurd. This passage has been discussed often,[3] but the issues and difficulties that it raises about explanations of weakness have not been sufficiently appreciated; I shall try to show that Plato's argument is at the very least a serious challenge to those who think that the phenomenon of human weakness, though perhaps common enough and familiar enough, can be easily understood. In section I, I set out the context and limitations of Plato's argument, and state the main questions that should be raised about it. In section II, I try to reconstruct the argument as we find it in the text, and in the next section I indicate briefly how the argument may be freed from the severe limitations set to it and thus generalised. Finally, in sections IV and V, I try to unravel the main ambiguities in Plato's argument, assess their consequences to the argument, and follow out their implications concerning different kinds of explanations in cases of weakness. Different sorts of explanations employed recently by philosophers and psychologists are discussed.

I

Towards the end of a lengthy discussion about the unity of the virtues, Socrates raises a (relatively) new issue within which the argument against explanations is set: the role of knowledge in action. At 352b (p. 31 above) he sets out before Protagoras two opposite hypotheses:

> The opinion generally held of knowledge is something of this sort – that it is not a strong or guiding or governing thing; it is not regarded as anything of that kind, but people think that, while a man often has knowledge in him, he is not governed by it, but by something else – now by passion, now by pleasure, now by pain, at times by love, and often by fear.

and

> knowledge is something noble and able to govern man, and that whoever learns what is good and what is bad will never be swayed by anything to act otherwise than as knowledge bids, and ... intelligence is a sufficient succour of mankind.

Protagoras, asked to reveal his own thoughts on the subject, politely agrees with the second hypothesis, which represents Socrates' own view, but Socrates is set on examining the first hypothesis – the hypothesis of the many – and proceeds to restate it with some additions and distinctions:

> Now you know that most people will not listen to you and me, but say that (*a*) many, while knowing what is best, refuse to perform it, though they have the power, and do other things instead. And whenever I have asked them to tell me what can be the reason for this, they say that (*b*) those who act so are acting under the influence of pleasure or pain, or under the control of one of the things I have just mentioned (352d-e).

In this restatement of the hypothesis of the many, Socrates has distinguished two parts: part (*a*) states that a certain phenomenon occurs, and part (*b*) is given as an explanation of the occurrence of that phenomenon. The significant point about this distinction is that Socrates proceeds to give an argument against (*b*), *not* (directly) against (*a*).[4] The conclusion of the argument that ends formally at 355b (p. 33 above) is *not* that no one acts contrary to what he knows to be best, but that (on the premises agreed on) the explanation 'overcome by pleasure' has been reduced to absurdity. Of course, Socrates (and Plato) believe that part (*a*) of the hypothesis is false, and he asserts this at the beginning and the end of the argument (352b, 357d); these assertion indeed provide the wider context within which the argument presented between 352d and 355c is set, but it is not these assertions (the denial of weakness) that the argument attempts to prove, but the absurdity of the explanation of weakness.

Understanding the argument in this way – as an argument against (*b*) – is very different from understanding it as an argument against (*a*). Aside from the fact that this interpretation is faithful to the text, it enables us to avoid a general difficulty, noticed by Professor Vlastos in his excellent introduction to the *Protagoras*, a difficulty that would seem to doom the argument to failure from the outset. Vlastos is commenting on Socrates' statements at 352a–c and 358d – statements which deny part (*a*) and which on the present interpretation form the wider context of the argument, *not* the conclusion of it. At 358d Socrates says that 'to pursue what one believes to be evil rather than what is good *is not in human nature*', and Vlastos writes:

> The words which are italicised show quite well what kind of statement Socrates is making here: the kind which we would

call an empirical one. [The Socratic doctrine that anyone who knows what is the best course of action open to him in any given situation cannot fail to follow it] . . . purports to tell us a fact of human nature – the kind of matter of fact that can only be found out by observation. Where then is the reference to such observation? Nowhere in the whole of this elaborate argument. Socrates . . . is quite content here with a purely *deductive* proof of it. Now anyone who could excogitate by pure deduction a fact of human nature would have to be more than a master of argument – he would have to be a wizard. And as Socrates is only human, we would not be risking much if we were to predict that his attempts will fail.

(Plato, *Protagoras* (New York, 1956) pp. xxxviii–xxxix)

I agree that it is difficult to see how one can show by a 'purely deductive proof' and no reliance on observations or empirical propositions that (*a*) is false. But there is no similar difficulty in showing that, given the description of weakness – as given in part (*a*) – and the hedonistic hypothesis, then the explanation given in (*b*) is absurd or untenable; for there is at least a possibility that the explanation in (*b*) is incompatible with the description of weakness and hedonism, and this of course could be shown by a purely deductive proof or by logical analysis alone. In interpreting the argument in this way I am not denying that Socrates was very much concerned to convince Protagoras and the *hoi polloi* (the vulgar) that (*a*) or some version of it is false; indeed his motive perhaps for attacking common explanations of weakness was to convince us that the weakness does not occur at all. But the falsity of (*a*) does not follow logically from the absurdity of the explanation (*b*); nor does Plato write that it does. The most we can say is that the absurdity of the common explanation paves the way to Socrates' own explanation, and that if we become convinced of the absurdity of the explanation (*b*) and of the other common explanations as well, we may reasonably come to doubt the truth of (*a*) or at least come to suspect its apparent innocence. In any case, Plato may not succeed here in convincing us that weakness does not occur, but he may succeed in showing that there are some difficulties with the ways we commonly explain weakness. (Here it is worth noting that Aristotle (pp. 64–8 below) in a passage that refers us to the present argument in the *Protagoras*, dismisses the question whether *akrasia* occurs, and concentrates on providing explanations that make its occurrence possible.)

There are two other points worth noticing about the actual argument that Socrates presents between 352d and 355c, and they are worth noticing because they constitute limitations on the scope and generality of the argument.

The first limitation is that, as Vlastos has pointed out, Socrates argues only against *one* of the five explanations of weakness that he first mentioned; he argues that 'overcome by pleasure' reduces to absurdity as an explanation of weakness, but he makes no clear move to show how his argument might be applied against the explanations 'overcome by' fear, love, hate, and passion. His argument, then, even if entirely successful, can refute only part of the opinion of the many; they might still be right about people being overcome by fear, love, and so forth.

The second important limitation of the argument is that it depends on the hedonistic hypothesis elaborated by Socrates between 353d and 354e (pp. 32–3 above). Not only is Socrates aware of this, but he emphasises it. At the end of this passage he says that 'it is still possible to retract if you can somehow contrive to say that the good is different from pleasure, or the bad from pain'. The argument then is not intended to show that 'overcome by pleasure' is absurd as an explanation of weakness, but only that it is absurd if one assumes hedonism; that is, it only shows that a hedonist is logically prevented from giving such an explanation. And incidentally, it is quite clear that Plato can argue this without being himself a hedonist. (This seems to me to settle the question whether 'the hedonism of the *Protagoras*' is compatible with the anti-hedonism of the *Gorgias* and other dialogues. As for the question why did Socrates use hedonistic premises in his argument, I see no mystery here at all, for the argument is in fact a perfect example of Socrates' favourite mode of argument; it attempts to show that one belief of the many, that in certain cases men are 'overcome by pleasure', is incompatible with another belief of theirs, the belief in hedonism.)

The point of setting out the context and limitations of Socrates' argument, aside from faithfulness to the text, is that we must, first, try to reconstruct and assess the soundness of the argument within its context and limitations. If the argument fails within these narrow bounds, we need to go no further, aside from determining the mistakes it contains. But if it has some measure of success, as I shall try to show, then we can, and must, raise the question whether it can be freed from those limitations, whether it can be freed from the hedonistic hypothesis, and whether it can be brought to bear

against the other explanations of weakness. This is the strategy I
follow in this paper.

II

The argument that Socrates offers between 352b and 356c divides
into three stages: (1) descriptions of cases of weakness and statements of the explanations commonly offered for the occurrence of
weakness so described (352b–353d; p. 31, line 7, to p. 32, line
7, above); (2) elaboration of the hedonistic hypothesis on which
Socrates' argument depends (353d–355a; p. 32, line 8, to p.
33, line 23, above); (3) substitution of 'good' for 'pleasure' in
the explanation 'overcome by pleasure', 'painful' for 'evil' in the
description of the case, and argument that on either substitution
the resulting explanation has been reduced to absurdity (355a–
356c; p. 33, line 24; to p. 34, line 27, above). From 356c to 358e
Socrates, apparently assuming that he has disposed of the explanations of the many, proceeds to elaborate his own familiar explanation, that what is called weakness is due to misestimation of
the values, of the alternatives due to their nearness or remoteness
in time.) I shall discuss each stage of the argument in turn, concentrating on stage (3), which is the source of all the important difficulties that arise in trying to understand and assess the success of
Socrates' argument. In doing this, I shall stay close to the text, but
at the same time I shall give Plato the benefit of the doubt in cases
of ambiguity and incompleteness of expression. My aim in this
section of the paper is to reconstruct the argument so that any
success that it may have, however limited, can be brought out, the
only limitations in this being the text and the nature of the case.

In stage (1) Socrates offers four different descriptions of cases of
weakness, and lists five possible explanations of cases so described,[5]
but at the beginning of stage (3) of the argument Socrates picks out
one of these descriptions and matches it with the explanation 'overcome by pleasure', and his subsequent argument about the absurdity
of the explanation concerns this pair:

> It is often the case that a man, knowing the evil to be evil [know-
> ing bad things to be bad things], nevertheless commits it [does
> them], when he might avoid it [them], because he is driven and
> dazed by his pleasures (355b).

The sorts of cases that the many have in mind when they give this sort of explanation, according to Socrates, are those in which a man is overcome by the pleasures of 'food or drink or sexual acts' (353c).[6] There are obvious ambiguities in Socrates' description of the case just quoted. In one sort of case a man may know (believe) that what he does (A) is bad, but he may also know that the alternatives to A open to him (B or C) are worse. This clearly is a case of doing the lesser of several evils, not a case of weakness. To get the latter we must suppose that the man thinks that either B or C is a good or at least a lesser evil than A; in short, we must suppose that he thinks that what he does is *bad in comparison to the alternatives.* In a second sort of case a man may think of the alternatives of what he is doing (A) as simply not doing or avoiding A (rather than doing something else), and he may think of the value of not doing A as simply the absence of the value contained in doing A (nothing lost and nothing gained). Here of course the man may think that A contains only good, or only evil, or both good and evil. In the last (mixed-type) case, he may think that the good outweighs the evil (so that A is *good on the whole*) or the converse (*bad on the whole*), or that neither outweighs the other. It is in fact this mixed type of case that Socrates seems to be discussing, since throughout the passage he finds it necessary to compare with each other only the values contained in what the agent does, not the value of what he does with the value of the alternatives open to him. And here quite clearly we must suppose that the case Socrates is considering is one in which the man knows that what he does is *bad on the whole*. (Within the second sort of case, if what a man does is bad on the whole, then it is also bad in comparison to the alternatives since the latter are thought of as nothing lost and nothing gained.)

In stage (2) of the argument we are invited to suppose that the people who give the explanation 'overcome by pleasure', the *hoi polloi*, are hedonists. What kind of hedonists? We do not have to classify them.[7] It is sufficient to notice that the following points about them are agreed to by Socrates and Protagoras. (1) When the *hoi polloi* assert that something which they say is pleasant is also bad, the only reason they can give is that it results in pain which outweighs the pleasure (so that it is painful on the whole); and when they judge something which they say is painful to be good, the only reason they can give is that it results in pleasure which outweighs the pain (so that it is pleasant on the whole) (354c–e; p. 32 above). (2) The *hoi polloi* pursue pleasure as a good,

and avoid pain as an evil (354c). (3) The *hoi polloi* cannot contrive
to say that the good is different from pleasure and the bad from
pain (if they could, the argument would not go through) (355a;
p. 33 above). (4) According to the hedonism of the *hoi polloi* we
have two things and four names: the names 'good', 'bad', 'pain',
and 'pleasure' (the point being that 'good' and 'pleasure' are names
for one and the same thing, and similarly with the other pair). In
the next stage of the argument Socrates indeed proceeds to *substitute* 'good' for 'pleasure' and 'painful' for 'evil'. (It looks as if we
must suppose that the agent, as well as the *hoi polloi*, is a hedonist,
since some of Socrates' substitutions are within intensional or
referentially opaque contexts; thus at 355e, in the sentence 'He
knows it to be bad', he substitutes 'painful' for 'bad'.)

We come now to the final stage (3) of the argument (355c–356c),
by far the most difficult. Plato's text here seems full of obscurities
and ambiguities, but there are a few signposts in it, which have not
been sufficiently noticed and which will help us to a sound interpretation of the passage and an appreciation of Plato's argument.
The first of these is that at the beginning of this stage of the argument, having already said that without assuming hedonism his
argument does not go through, Socrates says:

> I tell you that if this is so [that is, if we assume the hedonism
> described above], the argument becomes absurd, when you say that
> it is often the case that a man, knowing the evil to be evil,
> nevertheless commits it, when he might avoid it, because he is
> driven and dazed by his pleasures.

The complete dependence on hedonism in which Socrates places
his argument against the explanation 'overcome (or driven and
dazed by) pleasure' indicates clearly not only that this explanation
is to be reconstructed along hedonistic lines but also that the
alleged absurdity is to be found in a conjunction of the explanation
and hedonism, not simply in the explanation. Secondly, shortly
after the above passage, Socrates begins the long paragraph which
contains stage (3) of the argument by announcing:

> The absurdity of all this will be manifest if we refrain from using
> a number of terms at once, such as pleasant, painful, good, and
> bad; and as there appeared to be two things let us call them by
> two names – first good and evil, and then later on, pleasant and
> painful.

Socrates completes both of these substitutions by the end of this long paragraph, and after that (356c) the absurdity of the explanation 'overcome by pleasure' is not even mentioned once. This suggests quite clearly that the absurdity that Socrates has in mind must be sought in the text of this paragraph, not in later text (when Socrates elaborates his own explanation) as some writers have supposed.[8] Finally, though in several places the expressions that Socrates uses that have been translated by 'because he is overcome by pleasure' are ambiguous and could be rendered by 'being overcome by pleasure', in two passages (352d–e and 355c) Socrates makes it perfectly clear that being overcome by pleasure is given by the many as the reason or cause of the behaviour of acting contrary to one's knowledge; and hence '*because* he is overcome by pleasure' is the correct translation of the expressions that Socrates uses, suggesting as it does that 'overcome by pleasure' is given as an explanation of the behaviour of acting contrary to one's knowledge. The upshot is that – though Socrates does not *always* say this during stage (3) of his argument – it is the statement 'Sometimes men do what they know (or believe) is bad, when they can avoid it, *because* they are overcome by pleasure' that Socrates argues is absurd; not the statement 'Sometimes men do what they know (or believe) is bad, when they can avoid it, *and* (yet) they are overcome by pleasure.' These two statements are of course of different logical form; in conjunction with hedonism the former may turn out upon analysis to contain an absurdity, while the latter may not. Moreover, the former directs our attention to the fact that Socrates is arguing against an explanation, not simply against a statement of fact – an explanation that needs reconstruction.

These preliminaries out of the way, we come now to the difficult matter of locating the absurdity that Socrates has in mind; it is worth giving in full here Socrates' argumentation (following the last quotation) during the first substitution:

Let us then lay it down as our statement, that man does evil in spite of knowing the evil of it. Now if someone asks us: Why? we shall answer: Because he is overcome. By what? the questioner will ask us; and this time we shall be unable to reply: By pleasure – for this has exchanged its name for 'the good'. So we must answer only with the words: Because he is overcome. By what? says the questioner. The good – must surely be our reply. Now if our questioner chance to be an arrogant person he will laugh and exclaim: What a ridiculous statement, that a man does evil, knowing it to be evil, and not having to do it, because he is overcome by the good! Is this, he will ask, because the good is not worthy of conquering the evil in you, or because it is worthy? Clearly we must reply: Because it is not worthy; otherwise he whom we speak of as overcome by pleasures would not have offended. But in what sense, he might ask us, is the good unworthy of the bad, or the bad of the good? This can only be when the one is greater and the other smaller, or when there are more on the one side and fewer on the other. We shall not find any other reason to give. So it is clear, he will say, that by 'being overcome' you mean getting the greater evil in exchange for the lesser good. That must be agreed.

Socrates is here discussing a case of doing something or avoiding it (say, eating another serving of Athenian pastries or refusing to do so) where doing the thing in question contains both good and bad (harm and benefit) or both pleasure and pain (say, the pleasure of eating the pastries and the subsequent indigestion). Socrates is trying to give an analysis of 'overcome by good' so that it becomes absurd, on the hedonistic premises already agreed, as a reason or cause of weakness. Vlastos has correctly pointed out that 'worthy' (*axion*) is used by Socrates here as a value term, so that the good (benefit, pleasure) contained in a course of action is 'worthy of conquering' the evil (harm, pain) also contained in it if and only if the good exceeds the evil in quantity so that the course of action is good on the whole. Once we see this, it becomes clear from the two questions that Socrates raises and himself answers in this passage that he is taking 'overcome by good' in *one of two possible senses* – and this indeed is the most important ambiguity of the whole argument. In one sense (1) a man who does something that contains both good (benefit) and bad (harm) may be said to be 'overcome by the good' if the good is worthy of conquering the bad; that is, if the good outweighs the bad. In another sense (2) a man in similar circumstances may be said to be overcome by the good (pleasure) if his desire for the good (pleasure) that the course of action contains is *stronger* than his fear of (desire to avoid) the bad (pain) it contains. Socrates ignores the possibility of taking 'overcomes' in sense (2), and this is a serious fault in the argument. We must not be satisfied with this criticism, however; we need to follow out the argument with *each* of (1) and (2) if we are to appreciate the issues involved, and for the moment we must follow Socrates. Now once we grant

Socrates' interpretation of 'overcome by . . .', the explanation of the *hoi polloi* can be interpreted in three different ways, all untenable:

D1. Sometimes a man does something which is bad, knowing it to be bad, when he can avoid doing it

because

E1. the good contained in what he does is worthy of conquering – that is, outweighs – the bad contained in what he does.

E2. the good contained in what he does is worthy of conquering – that is, outweighs – the bad contained in what he does and the man knows this.

E3. the man takes (chooses, prefers, decides to take) the (known) greater harm (evil) contained in what he does in return for securing (as the price of) the (known) lesser good contained in what he does.

Socrates does not explicitly separate the first two interpretations, but this does not damage his argument, for both E1 and E2 contradict the description of the case; this is what Socrates is pointing out when he says that we must suppose that the harm contained in what the man does outweighs the benefit, otherwise the man would not have erred or (in our terms) he would not have done something which was *bad on the whole*; by hypothesis our man does something that contains good and bad where the bad outweighs the good and by hypothesis again he knows this. Once we rephrase the description so as to make this clear, the conjunction of the description with either E1 or E2 is self-contradictory:

D2. Sometimes a man does something which contains good and bad where the bad outweighs the good, knowing that this is so, when he can avoid doing it, because E1 and/or E2.

There is one way in which E1 can be saved, and that is by adding 'the man thinks or believes' in front of it, and deleting 'knowing it to be bad on the whole' from the description; but this way out is Socrates' own, and impossible for the many, for it amounts to a denial of weakness, since the man is now acting in accordance, and indeed on the basis of, his value beliefs (though mistaken ones, of course). We may notice that E1 and E2 would not contradict D2 if 'good' had not been substituted for 'pleasure' in E1 and E2.

Similarly with the second set of substitutions. Here we see clearly what exactly ethical hedonism contributes to Socrates' argument.

Explanation E3 does not contradict the description. The absurdity it involves consists in E3 (considered as an explanation of the case described in D2) contradicting one of the principles of the hedonism of the *hoi polloi*; but before we go into this we must consider more carefully the line in Plato's text of which E3 is a translation. This line is obscure mainly because of two difficulties, only the first of which has been resolved by writers on the passage. Gallop points out correctly that the preposition *anti*, normally rendered 'instead of' or 'in exchange for', cannot be so rendered here because both these expressions suggest that the agent does not 'take' the good or benefit contained in the case, whereas quite clearly Socrates is discussing a mixed case where the course of action the agent follows contains both harm and benefit (this is made quite explicit at 353c among other places). Following J. L. Stocks, Gallop correctly suggests that we take *anti* in the sense of 'as the price of' or 'in return for securing', and I follow this rendering which enhances our understanding of the argument.

The second and more serious difficulty is how to understand the crucial verb *lambanein* in this line (this is the verb that replaces 'overcome' in the whole sentence; this replacement I shall discuss later): it has been translated as 'gets', 'takes', 'chooses'.[9] Now *lambanein*, and its literal translation 'take', in the present context, may be understood in either one (or both) of two different ways: to refer to (1) what the agent in fact does, the actual execution of the action which contains more harm than benefit (say, the man's actual reaching for, taking hold of, and eating the pastries), or (2) to what the agent seeks, chooses, or possibly decides or prefers to do. In the latter case the use of the verb would introduce a referentially opaque or intensional context; in the former case it would not.

There are several excellent reasons for rejecting (1) and adopting *lambanein* in sense (2) as the correct interpretation of the text. The major reason against (1) is that if we were to understand *lambanein* in the sense of (1), then E3 would not be an explanation at all, for it would simply (do nothing more than) *repeat* part of what we already have in the description of the case, namely that the man does what (he knows) is bad on the whole. It is not that E3 so interpreted involves absurdity or contradicts hedonism; it is not an explanation at all. This is not what Plato is talking about. (A second reason against the interpretation of E3 with *lambanein* in sense (1) is that the preposition *anti* cannot with good sense be taken with a verb that refers only to the execution of an action (behaviour divorced from any intensional element.) The major reason in favour of understanding *lambanein* in the sense 'seeks to' or 'chooses' is that it enables us to see the relevance of what Socrates proceeds to do immediately after this line when he takes up the second substitution, and to bring out the absurdity that Socrates is talking about. On the second substitution we obtain:

D3. Sometimes a man does something which is painful on the whole, knowing that this is so, when he can avoid doing it,

because

E4. He takes (chooses, prefers, decides to have) the (known) greater pain contained in what he does in return for securing the (known) lesser pleasure.

Socrates repeats once more interpretation (1) of 'overcome', and immediately after that proceeds to elaborate a principle which is implied by the hedonism of the *hoi polloi* (which we may remember is a premise of the whole argument) and which contradicts the explanation E3 once we take the *lambanein* in the sense of 'seeks', 'chooses', or 'prefers'.

For if you weigh pleasant things against pleasant, the greater and the more are always to be preferred [*leptea*]: if painful against painful, then always the fewer and the smaller. If you weigh pleasant against painful, and find that the painful are outbalanced (outweighed) by the pleasant – whether the near by the remote or the remote by the near – that action must be (is to be) done to which the pleasant are attached; but if the pleasant are outweighed by the painful, that action is not (must not) be done (356b–c, p. 34 above).

The very last part of this hedonistic principle contradicts directly the explanation of the *hoi polloi* in its last substitution; and a similar principle, obtained by substituting 'good' for 'pleasant' and 'bad' for 'painful' in the above principle, contradicts directly the explanation of the *hoi polloi* that is obtained by the first substitution (that is, E3). This indeed is the absurdity that Socrates is talking about. But in order to appreciate this we must see at once that the hedonistic principle elaborated by Socrates does *not* assert a connection between a man's evaluations or ranking of the alternatives before him (the immediate results of the 'weighing' that Socrates is talking about) and his behaviour (the execution of a particular action), but rather a connection between his evaluations and what (presumably as a result of the evaluations) he seeks or chooses to do. If Socrates' hedonistic principle were interpreted as asserting the former connection, Socrates would indeed at this point be begging the wider issue at stake within which the argument against explanations is set: the relation of knowledge to action. But Socrates need not rely on this. All that he needs at this stage is the latter connection, between a man's evaluations or rankings of the alternatives and what he seeks or chooses (decides, prefers) to do. This interpretation of the hedonistic principle on which Socrates relies to obtain the absurdity, is perfectly consistent with – indeed it is suggested by – the psychological hedonism that Socrates and Protagoras earlier attribute to the masses: people 'pursue pleasure as being a good and avoid pain as being an evil' (354c). 'Pursue' and 'avoid' (*diokein* and *pheugein*) must be understood to refer to one's seeking to obtain pleasures and seeking to avoid pains, not to one's actually obtaining pleasures and successfully avoiding pains. The principle asserted is *not* that (1) people always act in a way that maximises their pleasures and/or minimises their pains, but that (2) people always seek to act in such a way as to maximise pleasure and/or to minimise pain, where 'seek' is clearly opaque. Principle (1) is clearly and obviously false, since people often make mistakes, or lack the opportunity or the ability, or are prevented from maximising and/or minimising their pleasures. And it is clear that the psychological hedonism on which Socrates is relying here would employ (2), not (1), as a principle of explanation of human behaviour: a typical explanation along these lines would include (2) as the operative principle, statements about the agent's knowledge or estimate of the amounts of pleasures and pains involved in the alternatives before him, and possibly statements about opportunity and ability to do or avoid the behaviour at issue.

(A model explanation along the lines suggested by the hedonism that Socrates attributes to the masses: Why did S do A at t_1?

(1) S did A at t_1

because

(2) All men seek to maximise their pleasure and/or minimise their pains

and

(3) S knew (believed) at t_1 that A would maximise his pleasures and not-A (avoiding A) would not (or A is pleasant on the whole and not-A is not).

This model (Model I) may be the model that Plato has in mind and it may properly be called a teleological model. It is to be noticed that (2) and (3) do *not* logically entail (1); this model does not satisfy Hempel's requirements for a scientific explanation.

Now this may happen: one may argue that only a limited number of factors can account for the possiblity of (2) and (3) being true and (1) being false – say, lack of physical ability to carry out the action (e.g. the man does not swim or ride a bike or is blind), lack of opportunity, or, finally, external, physical coercion. Now on the basis of *this*, one might argue that (2) implies a stronger generalisation: (2^1) Whenever a man is faced with two or more alternatives and he has the physical ability and the opportunity to do either and is not physically coerced to do any, he will do the one which he knows or believes at the time will maximise his pleasures and/or minimise his pains.

(2^1) together with appropriate factual premises entails (1), and makes it possible to have, in logical form, a deductive-type explanation of a certain sort (II). Whether Socrates would go on to attribute (2^1) as well as (2) to hedonists is not clear; what is clear from the text is, first, that he does not in fact do so, and second that he does not need to for his argument. For his argument, all that he needs to suppose is that hedonists hold (2) and that their model of explanation of behaviour is (I). For once 'overcome by . . .' is interpreted in Socrates' way, the explanation contradicts (2), and that is enough.)[10]

What Socrates has shown is that on the assumption of hedonism (ethical and psychological), one explanation of weakness commonly given by the masses, 'overcome by pleasure', reduces to absurdity in the sense that (once we make the substitutions allowed by ethical hedonism and interpret 'overcome' in the sense indicated) it contradicts the very principle of psychological hedonism which is universally employed by hedonists in the explanation of behaviour.

In summarising this section of the paper, we may say that Socrates is indeed successful in reducing the explanation of weakness commonly given by the masses, 'overcome by pleasure', to absurdity provided (1) that we allow him as premisses the combination of ethical and psychological hedonism that he attributes to the masses, (2) that we grant him his interpretation of 'overcome', and (3) that we understand the main verbs used in the various statements of psychological hedonism ('take', 'pursue', 'avoid') in an opaque sense. But the success of Socrates' argument is clearly very limited. To begin with, as an argument against non-Socratic (and non-early Platonic) explanations of weakness, Socrates' argument is limited *to* 'overcome by pleasure' and *by* its hedonistic premises; what about the other explanations Socrates mentioned at the outset, and what about any of these explanations offered by non-hedonists? In the second place, what happens to Socrates' argument and, more generally, to the explanations commonly given by the masses, when we interpret 'overcome' in the sense Socrates has ignored – that is, the sense in which 'overcome' refers to the relative *strength* of the desires (feelings, passions) for or against the alternatives before the agent (rather than to the relative values of the alternatives)? Finally, why should Socrates (and Plato) have ignored this important, and indeed more plausible, sense of 'overcome'? In the remaining sections of this paper I take up each of these questions in turn.

III

Can Socrates' argument against 'overcome by pleasure', as reconstructed above, be generalised so as to apply to the other explanations originally mentioned by Socrates – 'overcome by' passion, love, pain, fear? And can Socrates' argument be 'freed' from its hedonistic premises, in the sense that some other plausible Platonic non-question-begging premises can be found which can be successfully substituted for the hedonistic premises? If we can show that the answers to these questions are affirmative, we thereby show that the success of Socrates' argument is not so limited after all, and that his argument is of some general significance. I shall try to show in *one move* that the answers to both questions are affirmative by constructing an argument, parallel to Socrates', against the explanation 'overcome by fear' without relying on hedonistic premises. The case of weakness and its explanation before us now is as follows:

Sometimes a man fails to do something which is good, and which he knows to be good, when it is in his power to do it, because

> he is overcome by fear.

The main reason I have selected the explanation 'overcome by fear' is that Socrates later on in the *Protagoras*, when he begins a discussion of courage at 358d, provides us with a definition of fear:

> Well, I said, is there something you call dread or fear? And is it – I address myself to you, Prodicus – the same as I have in mind – something I describe as an expectation of evil, whether you call it fear or dread?

In the argument we are about to construct, this definition of fear can take the place that ethical hedonism had in Socrates' argument: that is, if granted as a premise in the new argument, it allows us to substitute 'expectation of evil' for 'fear' in the explanation:

> Sometimes a man fails to do something which is good, and which he knows to be good, when it is in his power to do it,

because

> he is overcome by the evil he expects.

Socrates can now argue that this explanation is absurd for reasons similar to the ones we attributed to him for arguing that the explanation obtained after the first substitution in his own argument is absurd; that was, it may be remembered:

> Sometimes a man does something which is bad, knowing that it is bad, when it is in his power to avoid it

because

> he is overcome by the good.

To see the parallel absurdity of the explanation 'overcome by the evil he expects' we need do only two things: eliminate the ambiguities of the statement, and indicate what principle is to take the place and perform the function of psychological hedonism. Eliminating the ambiguities (that is, eliminating interpretations analogous to E_1 and E_2 for analogous reasons) we obtain:

Sometimes a man fails to do something which is good on the whole, knowing that it is good on the whole – that is, knowing that the good that it contains outweighs the evil (bad) that it contains – when it is in his power to do it.

because

he seeks to (chooses, prefers, decides to) avoid the greater good in return for (as the price of) avoiding the lesser evil.

Well, what principle can take the place of psychological hedonism here? A principle, which Socrates (and Plato) argues for in many early dialogues (e.g. *Meno*, 77b–78b; *Gorgias*, 468c) and which can be assumed here without begging any of the questions at issue: that every man desires or seeks (pursues) to get good things and seeks or desires to avoid getting bad or evil things; and the consequent principle that everyone pursues (or desires to do) things which are good on the whole or good in comparison to the alternatives, and seeks to avoid things that are bad in comparison to the alternatives and/or bad on the whole. It is this last part of the principle that contradicts the explanation 'overcome by fear' as reduced above.

IV

What happens to Socrates' argument against explanations of weakness and, more important, what happens to these explanations themselves when we take 'overcome by . . .' to refer to the relative *strengths* of the agent's desires for and against the course of action before him?

Let us begin by noticing a point in the argument that we have so far ignored. At 356a (p. 34 above), during the second substitution at the last stage of the argument, Socrates briefly raises and answers an objection to his argument:

For if you should say: But, Socrates, the *immediately* pleasant differs widely from the *subsequently* pleasant or painful, I should reply: Do they differ in anything but pleasure and pain? That is the only distinction. Like a practice weigher, put pleasant things and painful on the scales, and with them the *nearness* and *remoteness*, and tell me which count for more [italics mine].

On the basis of Socrates' answer here, the immediately subsequent passage, and the analogy of size at 356d, we can confidently interpret Socrates' answer as follows. This feature of the case, the pleasure being near in time and the pain remote in the future, does indeed make a difference in the explanation, it is not an irrelevant feature; but the only difference this feature can make is a difference in pain or pleasure or rather in the quantities of pleasure and pain. It is not, however, a difference in the *actual* quantities of pleasure and pain involved in the case (we are not to suppose that the further the pain is in the future the smaller it will be!), but in the *estimated* or *believed* (by the agent) quantities of pleasure and pain. This answer leads Socrates to *his own* explanation of the case, elaborated after the last stage of the argument we have examined: that just as in the case of size and variation of distance, so here also because the pleasure is near the agent in time and the pain far he misestimates the quantities and supposes that the pleasure outweighs the pain; so that he was acting in accordance with, indeed on the basis of, his hedonistic principle, even though he made a mistaken application of it. Socrates' answer to the objection and his own explanation are of course once more predicated on the assumption that 'overcome by pleasure' must refer to the pleasure outweighing the pain (in the agent's estimate).

But it is possible to give a quite different answer to Socrates' question – not an answer that Plato rejects, but one which he seems to ignore. We may suppose, without contradicting anything that Plato says: (*a*) that the agent, Agathon, knowing or believing what he did, had a desire for the pleasure he expected from eating the pastries and a desire to avoid (or a fear of) the pain he also expected afterward; (*b*) that these two desires (or the desire and the fear) may be considered as conflicting desires, and conceived as causes; (*c*) that these desires, considered as causes of behaviour, can be supposed to have degrees of causal strength. Making the common additional assumption which is usually treated as a kind of law, that the behaviour that issues from conflicting desires is that in accordance with the stronger desire (or the subject always acts in accordance with the stronger desire), we can now construct a causal explanation of our case as follows:

1. Agathon was faced with the alternatives of eating or not eating Athenian pastries.
2. Agathon had a desire to eat the pastries and a desire to avoid eating (or a fear of eating) the pastries.

3. Agathon's desire to eat and desire not to eat the pastries (or the fear of eating) are conflicting desires.
4. No other (interfering) desires or motives were present that were connected with the two alternatives.
5. In every case of conflicting desires (and no interfering motives or external forces) the subject satisfies (acts in accordance with) the stronger desire.
6. Agathon's desire to eat the pastries was stronger than his desire not to eat them.[11]
7. Agathon ate the pastries.

The phrase 'overcome by pleasure' is now understood as a shorthand for this explanation, and in particular as referring to (6) and (5)

Explanations of this kind – that is, those that use (5) or some version of it as the main explanatory principle – are always logically relevant to cases of weakness (even though we may sometimes prefer other kinds of explanations) since conflicting motivations are characteristic of such cases, whether the conflicting motives be practical beliefs (or knowledge) and desires, as in Plato, or calm and violent passions, as in Hume.

It should be noticed at once that an explanation of this kind can be perfectly respectable provided that we have ways of determining the relative strength of the conflicting desires independently of knowledge or information as to what action ensues from the conflict.[12] This condition (let us call it A) *must* be satisfied: otherwise, if our only way of telling which desire is stronger were to wait and see what action ensues, the main principle of the explanation (5) would be empty of empirical content, and the explanation would be trivial. Applied to our example, condition A requires that we be able to determine whether (6) is true independently of knowledge or information that (7) is true.

Now, so far as explanations of weakness are concerned, it is important to realise that condition A must be satisfied in at least two significantly different ways. (I) One way is to suppose that there is some consistent correlation between the agent's evaluation or rankings of the alternative before him and the strength of the conflicting desires that attach to these alternatives. This supposition would satisfy condition A since it is certainly possible to ascertain the agent's rankings (for example, by asking him) of the alternatives independently of knowing what alternative he actually takes (and, in addition, it is of course possible to rank alternatives without actually acting on the rankings because, say, one is prevented from doing so). Applied to our case, the supposition that would satisfy condition A is that if Agathon believes that the pleasure of eating the pastries outweighs the subsequent pain, then his desire to eat the pastries is stronger than his desire not to eat (or his fear of eating). It is conceivable that some such supposition is true, given some appropriate restriction of its scope; but whether or not this is so, it is certainly plausible, and its plausibility is perhaps enhanced by the difficulty of finding some *other* way to satisfy condition A. We may notice further that if we satisfy condition A in the way just indicated, the ground or evidence for (6) will usually be a belief statement such as (6') Agathon believes that the pleasure of eating the pastries outweighs the subsequent pain. The success of such an explanation depends on (6') being true, but not on what Agathon believes being true (Agathon may indeed be mistaken in his ranking and the reason for this may be that the pleasure was near and the pain much later – all this is consistent with the success of the explanation in question).

Before proceeding to the second way of satisfying condition A, I wish to point out an important consequence of the first way of satisfying condition A. If one assumed or supposed (whether explicitly or implicitly) that (5) or some version of it is the relevant explanatory principle in cases of conflicting motives or desires or drives, and further that the first way (I) is the *only* way to satisfy condition A, then clearly the occurrence of *akrasia* or weakness will appear an impossibility to him (or, at least, *akrasia* will appear inexplicable). For in cases of *akrasia* the agent is supposed to be acting contrary to his knowledge or belief of which alternative is best (or better) – that is, contrary to *his* own ranking of the alternative; but, given our present supposition, this implies that he acts in accordance with the weaker, not the stronger, of the conflicting motives! At the same time, the present suppositions are quite inconsistent with the agent's acting against *the correct* ranking (correct even according, for example, to the agent's hedonistic principles); and this will be the case precisely when the belief in (6'), not (6') itself, is false. The explanation will work equally well here; and the inclination will be to say that what occur are cases where the agent acts against the correct (even by his own value principle) ranking, not his own ranking. There is some evidence in the argument in the *Protagoras*, not that Plato thought of the matter explicitly in this way, but that he was thinking of it in this kind of context. For he begins the whole argument by asking which is stronger or more powerful in directing human conduct, knowledge of good and evil or such things as pleasure, pain, fear, love and so forth; and this language suggests (5) or some version of it as the relevant explanatory principle. And when, as we have seen, he comes to interpreting 'overcome by pleasure', he does so by referring us to the hedonistic values of the alternatives, and this suggests that the strength of the motive is to be inferred from the value ranking of the alternatives.

(II) A significantly different manner of satisfying condition A would obtain if we had ways of determining the relative strength of the conflicting motives independently of any knowledge (or information) of the agent's evaluations or rankings of the alternatives to which the conflicting motives refer and of course independently of information of what behaviour in fact ensues. If condition A can be satisfied in this manner, this allows, at the very least, for the possibility that the stronger (strongest) desire is not always the desire referring to the alternative that has the agent's higher (highest) ranking. Indeed, on the present supposition, there would be no *a priori* reason to expect that 'stronger motive' correlates consistently with 'higher ranking'; we might well find out that under certain conditions (for example, when the agent is in some state of emotional excitement), there is no correlation at all between 'stronger motive' and agent's 'higher ranking'. Now the supposition that sometimes, even quite often, people act against their own rankings or evaluations of the alternatives before them (even though they are not externally forced or compelled to, and have the opportunity to act in accordance with their own evaluations) will not be puzzling at all; for such behaviour will no longer appear inexplicable.

Can condition A be satisfied in the second way? It seems that it has been satisfied in cases of explanations of animal behaviour resulting from conflicting motives or drives, where the model of explanation used is similar to the one I have outlined, and the explanatory principle (5) or some variant of it is explicitly used.[13] Roughly speaking, it has been possible to show that the strength of two conflicting drives or motives – say, the desire for certain food (approach drive) and the fear of the electric shock that accompanies the obtaining of the food (avoidance drive) – increases as the animal approaches the goal, and that in fact the rate of increase of the avoidance drive is always greater than that of the approach drive (and it has been possible to measure the rate of increase of strength by measuring pull or speed at different points). In addition it has been possible to determine the initial strength (under controlled conditions) of the approach and avoidance drives (by vary-

ing such things as the time of deprivation of food or the intensity of
the electric shock). In consequence, it has been possible (under controlled conditions) to plot and predict the relative strengths of the approach and avoidance drives or motives at any given distance from
the goal, and to predict what behaviour will result (reaching the goal
or not) in accordance with the principle that the animal's behaviour
at any given point (and at the end) will be in accordance with the
stronger motive. More recently, exactly the same explanatory
model has been used, perhaps without enough caution, in cases of
human behaviour resulting from conflicting motives; but it is not
clear to me in this case (of human behaviour) that condition A has
been satisfied.[14] In any case, the success of the explanatory model
in the case of animal behaviour seems to point to the possibility
that explanations of the same kind, satisfying condition A in the
second (II) way, can be given of human behaviour in cases of conflicting motives.

V

We have seen that Plato uses the language of strength and yet overlooks the possibility of interpreting the various explanations of
weakness, 'overcome by . . .', in terms of the strength of the conflicting desires. How can we account for this? One possibility of
course is that Plato did not distinguish the concepts of strength and
value or value estimate. It is difficult enough to find a way of
determining the strengths of conflicting desires (passions, feelings)
independently of knowledge of ensuing behaviour (condition A) and
independently of knowledge of the agent's rankings or value estimates of the objects of his desires – the second way (II) of satisfying
A (p. 58 above). The very possibility of doing either or both of
these might not occur to one unless he encounters certain difficulties
(of which the denial of weakness may be one). William McDougall's
discussion is a good illustration of this point.[15] Or the necessity to
satisfy condition A may be forced on one but he may not see further
any need to satisfy condition A in any way other than (I) (p. 56
above), as Mill's discussion illustrates.[16] I know of no explicit
evidence that Plato saw any necessity to satisfy condition A at all,
certainly none that condition A is to be satisfied in any other way
than (I). He seems to run together strength and value estimate;
when, for instance, he considers an objection that might be under-

stood to imply that strength of desire varies with variation of distance from the object of the desire, he understands it rather to imply that the agent's estimate of the value of the object varies with distance. The whole confusion is made easier to fall into by the fact that strength is not entirely independent of value estimate.[17]

A second possible line of explanation relates to two hitherto unnoticed features of the passage we have examined. One of these is a shift in Plato's language, from the language of strength to the language of value estimates, of which the turning point is at 355d (p. 33 above) where the passive 'overcome by' is replaced by 'to take' or 'to choose'. A list of the relevant phrases in the order in which they occur is sufficient to confirm this: 'dragged about' (352bc), 'under the control', 'being overcome by' (repeated five times before 355d), 'being overpowered by', 'being driven and dazed'; 'take', 'choose', 'weigh', 'choose', 'choice of odd and even', 'right choice of pleasure and pain' (357b). This shift from the language of strength (all in the passive voice) to the language of value estimate (all in the active voice) suggests the possibility of another shift during the passage, a shift in the sorts of cases being considered: from cases where the agent is acting in the heat of passion, 'driven out of his senses' (as Wayte says),[18] where he has lost control of himself, to cases of calm and cool choice and action. Indeed the radical shift in the language cannot but remind one of Austin's charge:

Or we collapse succumbing to temptation into losing control of ourselves – a bad patch, this, for telescoping . . . Plato, I suppose, and after him Aristotle, fastened this confusion upon us, as bad in its day and way as the later, grotesque, confusion of moral weakness and weakness of will. I am very partial to ice cream, and a bombe is served divided into segments corresponding one to one with the persons at High Table: I am tempted to help myself to two segments and do so, thus succumbing to temptation and even conceivably (but why necessarily?) going against my principles. But do I lose control of myself? Do I rave, do I snatch the morsels from the dish and wolf them down, impervious to the consternation of my colleagues? Not a bit of it. We often succumb to temptation with calm and even with finesse.

('A Plea for Excuses', in *Philosophical Papers*
(Oxford, 1961) p. 146)

The second unnoticed feature of the passage is that Plato repeats three times (up to 355d), as part of the description of cases of weakness, that the agent 'could avoid' what he did or 'did not have to do' what he did. Plato does not say what he means by this; he could be referring to physical ability, lack of physical coercion, or opportunity. It is also possible, I suggest, that he is referring to psychological ability to do or refrain from doing or to lack of psychological compulsion. This concept is of course difficult and in need of analysis; but if for the moment we suppose that this suggestion is near the mark, a new and interesting line of conjecture opens up that makes more intelligible Plato's treatment of weakness in the *Protagoras*, and perhaps even gives new life to his argument. The conjecture is that when a man acts contrary to his knowledge or belief of what is best (for him), *and* the true explanation of his action is in terms of the strength of his conflicting desires (passions, feelings) – an explanation of the sort outlined above (pp. 55–6) – *and* condition A is satisfied in manner (II), then the agent acted under psychological compulsion or was not psychologically able to refrain from doing what he did. Thus if a man, say, knows or believes that eating another serving of Athenian pastries would give him pleasure but would also harm him, and also believes that the harm outweighs the pleasure (so that he believes the pleasure is not worth the harm), but he eats nevertheless, and the true explanation of his eating is that his desire for the pleasure was stronger than his fear of the harm, and we can determine this independently of knowledge of his action and knowledge of his value estimate, then he was not psychologically able to refrain from eating. The plausibility of connecting this type of explanation with psychological compulsion is enhanced by two considerations. First, when all these conditions are (accepted as) satisfied we have the feeling that our man is no longer an agent; he is not *doing* anything, something is happening to him – the very point suggested by Plato's passive language of strength (overcome, overpowered, dazed, and driven). The second point is that if we accept the explanation and still say that the man *could* (psychologically) have refrained from eating, it seems that the only thing we can mean is that he *would* have refrained *if* his *fear* had been stronger instead. Now we are faced with the question whether the man had control, in any clear sense, over the *strength* of his feelings (and whether in general one can be said to have any such control). Until a clear affirmative answer can be given to this question, the verdict that the man was not (psychologically) able to refrain will have to stand. Until such an answer is given, we can say, tentatively, that this sort of explanation in terms of strength can be used to give *one* clear sense to the notion of psychological ability or at least psychological compulsion.[19]

Finally, if this conjecture is accepted, it constitutes a defence of Plato's argument. For it follows from it that if we interpret the explanations of the masses, 'overcome by . . .', in terms of strength (the interpretation that Plato ignores or overlooks, thus weakening his argument), then one of the conditions included in the description of the case explained is contradicted: namely, the condition that the man could or was able (psychologically) to refrain from acting contrary to his knowledge of what is best (for him). The 'wider' issue in the whole passage in the *Protagoras* was whether it is possible for men to act contrary to their knowledge of what is best when they can refrain. The 'narrower' issue, what the argument was all about, was whether, assuming that this is possible, the explanation can be that men are overcome by their passions, pleasure, pain, fear, love, and so forth. By interpreting 'overcome by' as referring to the value estimates or rankings of the agent, Socrates succeeded in showing that one such explanation leads to contradiction (taking hedonism as a premise). This paved the way to his own explanation (ignorance of what is best) which in effect answers the wider issue negatively, since the explanation cancels out one of the conditions in the description of weakness. It now results that if we remedy the most serious weakness in Socrates' argument, and construe 'overcome by . . .' on the model of explanations in terms of strength, the wider issue is answered negatively once more since we now cancel out another condition, namely that the agent could (psychologically) have refrained from acting contrary to his knowledge. That this condition is included in descriptions of weakness is fair enough. For the philosophically puzzling cases of (prudential and moral) weakness, in so far as their occurrence reflects on the notion of having or holding (or 'assenting to') a practical principle, rule, or belief, are the cases where the man was *not* under (psychological as well as physical) compulsion. The cases where he was are after all understandable enough – at least if our concept of compulsion is clear enough.[20]

III Continence and incontinence

Aristotle

Six Varieties of Character; Method of Treatment; Current Opinions

1. Let us now make a fresh beginning and point out that of moral states to be avoided there are three kinds – vice, incontinence, brutishness. The contraries of two of these are evident – one we call virtue, the other continence; to brutishness it would be most fitting to oppose superhuman virtue, a heroic and divine kind of virtue, as Homer has represented Priam saying of Hector that he was very good,

> For he seemed not, he,
> The child of a mortal man, but as one that of
> God's seed came.[1]

Therefore, if, as they say, men become gods by excess of virtue, of this kind must evidently be the state opposed to the brutish state; for as a brute has no vice or virtue, so neither has a god; his state is higher than virtue, and that of a brute is a different kind of state from vice.

Now, since it is rarely that a godlike man is found – to use the epithet of the Spartans, who when they admire anyone highly call him a 'godlike man' – so too the brutish type is rarely found among men; it is found chiefly among barbarians, but some brutish qualities are also produced by disease or deformity; and we also call by this evil name those men who go beyond all ordinary standards by reason of vice. Of this kind of disposition, however, we must later make some mention[2] while we have discussed vice before;[3] we must now discuss incontinence and softness (or effeminacy), and continence and endurance; for we must treat each of the two neither as identical with virtue or wickedness, nor as a different genus. We must, as in all other cases, set the observed facts before us and, after first discussing the difficulties, go on to prove, if possible, the truth of all the common opinions about these affections of the mind, or, failing this, of the greater number and the most authoritative; for if we both refute the objections and leave the common opinions undisturbed, we shall have proved the case sufficiently.

Now (1) both continence and endurance are thought to be included among things good and praiseworthy, and both incontinence and softness among things bad and blameworthy; and the same man is thought to be continent and ready to abide by the result of his calculations, or incontinent and ready to abandon them. And (2) the incontinent man, knowing that what he does is bad, does it as a result of passion, while the continent man, knowing that his appetites are bad, refuses on account of his rational principle to follow them. (3) The temperate man all men call continent and disposed to endurance, while the continent man some maintain to be always temperate but others do not; and some call the self-indulgent man incontinent and the incontinent man self-indulgent indiscriminately, while others distinguish them. (4) The man of practical wisdom, they sometimes say, cannot be incontinent, while sometimes they say that some who are practically wise and clever *are* incontinent. Again, (5) men are said to be incontinent even with respect to anger, honour, and gain. These, then, are the things that are said.

Contradictions Involved in the Current Opinions

2.   Now we may ask (1) how a man who judges rightly can behave incontinently. That he should behave so when he has knowledge, some say is impossible; for it would be strange – so Socrates thought – if when knowledge was in a man something else could master it and drag it about like a slave. For *Socrates* was entirely opposed to the view in question, holding that there is no such thing as incontinence; no one, he said, when he judges acts against what he judges best – people act so only by reason of ignorance. Now this view plainly contradicts the observed facts, and we must inquire about what happens to such a man; if he acts by reason of ignorance, what is the manner of his ignorance? For that the man who behaves incontinently does not, before he gets into this state, *think* he ought to act so, is evident. But there are *some* who concede certain of Socrates' contentions but not others; that nothing is stronger than knowledge they admit, but not that no one acts contrary to what

has seemed to him the better course, and therefore they say that the incontinent man has no knowledge when he is mastered by his pleasures, but opinion. But *if* it is opinion and not knowledge, if it is not a strong conviction that resists but a weak one, as in men who hesitate, we sympathise with their failure to stand by such convictions against strong appetites; but we do not sympathise with wickedness, nor with any of the other blameworthy states. Is it then *practical wisdom* whose resistance is mastered? That is the strongest of all states. But this is absurd; the same man will be at once practically wise and incontinent, but *no one* would say that it is the part of a practically wise man to do willingly the basest acts. Besides, it has been shown before that the man of practical wisdom is one who will act[4] (for he is a man concerned with the individual facts)[5] and who has the other virtues.[6]

(2) Further, if continence involves having strong and bad appetites, the temperate man will not be continent nor the continent man temperate; for a temperate man will have neither excessive nor bad appetites. But the continent man *must*; for if the appetites are good, the state of character that restrains us from following them is bad, so that not all continence will be good; while if they are weak and not bad, there is nothing admirable in resisting them, and if they are weak and bad, there is nothing great in resisting these either.

(3) Further, if continence makes a man ready to stand by any and every opinion, it is bad, i.e. if it makes him stand even by a false opinion; and if incontinence makes a man apt to abandon any and every opinion, there will be a good incontinence, of which Sophocles' Neoptolemus in the *Philoctetes* will be an instance; for he is to be praised for not standing by what Odysseus persuaded him to do, because he is pained at telling a lie.

(4) Further, the sophistic argument presents a difficulty; the syllogism arising from men's wish to expose paradoxical results arising from an opponent's view, in order that they may be admired when they succeed, is one that puts us in a difficulty (for thought is bound fast when it will not rest because the conclusion does not satisfy it, and cannot advance because it cannot refute the argument). There is an argument from which it follows that folly coupled with incontinence is virtue; a man does the opposite of what he thinks right, owing to incontinence, but thinks what is good to be evil and something that he should not do, and in consequence he will do what is good and not what is evil.

(5) Further, he who on conviction does and pursues and chooses

what is pleasant would be thought to be better than one who does so as a result not of calculation but of incontinence; for he is easier to cure since he may be persuaded to change his mind. But to the incontinent man may be applied the proverb 'When water chokes, what is one to wash it down with?' If he had been persuaded of the rightness of what he does, he would have desisted when he was persuaded to change his mind; but now he acts in spite of his being persuaded of something quite different.

(6) Further, if incontinence and continence are concerned with any and every kind of object, who is it that is incontinent in the unqualified sense? No one has all the forms of incontinence, but we say some people are incontinent without qualification.

SOLUTION OF THE PROBLEM, IN WHAT SENSE THE INCONTINENT MAN ACTS AGAINST KNOWLEDGE

3.   Of some such kind are the difficulties that arise; some of these points must be refuted and the others left in possession of the field; for the solution of the difficulty is the discovery of the truth. (1) We must consider first, then, whether incontinent people act knowingly or not, and in what sense knowingly; then (2) with what sorts of object the incontinent and the continent man may be said to be concerned (i.e. whether with any and every pleasure and pain or with certain determinate kinds), and whether the continent man and the man of endurance are the same or different; and similarly with regard to the other matters germane to this inquiry. The starting-point of our investigation is (*a*) the question whether the continent man and the incontinent are differentiated by their objects or by their attitude, i.e. whether the incontinent man is incontinent simply by being concerned with such-and-such objects, or, instead, by his attitude, or, instead of that, by both these things; (*b*) the second question is whether incontinence and continence are concerned with any and every object or not. The man who is incontinent in the unqualified sense neither is concerned with any and every object, but with precisely those with which the self-indulgent man is concerned, nor is he characterised by being simply related to these (for then his state would be the same as self-indulgence), but by being related to them in a certain way. For the one is led on in accordance with his own choice, thinking that he ought always to pursue the present pleasure; while the other does not think so, but yet pursues it.

(1) As for the suggestion that it is true opinion and not knowledge against which we act incontinently, that makes no difference to the argument; for some people when in a state of opinion do not hesitate, but think they know exactly. If, then, the notion is that owing to their weak conviction those who have opinion are more likely to act against their judgement than those who know, we answer that there need be no difference between knowledge and opinion in this respect; for some men are no less convinced of what they think than others of what they know; as is shown by the case of Heraclitus. But (*a*), since we use the word 'know' in two senses (for both the man who has knowledge but is not using it and he who is using it are said to know), it *will* make a difference whether, when a man does what he should not, he has the knowledge but is not exercising it, or *is* exercising it; for the latter seems strange, but not the former.

Further (*b*), since there are two kinds of premisses, there is nothing to prevent a man's having both premisses and acting against his knowledge, provided he is using only the universal premiss and not the particular; for it is particular acts that have to be done. And there are also two kinds of universal term; one is predicable of the agent, the other of the object; e.g. 'dry food is good for every man', and 'I am a man', or 'such-and-such food is dry'; but whether 'this food is such-and-such', of this the incontinent man either has not or is not exercising the knowledge.[7] There will then be, firstly, an enormous difference between these manners of knowing, so that to know in one way when we act incontinently would not seem anything strange, while to know in the other way would be extraordinary.

And further (*c*) the possession of knowledge in another sense than those just named is something that happens to men; for within the case of having knowledge but not using it we see a difference of state, admitting of the possibility of having knowledge in a sense and yet not having it, as in the instance of a man asleep, mad, or drunk. But now this is just the condition of men under the influence of passions; for outbursts of anger and sexual appetites and some other such passions, it is evident, actually alter our bodily condition, and in some men even produce fits of madness. It is plain, then, that incontinent people must be said to be in a similar condition to men asleep, mad, or drunk. The fact that men use the language that flows from knowledge proves nothing; for even men under the influence of these passions utter scientific proofs and verses of Empedocles, and those who have just begun to learn a science can string together its phrases, but do not yet know it; for it has to become part of themselves and that takes time; so that we must suppose that the use of language by men in an incontinent state means no more than its utterance by actors on the stage.

Again (*d*), we may also view the cause as follows with reference to the facts of human nature. The one opinion is universal, the other is concerned with the particular facts and here we come to something within the sphere of perception; when a single opinion results from the two, the soul must in one type of case[8] affirm the conclusion, while in the case of opinions concerned with production it must immediately act (e.g. if 'everything sweet ought to be tasted', and 'this is sweet', in the sense of being one of the particular sweet things, the man who can act and is not prevented must at the same time actually act accordingly). When, then, the universal opinion is present in us forbidding us to taste, and there is also the opinion that 'everything sweet is pleasant', and that 'this is sweet' (now this is the opinion that is active),[9] and when appetite happens to be present in us, the opinion bids us avoid the object, but appetite leads us towards it (for it can move each of our bodily parts); so that it turns out that a man behaves incontinently under the influence (in a sense) of a rule and on opinion, and of one not contrary in itself, but only incidentally – for the appetite is contrary, not the opinion – to the right rule. It also follows that this is the reason why the lower animals are not incontinent, viz. because they have no universal judgement but only imagination and memory of particulars.

The explanation of how the ignorance is dissolved and the incontinent man regains his knowledge is the same as in the case of a man drunk or asleep and is not peculiar to this condition; we must go to the students of natural science for it. Now, the last premiss being an opinion about a perceptible object, and being also what determines our actions, this a man either has not when he is in the state of passion, or has it in the sense in which having knowledge did not mean knowing but only talking as a drunken man may mutter the verses of Empedocles. And because the last term is not universal nor equally an object of scientific knowledge with the universal term, the position that Socrates sought to establish actually seems to result; for it is not in the presence of what is thought to be knowledge proper that the affection of incontinence arises (nor is it this that is 'dragged about' as a result of the state of passion), but in that of perceptual knowledge.[10]

This must suffice as our answer to the question of action with and without knowledge, and how it is possible to behave incontinently with knowledge.

IV Aristotle on moral weakness

W. F. R. Hardie

In book vii of the *Nicomachean Ethics* Aristotle, making a fresh start (1145 a15 ff.; p. 63 above),[1] distinguishes three kinds of 'moral states to be avoided': vice, incontinence (*akrasia*), and brutishness (*thēriotēs*). The opposed good states are virtue, continence (*enkrateia*), and superhuman virtue. The difference between continence and the vice of the self-indulgent man, are stated as follows in ch. 9.

> both the continent man and the temperate man are such as to do nothing contrary to the rule for the sake of the bodily pleasures, but the former has and the latter has not bad appetites, and the latter is such as not to feel pleasure contrary to the rule, while the former is such as to feel pleasure but not to be led by it. And the incontinent and the self-indulgent man are also like one another; they are different, but both pursue bodily pleasures – the latter, however, also thinking that he ought to do so, while the former does not think this (1151 b34–1152 a6).

The virtuous man, then, is described as having no bad desires; he feels no desires or emotions either more or less than he should. It is not easy to see what additional moral stature could make a man more than virtuous, more than a man. Has not Aristotle said that 'with regard to what is best' virtue itself is an extreme? (1107 a6–8). It is not surprising that Aristotle has nothing to tell us about heroic virtue. Its opposite, brutishness or bestiality, may be either inborn or a consequence of disease. 'The man who is by nature apt to fear everything, even the squeak of a mouse, is cowardly with a brutish cowardice, while the man who feared a weasel did so in consequence of disease' (1149 a7–9). Corresponding to the brutish and morbid forms of vice there are also brutish and morbid forms of incontinence: There are people who yield to such desires or impulses knowing them to be wrong (1149 a16–20).

At the beginning of his ch. 3 (p. 66 above) Aristotle says that there are two main topics to be considered: a problem or problems concerning the analysis of incontinence, and a problem or problems

concerning its sphere. Aristotle's main concern is with the problem
of analysis, 'whether incontinent people act knowingly or not, and
in what sense knowingly' (1146 b8–9). Aristotle discusses the problem of analysis as if it were primarily a question about the conduct
of men who, although knowing better, indulge bodily desires. But, in
asking and answering his question about the sphere of incontinence,
he recognises implicitly that the problem has a wider scope. He asks
'with what sorts of object the incontinent and the continent man
may be said to be concerned (i.e. whether with any and every
pleasure and pain or with certain determinate kinds), and whether
the continent man (enkratēs) and the man of endurance (karterikos)
are the same or different' (1146 b9–13). To take the second point
first, Aristotle elucidates the difference between continence and
endurance at the beginning of ch. 7: the continent man overcomes,
the incontinent fails to overcome, the temptations of pleasure; the
man of endurance holds out, the soft man (malakos) fails to hold out,
against pain (1150 a13–15). It seems plain that these are different
types, and that Aristotle thinks so: a hardy man might be incontinent, a continent man might be soft. The question about the sphere
of incontinence is reformulated by Aristotle at the beginning of ch. 4:
'whether there is anyone who is incontinent without qualification,
or all men who are incontinent are so in a particular sense, and if
there is, with what sort of objects he is concerned' (1147 b220–1).
Aristotle's answer to this question is based on the following classifi-
cation of pleasures: (1) The bodily pleasures, those connected with
food and sex, which are 'necessary' – these are the pleasures with
which temperance (sōphrosunē) and intemperance (akolasia) are by
definition concerned (b23–8); (2) pleasures which are not necessary
but 'are worthy of choice in themselves but admit of excess', e.g.
'victory, honour, wealth, and good and pleasant things of this sort'
(b29–31); (3) to these two classes of pleasures Aristotle adds a third
in ch. 5, bestial and morbid pleasures which are not naturally felt
as pleasant but can be so felt as a consequence of mutilation, bad
habits, or natures originally bad (1148 b17 ff.). Aristotle's answer
to his question is that unqualified incontinence is concerned with
pleasures of the first class. This conclusion is stated at the end of
ch. 5: 'that continence and incontinence, then, are concerned only
with the same objects as self-indulgence and temperance and that
what is concerned with other objects is a type distinct from incontinence, and called incontinence by a metaphor and not simply, is
plain' (1149 a21–4). Aristotle goes on to argue in ch. 6 that 'incontinence in respect of anger is less disgraceful than that in
respect of the appetites'. In the final section (§7) of ch. 6 he main-

tains that 'brutishness is a lesser evil than vice, although it is more
terrifying; for it is not that the better part has been perverted . . .
they *have* no better part'. 'A bad man will do ten thousand times as
much evil as a brute' (1150 a7–8).

Aristotle's treatment of the scope of incontinence is liable to
strike us as perverse. He seems to be trying, somewhat arbitrarily,
to narrow the scope of the term, restricting the problem as if it
concerned only carnal appetites and pleasures. Surely what he ought
to insist on is that the concept has application to any impulse or
desire or emotion which is liable, by inappropriateness or again by its
excess or defect, to conflict with a man's understanding of what is
right and good. There are two points to be made in answer to this
criticism. The first is that Aristotle's restriction of the term is not
arbitrary but an expression of his conviction that the apparent facts
should be handled with care and delicacy. In ch. 1 he makes the
following important statement on method: 'We must, as in all other
cases, set the observed facts [*ta phainomena* – I quote the Oxford
translation] before us and, after first discussing the difficulties, go on
to prove, if possible, the truth of all the common opinions about these
affections of the mind, or, failing this, of the greater number and
the most authoritative; for if we both refute the objections and leave
the common opinions undisturbed, we shall have proved the case
sufficiently' (1145 b2–7; pp. 63–4 above). Among the 'phenomena'
to be considered is the fact that we are prepared to apply the term
akrasia simply to those who are induced by carnal desires to stray
from their chosen paths, to apply it only in a qualified sense, by a
conscious extension or metaphor, to those led astray by desires of
other kinds. We add the qualification 'in respect of this or that',
e.g. anger (1148 a10). Somewhat similarly there is a use in English
of 'immoral' in which the word refers exclusively to sexual ir-
regularity. Such facts may or may not be significant, and may be
significant in different degrees. But, on Aristotle's principles, we
should assume that they are significant unless they are shown not
to be. The second point to make is that Aristotle does not say, or
suggest, that the problems raised by incontinent behaviour are confined to *akrasia* in its proper or unqualified sense. In particular, the
questions whether, and in what sense, the incontinent man acts
against 'knowledge' may be asked about all kinds of *akrasia*, even
including the *akrasia* which is a fault (*hamartia*) rather than a vice
(*kakia*) (1148 a3). Presumably the answer which is good for *akrasia*
in its unqualified sense will be good also, *mutatis mutandis*, for other
varieties.

But Aristotle's treatment of unqualified *akrasia* has incurred a further criticism to which there is, perhaps, no satisfactory answer. It is said that he presents too crude and simple a view of the temptations which spring from bodily appetites. He insists on their power to knock a man off his balance, to drive him out of his right mind. The incontinent man is like one who is asleep or mad or drunk (1147 a17–18; p. 67 above). But, in the life of a being capable of complex social and intellectual enjoyments, these appetites rarely operate alone; the threat to virtue comes not so much from their intensity as from their fusion with more subtle satisfactions. I quote from T. H. Green:

> The conflict of the moral life would be a much simpler affair than it is if it were mainly fought over those bodily pleasures in dealing with which, according to Aristotle, the qualities of continence and incontinence are exhibited. The most formidable forces which right reason has to subdue or render contributory to some 'true good' of man are passions of which reason is in a certain sense itself the parent. They are passions which the animals know not, because they are excited by the conditions of distinctively human society. They relate to objects which only the intercourse of self-conscious agents can bring into existence. This is often true of passions which on first thoughts we might be inclined to reckon merely animal appetites. The drunkard probably drinks, as a rule, not for the pleasure of drinking, but to drown pains or win pleasures – pains, for instance, of self-reproach, pleasures of a quickened fancy or of a sense of good fellowship – of which only the thinking man is capable.
>
> (*Prolegomena to Ethics*, § 126)

I turn now to Aristotle's central problem (*aporia*) about incontinence. The problem is formulated at the beginning of ch. 2. The first part of this chapter contains a preliminary discussion of the question, and some answers to it are rejected as inadequate. The problem is reformulated at the beginning of ch. 3, and what the chapter contains is prima facie an exposition by Aristotle, in a series of stages, of his own solution. But we must not assume that this is what the chapter does contain. For Cook Wilson, whose opinion has much weight, maintained that the chapter as it stands is not a continuous discourse but a conflation of at least two similar versions.[2] Moreover, Cook Wilson's thesis, as he stated it in 1879, was that neither component of the chapter can have been written by Aristotle, if Aristotle is the author of the rest of ch. vii of the *Nicomachean Ethics* (EN), and of the *Eudemian Ethics* (EE). His

reason for holding this view was that, whereas Aristotle clearly believed that men do act in ways which they know at the time of acting to be wrong, the solution reached in ch. 3 asserts or implies that
Socrates was right when he said that this could not happen. In the
1912 postscript Cook Wilson adhered to the view that two parallel
versions are conflated in EN vii. 3, but was doubtful about the
adequacy of his reasons for having denied that Aristotle wrote
them. He was led to this change of view by reflection on modern
writings of known authorship. This convinced him 'that the possibilities of incoherence are not merely greater than what I may
have thought when I wrote this study of EN vii, but far beyond
what is usually admitted in contemporary criticism (pp. 88, 89).
But he still thought that the doctrine of the chapter should never
have been held by Aristotle and that it is inconsistent with 'everything else relevant' in his writings. 'It is a question of degree; and
while, in face of the facts I have observed, I would not say the
thing is impossible, I do not find it easy to credit Aristotle with so
grave a lapse as this' (p. 90). Cook Wilson is not alone in finding
incoherence in Aristotle's treatment, as it has come down to us, of
this subject. Ross complains that Aristotle's 'formal theory' fails to
recognise the fact, of which he elsewhere shows himself to be aware,
that 'incontinence is due not to failure of knowledge, but to weakness of will' (*Aristotle*, p. 244). It is clear that there is a formidable
case for this criticism. I think that there is some incoherence, as
well as much that is illuminating and suggestive, in Aristotle's discussion. But the difficulty has been exacerbated, mis-stated if not
over-stated, as the result of a failure to notice the precise terms in
which the problem is formulated by Aristotle. The misunderstanding
to which I refer has arisen in fact as a consequence of a mistransla-
tion of the first sentence of ch. 2 and a translation which is at least
highly questionable of the fourth sentence of the chapter. Our first
task, then, is to look closely at Aristotle's formulation of the
problem.

The problem is set, as Aristotle implies in the passage on method
already quoted (1145 b2–7), by the contradictory opposition of
two strongly supported opinions (*endoxa*): on the one hand, the
universally held view that men do in fact sometimes perform
actions which they know to be wrong and do not perform actions
which they know to be required; on the other hand the denial,
attributed to Socrates, that this could happen. 'For Socrates was
entirely opposed to the view in question, holding that there is no
such thing as incontinence; no one, he said, when he judges acts
against what he judges best – people act so only by reason of

ignorance' (1145 b25–7). The view which Socrates rejected is
implicit in the meaning of *akrasia* as ordinarily understood. 'The
incontinent man, knowing that what he does is bad, does it as a
result of passion, while the continent man, knowing that his
appetites are bad, refuses on account of his rational principle to
follow them' (1145 b12–14). Similar descriptions of the phenomenon, none of them conveying any doubts about their own
accuracy, are given by Aristotle in other passages in the EN and in
the *De Anima*.[3] Such passages made it seem obvious to Cook
Wilson and Ross that Aristotle was not himself in any doubt about
the occurrence of an 'active struggle' (Cook Wilson) between
reason and desire in which reason might be the loser. The passage
which supports this most strongly is, perhaps, the one in EN vii. 7 in
which Aristotle distinguishes two kinds of incontinence:

> Of incontinence one kind is impetuosity (*propeteia*), another
> weakness (*astheneia*). For some men after deliberating fail,
> owing to their emotion, to stand by the conclusions of their
> deliberation, others because they have not deliberated are led by
> their emotion; since some men (just as people who first tickle
> others are not tickled themselves), if they have first perceived
> and seen what is coming and have first roused themselves and
> their calculative faculty, are not defeated by their emotion,
> whether it be pleasant or painful (1150 b19–25).

It seems clear that, if there are facts which these sentences describe
with complete accuracy, then Socrates is wrong and the assumptions or convictions which he rejected are correct.

But does not Aristotle *say* that Socrates was wrong, and obviously
wrong? The words in the text which immediately follow the statement, quoted above, of the Socratic view are translated as follows by
Ross: 'Now this view plainly contradicts the observed facts . . .'
(*amphisbētei tois phainomenois enargōs*) (1145 b27–8). Most of the
commentators offer a similar rendering of 'phenomena' or else
straddle, as the Greek term can, between observed facts and
accepted opinions. The question has helpfully been brought to a
head in an article by G. E. L. Owen.[4] He points out that, while
there are passages in which *phainomena* seems to mean 'facts' or
'empirical observations', it can hardly have this meaning in 1145 b3.
Moreover Ross's rendering in 1145 b28 ('the observed facts') makes
the whole sentence inconsequent. For the sentence continues: '. . .
and we must inquire about what happens to such a man; if he acts
by reason of ignorance, what is the manner of his ignorance?' But,

if it is false that we act 'by reason of ignorance', the question what kind of ignorance it is cannot arise. Yet Aristotle is apparently here willing to consider the possibility that conduct of the kind which would conventionally be described as sinning against knowledge might be due to some kind of ignorance. Finally the solution actually offered in ch. 3 involves attributing to the incontinent man ignorance of a kind, although not ignorance of moral principles (1147 b6–17; p. 68 above). Owen draws the following conclusion from his examination of the passage (1145 b27–9): 'So Socrates' claim conflicts not with the facts but with what would commonly be said on the subject, and Aristotle does not undertake to save everything that is commonly said' (p. 86).

In order to make good Owen's interpretation of the passage, with which I agree, it is not, I think, *necessary* to reject Ross's translation of 'phenomena' in 1145 b28 as 'observed facts'. For there are different 'facts' with which the view of Socrates might be held to conflict. Some would claim to refute the view by saying that in fact men do wrong actions in full awareness that they are wrong. But a less drastic criticism of the view might be that, as stated by Socrates or one of his followers, the view conflicted with the fact that there are cases or stretches of human conduct which it is natural to describe, even if mistakenly, as acting wrongly against knowledge and which in fact are so described. It is convenient to use the expression 'ostensible incontinence' as an abbreviation of what I have just said. The Socratic doctrine is a direct denial that incontinence occurs . . . *hōs ouk ousēs akrasias* (1145 b25–6). But, as stated, it is inconsistent even with ostensible incontinence. In order to make it consistent it would be necessary to answer the question what manner of ignorance is involved, and this would be an amending qualification of the doctrine as first stated. I must make it clear that what I am considering at present is Aristotle's *formulation* of the problem concerning incontinence. I am not saying anything on the question whether Aristotle believes, or says that he believes, that all incontinence is merely ostensible and not actually, in a strict sense, what it seems or purports to be. Our present question is about Aristotle's question, not about his answer.

We are now in a position to see why it is necessary to reject a widely accepted translation and interpretation of Aristotle's formulation of his problem in the first sentence of ch. 2. I take this to mean that there is a problem about the sense in which the man who acts incontinently has 'right understanding'. I agree with the rendering by D. P. Chase in the Everyman Translation: 'Now a man may raise a question as to the nature of the right conception in violation of which a man fails of self-control.' For Aristotle proceeds to consider whether the understanding is in the form of knowledge (*epistēmē*), opinion (*doxa*), or prudence (*phronēsis*); three possible varieties of understanding according to the *De Anima* (Γ3, 427 b24–6). The interpretation is confirmed by the fact that, at the beginning of ch. 3, the problem is reformulated as 'whether incontinent people act knowingly or not, and in what sense knowingly' (1146 b8–9). In ch. 2 also, as we have seen, Aristotle is prepared to *consider* the possibility that incontinence is only ostensible, that the incontinent man understands that what he is doing is wrong only in some more or less Pickwickian sense of 'understands'. And yet both Cook Wilson and Ross, as well as other scholars, understand the first sentence of ch. 2 in a way which makes Aristotle imply, inconsistently with what he goes on to say, that incontinence is certainly real and not merely ostensible. According to Cook Wilson, the question at issue is 'How is it that a man knowing the right can do the wrong?' (*Aristotelian Studies*, pp. 48–9). Ross translates: 'Now we may ask how a man who judges rightly can behave incontinently.' According to this formulation, there is no puzzle as to whether, or in what sense, the incontinent man knows what is right. The only puzzle is as to how, having this knowledge, he can go wrong. As we have seen, both Cook Wilson and Ross are perplexed by the fact that in ch. 3 Aristotle seems to end by defending a solution which partially vindicates the view of Socrates: 'the position that Socrates sought to establish actually seems to result' (1147 b14–15). I suggest that a factor in this preplexity is their misunderstanding of Aristotle's formulation of the problem at the beginning of ch. 2. I do not, of course, mean that there is no other evidence suggesting that Aristotle agreed with the popular view, rejected by Socrates, that the incontinent man knows very well that what he is doing is wrong. Indeed we have already seen that there is such evidence, although we have kept open the question whether it is decisive. But I propose to take it as certain that Aristotle does not, from the start, so formulate the question as to beg it against Socrates.

It seemed evident to Cook Wilson, and has seemed evident to many philosophers as well as to commentators on Aristotle, that the Socratic view 'plainly contradicts the observed facts'. To the question how these facts are known the answer would be that we find them when we look into ourselves: we can observe in ourselves the 'active struggle' between our knowledge of principles and our desires; we can catch ourselves in the act of following the worse when we see the better course. Now this contention is certainly plausible, and perhaps in the end its correctness can be vindicated and accepted with confidence. In the end but not at the beginning. The victory is too easy; too easy certainly to have satisfied Aristotle, or to satisfy any contemporary philosopher. Before we go on to try to follow Aristotle's discussion in detail it may be helpful to take a quick look at some considerations which would naturally incline Aristotle to shrink from flatly contradicting the Socratic doctrine, and to take seriously the question in what sense the incontinent man knows, or is convinced, when he acts or refrains from acting, that he is wrong.

Knowledge or judgement about what it is right and wrong to do differs from knowledge or judgement on matters of historical or scientific fact in ways which can tempt plain men, as well as philosophers, to say that a man cannot really know, cannot sincerely judge, that an action is right and not do it, or that it is wrong and do it. The man who, while professing principles of moderation, drinks or smokes too much does not *know* how to behave. The very fact that he goes wrong betrays lack of *sincerity* in his conviction of right. Is it then *logically* impossible that a man who knows how to behave should misbehave? If a man who is doing wrong says that he is doing wrong, is he insincere by the *definition* of sincerity? R. M. Hare, in *The Language of Morals*, propounds stipulative definitions which would make it 'analytic to say that everyone always does what he thinks he ought to (in the evaluative sense)' (p. 98 below). For he proposes 'to say that the test whether someone is using the judgement "I ought to do X" as a value-judgement or not is "Does he or does he not recognise that, if he assents to the judgement, he must also assent to the command 'Let me do X'?"' And Hare has said earlier that it is logically impossible to assent to a command and at the same time disobey it: sincerely assenting involves doing something (pp. 97–8 below). We cannot, indeed, as Hare would agree, make the Socratic paradox more acceptable *merely* by passing linguistic legislation, merely by choosing to define the 'sincerity' of belief in terms of practical conformity and thus making it impossible to *say* that the paradox is false. But the point to notice here is that there is something about 'value-judgements', their 'prescriptive' character, which makes it tempting to represent the contradictory of the Socratic view as not false, but absurd.

Does Aristotle show any inclination to yield to such a temptation? Plainly yes, in so far as he defines wisdom concerning practice as wisdom which is practical. If there is such a thing as acting

contrary to our better judgement, it would be natural to suppose that
the judgement involved was the faculty, *phronēsis*, of knowing
right from wrong in matters of conduct. Yet in ch. 2 this supposition
is dismissed as (logically) absurd.

> Is it then *phronēsis* whose resistance is mastered? That is the
> strongest of all states. But this is absurd (*atopon*); the same man
> will be at once practically wise and incontinent, but no one
> would say that it is the part of a practically wise man to do
> willingly the basest acts. Besides it has been shown before that the
> man of practical wisdom is one who will act (1140 b4–6, 1141
> b21); for he is a man concerned with individual facts (1141 b16,
> 1142 a24) and who has the other virtues (1144 b30–1145 a2, 1146
> a4–9).

If *phronēsis* is essentially practical, it is logically impossible for a
wise man to be incontinent. The doctrine is difficult, but discussion
of the difficulties is proper to a commentary on bk vi rather than
bk vii. But when we come to ch. 3 of bk vii, we shall have to consider a striking, if perhaps cryptic and unacceptable, expression of
the doctrine in the passage where Aristotle seems to say that what
in practical thinking corresponds to a conclusion in theoretical
thinking is an action (1147 a26–8; p. 68 above). If so, then it would
again be 'absurd' to suggest that we could act against a conclusion
of our practical thinking.

It is suggested, then, that there is a general difficulty about
holding that a practical principle can be understood and accepted
without being put into practice. The general difficulty would naturally take different forms in relation to different systems of moral
principles. For Aristotle the supreme principle is that a man
should seek his natural end, the highest form of happiness (*eudai-
monia*) of which he is capable. In its application to this principle the
Socratic doctrine would be that, if a man truly understands, or
judges rationally, that some course of action will be for his happiness, he will inevitably take it; if he does not, this can be due only
to lack of understanding, to ignorance. It may occur to him that
some other action will bring him immediate, or at least earlier,
gratification or enjoyment. But *ex hupothesei* he is convinced that, if
he lets this go, he will secure something better. It may occur to
him that the immediate enjoyment is a bird in the hand; his
calculation concerning his own future welfare may go wrong; he
may not survive to enjoy the fruits of his own righteousness or
prudence. But, again *ex hupothesei*, in making his original assess-

ment of what is best for him to do, due account has been taken of these considerations. How then can he go wrong, unless something happens which blinds, or at least dims, his moral vision?

This line of thought can be formulated in terms of Aristotle's account of the thought which leads to action. Aristotle has tried to show, in his treatment of practical wisdom in bk vi, that there is inevitably a close connection between correctness of understanding in practical matters and rightness of desire. We needs must love the highest when we see it. The man of practical wisdom has an under-'standing of the end which he wishes to achieve as well as the ability to make plans for achieving it (vi. 9, 1142 b31–3). There is a parallel between practical wisdom and theoretical wisdom, the excellences of the two intelligent parts of the soul (2, 1139 b12–13). It is proper to the theorist not only to deduce conclusions from premisses supplied to him but also to grasp intuitively the first principles from which, in the theoretical sciences, deduction starts (7, 1141 a17–20). In the practical science of politics (8, 1141 b23–33) the definition of the end corresponds to the first principles in the theoretical sciences (12, 1144 a31–6). The end envisaged by the wise man is the object of wish (*boulēsis*, iii. 5 1113 b3–4), a species of desire, and moves to action because, in being understood, it is also desired. If we are not good enough to desire it, we shall not be intelligent enough to grasp it. 'For wickedness perverts us and causes us to be deceived about the starting-points of action. Therefore it is evident it is impossible to be practically wise without being good' (12, 1144 a34–b1). On the basis of these conclusions Aristotle thinks, as we have seen, that he can refute in six lines the suggestion that a man could act incontinently if he had understood what he was doing in the sense in which the man of practical wisdom understands (vii. 2, 1146 a4–9).

We must now follow the course of the discussion in chs. 2 and 3 of bk vii. James J. Walsh, who has written a book of two hundred pages on Aristotle's analysis of *akrasia*,[5] draws 'a distinction between narrowly contextual and broadly integrative interpretations, according to whether or not the analysis should be taken as a whole and related to wider issues in Aristotle's philosophy' (p. 118). What I have so far tried to show, on the basis of considerations of the kind which Walsh calls 'integrative', is that it would be a mistake to start an examination of Aristotle's treatment of the subject with the assumption that he sets out primarily to refute the Socratic denial of the reality of *akrasia*. Aristotle, on the contrary, is anxious to open the proceedings in a strictly neutral way, and some eminent scholars, especially Cook Wilson, have failed to see this. It would

be surprising, in view of the conflicts of opinion noted by Walsh on
the interpretation of Aristotle's doctrine, if a 'contextual interpretation' of ch. 3 could demonstrate that the outcome of Aristotle's
discussion is decisively either for or against the Socratic denial. Our
aim can be only to get as clear as possible on the meaning of what
is said, and hence to limit as closely as possible the range of legitimate disagreement on the interpretation of the doctrine.

The first part (1145 b21–1146 a9) of ch. 2 contains, as we saw
earlier, a preliminary discussion of the question in what sense of
'understanding' the incontinent man understands, if he does understand, that what he is doing is wrong. In ch. 3, prima facie, Aristotle
expounds his own solution in a series of stages, but we have to keep
in mind the possibility that the chapter is an editor's conflation of
two parallel versions. The discussion in ch. 2 is based on the division
of 'understanding' (*hupolēpsis*) into three specific forms; knowledge (*epistēmē*), opinion (*doxa*), and practical reason (*phronēsis*).[6]
Three different possible interpretations of *akrasia* correspond to
these three kinds of understanding.

On the suggestion that the incontinent man acts against knowledge Aristotle remarks that some agree with Socrates that it would
be shocking if knowledge were 'overcome and dragged about like
a slave' by appetite (1145 b22–4). On the other hand Socrates' unqualified denial of *akrasia* conflicts with the apparent facts (1145
b27–8). We have already discussed the interpretation of this remark.
At the end of ch. 3 Aristotle says that in a sense Socrates seems to
have been right after all. He was right because the knowledge
against which the incontinent man acts is not 'knowledge proper'
but perceptual knowledge. The meaning of this difficult and (it
seems) textually corrupt passage will be discussed when we come
to it.

In the next section of ch. 2 (1145 b31–1146 a4), and again in
ch. 3 (1146 b24–31), Aristotle considers the suggestion that, while
Socrates was right to deny that a man could yield to desire if he
knew that it was wrong to do so, he might yield if his intellectual
state were not knowledge but belief or opinion. The section of ch. 3
is repetitive, but not so much so as to make it necessary to accept
Cook Wilson's view that it is a conflation of two versions. Taken
together the discussions of the suggestion in the two chapters pose
a dilemma. In ch. 2 Aristotle takes *doxa* (opinion) as being a judgement more tentative and less assured (*ēremaia*) than that of knowledge (1146 a1). But, on this interpretation, *akrasia* would be
excusable and not, as it is, blameworthy. In ch. 3 he remarks that
doxa (belief), although not knowledge, may be held with the same

degree of conviction, or the same absence of doubt, as in the case of Heraclitus. The apparent fact of *akrasia* is not made easier to accept at its face value by the substitution of belief in this sense for knowledge.

We need not understand Aristotle as implying here that the distinction between knowledge and belief makes no contribution to the understanding of the facts about ostensible *akrasia*. One of the horns of the dilemma might be grasped. It may be true that when we are not quite sure, but are of the opinion, that what we are doing is wrong, the wrongdoing is excusable. Perhaps incontinent behaviour often is excusable. Who is not ready to think this of his own *akrasia*? But the excuse cannot be made in all cases. Sometimes no doubt is entertained. If so, the problem is still on our hands even if its scope is diminished.

In the next section of ch. 2 (1146 a4–9), a passage we have already considered, Aristotle rejects as absurd the suggestion that the incontinent man acts against practical wisdom (*phronēsis*). For the same man would then be incontinent and practically wise. Besides, 'it has been shown that the man of practical wisdom is one who will *act*; for he is a man concerned with individual facts, and who has the other virtues'. We might express Aristotle's doctrine here by saying that practical wisdom necessarily involves commitment, and that an incontinent man could not count as committed to right conduct.

Aristotle's next suggestion (1146 b31–5) is that the solution of the problem might be found in the distinction between two senses in which a man may be said to 'know' something; the sense in which the geometer knows the theorem of Pythagoras when he is not thinking about geometry and the sense in which he can be said to know it only when he is actively engaged in proving it to himself or someone else. It will 'make a difference whether, when a man does what he should not, he has the knowledge but is not exercising it, or *is* exercising it; for the latter seems strange but not the former' (1146 b33–5). The distinction which Aristotle is here applying to the problem of incontinence, the question in what sense the incontinent man understands or knows, is the distinction, familiar and fundamental in his philosophy, between a capacity or potentiality, which may or may not be a state acquired by training or learning, and the actualisation, or actual exercise, of such a capacity. Aristotle here speaks of 'having' knowledge and 'using' it, and elucidates 'use' in terms of 'contemplation'. When he speaks of 'use' he means not the application of knowledge in practice but the exercise of dispositional knowledge in actual thinking.

Aristotle does not say at this point whether, in his view, the distinction between dispositional knowledge and activated knowledge solves, or contributes to solving, his problem. He goes on immediately to propound a new and more complex solution in which the distinction plays a part. The natural inference is that the distinction, even if it contributes something, does not, in Aristotle's view, solve the problem. Why not? In terms of our preceding discussion the reason must be that the distinction does not by itself account for, or 'save', the fact of ostensible *akrasia*; at least the form of *akrasia* which Aristotle calls 'weakness' (*astheneia*) as opposed to the impetuosity (*propeteia*) (7, 1150 b19–28). If the whole of the knowledge to which the incontinent man failed to conform were throughout only dispositional, he would not even be tempted to describe his own conduct as open-eyed wrongdoing or failure to do what he knew to be right. He might deplore his own blindness or amnesia, but his conduct would not even be ostensibly akratic.

Richard Robinson, in his essay, 'L'acrasie, selon Aristote',[7] expresses the opinion that Aristotle regards the distinction between potential and actual knowledge as solving his problem: the distinction 'contains virtually all that is needed for the explanation of *akrasia*' (p. 263). But Robinson does not overlook the objection that, if so, Aristotle would not be able, any more than Socrates, to account for ostensible *akrasia*. In effect he gives his answer when he remarks that there is an important difference between the position of Aristotle and that of Socrates: Aristotle recognised that, in the unfolding of a situation terminating in *akrasia*, the state of knowledge might change significantly. Thus the *akratēs*, before and after his lapse, might know perfectly well the nature of his act but not at the actual moment of commission (p. 265). Similarly Robinson attributes to Aristotle the view that the weak man, 'l'acratique faible', knows as the result of deliberation that the action which he is tempted to do is wrong, but actually does it at a time, 'pendant quelques instants', when passion has driven the knowledge from his mind (p. 274). If it is the case that the knowledge which is merely potential when *akrasia* occurs is actual at other times, this would indeed help to account for the belief that ostensible *akrasia* is not merely ostensible. But it does not answer the objection, urged by Ross against Aristotle, which Robinson is discussing when he offers his interpretation of 'l'acrasie faible'. Ross objects that Aristotle explains away the moral struggle, but that his explanation presupposes that it occurs at an earlier stage. 'And the account which explains how the wrong can be done in the absence of this knowledge cannot explain how the knowledge has come to be absent' (*Aristotle*, p. 224). We shall have to consider whether the further development of Aristotle's view in ch. 3 suggests that he anticipated this objection, and, if he did, how he would answer it. The fact that, if Aristotle held the view which Robinson attributes to him, he would have been open to criticism does not show that Robinson is wrong in attributing it to him. But I think that Walsh is justified in complaining that Robinson does not seem to notice the difficulty, and does not discuss it. 'Unfortunately, Robinson does not consider the condition of the morally weak man while one of his premisses is being driven out. Presumably he is in some state of conflict' (p. 120).

So far Aristotle has spoken of knowing what is better or best without saying precisely what it is that a man who has such knowledge knows. In the next section (1146 b35–1147 a10; p. 67 above) he offers as an analysis, or partial analysis, of such knowledge the doctrine of the practical syllogism. Aristotle reintroduces this doctrine, after a section on another aspect of the problem (1147 a10–14), in the section which begins at 1147 a24.

Two kinds of premiss (*protasis*), universal and particular, are involved in knowledge of what it is right to do. The universal premiss is a rule stating that everything of a certain sort is good; the particular premiss states that here is something of that sort.[8] Aristotle suggests that the incontinent man 'uses', i.e. actively contemplates, the universal premiss but not the particular. Without pausing to examine this suggestion he proceeds to refine it. The universal premiss contains both a personal reference to the agent and an impersonal reference to the object or the act; e.g. 'for every man dry food is expedient'. The elaboration of this example is complicated, if the text is sound, by the mention of an intermediate premiss, 'such and such food is dry'. But the suggestion which emerges from the example is clear: it is that the syllogism, or sorites, of action is complete, and actively known, with the exception of the particular, or singular, premiss in its reference to the action or thing as opposed to the agent; at this point the knowledge of the incontinent man is at most potential – 'but whether this food is such and such, of this the incontinent man either has not or is not exercising the knowledge' (1147 a7). The incontinent man fails to recognise the application of the rule in its impersonal reference.

This suggestion, considered as an attempt to save the phenomena of ostensible *akrasia*, is an advance on the preceding solution which relied exclusively on the distinction between dispositional and activated knowing. For, if certain parts of the thinking proper to the virtuous man are actual and not merely potential, this will help to account for the fact that akratic conduct looks, or feels, like acting against knowledge, or is remembered as acting against knowledge, even if, at the moment of action, there is no actual knowledge that the action is wrong.

The solution offered in this section (1146 b35–1147 a10), that the incontinent man does not realise the truth of the minor premiss, raises questions about the location of incontinence in relation to the distinction between the voluntary and the involuntary which Aristotle has elaborated in bk iii. Ross points out that, according to the doctrine of bk iii (1110 b31–1111 a24), an action which is due to ignorance of particular fact is involuntary (*Aristotle*, p. 223). The incontinent man gratifies his desire voluntarily, although his action does not spring from deliberate choice. But an action which is voluntary considered in terms of one description may be involuntary in relation to another. For, when A voluntarily gives B a drink, he may be poisoning him involuntarily. Thus Aristotle might say that, considered as a case of wrongdoing, the incontinent act is involuntary. But Ross points out that, in the terminology of bk iii, the incontinent action is done not through ignorance but rather in ignorance. 'Acting by reason of ignorance seems also to be different from acting *in* ignorance; for the man who is drunk or in a rage is thought to act as a result not of ignorance but of one of the causes mentioned, yet not knowingly but in ignorance' (1110 b24–7). It is clearly true, if we follow the analysis of this section, that the incontinent man is ignorant when he acts, and the fuller analysis which follows shows that he is responsible for his ignorance as a man whose ignorance is due to drink or anger is responsible. Reginald Jackson argues against Ross that incontinence is not action in ignorance on the ground that the ignorance involved is ignorance of the minor premiss.[9] But Aristotle does not say that the description 'acting in ignorance' is applicable only when the ignorance is ignorance of principles. He implies that he has in mind also ignorance of fact. As Walsh remarks, 'a drunken man is as responsible for his inability to tell pumice from granite as he is for his inability to remember that it is wrong to throw rocks at people' (p. 116). But, if Ross is right in saying that Aristotle here represents the incontinent man as acting in ignorance, this does not mean that there are not important differences between acting in ignorance in the kind of circumstances Aristotle has in mind in bk iii and incontinence. Thus the man who, because he is drunk, fails to notice that a gun is loaded would not, if he knew this fact, have any inclination to fire the gun. But the incontinent man, if he realised the consequences of drinking, would still feel a desire to drink. What is peculiar to his case, as we are to see, is that he is distracted between two different principles of action.

One further comment is appropriate at this stage. Why does Aristotle not consider, or even mention, the possibility of a failure to know effectively the universal premiss? If passion can confuse and darken the mind, make us liable to wishful thinking, we should expect the tendency to show itself in connection with either premiss. And the facts seem to confirm this expectation. The man taking a drink too many may persuade himself that the extra one will not be harmful to his digestion. But he may also lapse into thinking that it is not wrong to incur a hangover once a year. Sidgwick suggests that in the case of anger, it sometimes happens that 'the rule is simply forgotten for a time, just as a matter of fact might be'.[10] Aristotle ought perhaps to recognise that the *akratēs* may fail to 'use', actively to contemplate, either the particular premiss or the universal principle.

Aristotle now goes on to distinguish different kinds of dispositional knowledge (1147 a10–24). The man who is asleep or mad or drunk 'has' knowledge in one way but in another not: his knowledge is not on tap until he wakes up, or recovers his sanity or sobriety. It is not always possible to activate a formed disposition at a moment's notice: 'a sleeping geometer is at a further remove than one who is awake, and a waking one than one who is busy at his studies' (*De Generatione Animalium*, 735 a9–11). Aristotle adds that anger and physical appetite produce changes in the body similar to the changes involved in these states; they even make men mad. The condition of the *akratēs* is similar to these conditions. Aristotle next observes that ability to repeat moral maxims 'does not prove anything'. Men in these abnormal states may recite geometrical proofs or verses of Empedocles without, it is implied, knowing what they are saying. Two other examples are given of words used without understanding: the utterances of those who have 'just learned' something and the utterances of actors. The sequence of the argument in this section is not very clear or explicit, but I think that it is this. The drunken geometer, or the moral man drunk with passion, must first become sober before he is in a position to activate his dispositional knowledge. It would not be a valid objection to this, Aristotle is suggesting, to point out that, before he becomes sober, the geometer may recite a proof or the moral man repeat his maxim. The objection would be valid only if the hypothetical geometer and moral man knew what they were saying. So understood, the argument is consecutive. But I think that in this section Aristotle slides from the point from which he starts to a quite different point

without making the transition fully clear. He starts from the point
that a disposition may be more or less removed from actualisation.
He ends with the point that words may be used with less or more
understanding. Prima facie the second point may have more
relevance than the first to the main problem which he is considering
about *akrasia*.

'Again, we may also view the cause as follows with reference to
the facts of human nature' (1147 a24–5). What does Aristotle mean
by a 'physical' explanation, and to what does he oppose it? Burnet
quotes passages in which 'physical' (*phusikōs*) is opposed to 'logical' (*logikōs*).[11] The examination of a question is 'logical' if it makes
use of principles or distinctions which, like the distinction between
potential and actual, have applications to many different subjects.
The treatment of a topic is 'physical', at least if the topic falls within
physics, when it is in terms of principles proper and peculiar to the
topic treated. Joachim rightly points out that the phenomena of
akrasia, being occurrences in the embodied soul or besouled body of
a man, belong to the subject-matter of what Aristotle calls 'physical'
science. In the *Posterior Analytics* (A, 84 a7–9) 'logical' is opposed
to 'analytical', 'because the science in question is the science concerned with the facts of demonstrative knowledge'. When Aristotle
states here that the view he is about to expound is a 'physical' one,
he is implying that the earlier solutions were, indeed, inadequate but
not that they were on the wrong track. As Burnet remarks, the
earlier solutions 'have gradually prepared us for this one'. There is
no sharp contrast between the logical and the physical discussion,
but rather a step-by-step transition from the one to the other. It
should be noted that Robinson, while he does not dissent from the
generally accepted account of what Aristotle means by 'physical'
and 'logical', takes the view that the problem of *akrasia* is primarily
logical and that Aristotle, therefore, attaches relatively little importance to the psychological or psychophysical treatment of the
question (pp. 271, 272). But it is surely clear that, in the last part of
the chapter, Aristotle is offering an account which is a synthesis of
suggestions made earlier. Moreover, Joachim is surely right in saying
that the analysis of *akrasia* is a problem which is 'physical' in
Aristotle's sense.

The section starts from a recapitulation, and development, of the
doctrine of the practical syllogism. Two judgements are involved,
one which is universal and another which is concerned with the
particular facts and is in the sphere of perception (1147 a25–6).
'When a single judgement results from the two, the soul must in
one type of case affirm the conclusion, while in the case of judge-

ments concerned with production it must immediately act' (1147 a26–8). Aristotle proceeds to give an example of a syllogism issuing in action: 'if everything sweet ought to be tasted, and this is sweet, in the sense of being one of the particular sweet things, the man who can act and is not prevented must at the same time actually act accordingly' (1147 a29–31). This, as Ross points out, is the syllogism not of an incontinent (*akratēs*) but of a profligate man (*akolastos*). Aristotle proceeds immediately to a description of what happens in the incontinent man.

So far Aristotle has distinguished two kinds of syllogism, and has said that, in the case of both, the drawing of the conclusion follows necessarily when the premisses are apprehended together. The two kinds of syllogism resemble each other in having one universal premiss and one singular premiss. When the universal premiss is factual, the conclusion is a proposition which is believed. When the universal premiss is practical, the conclusion is an action which is done. We might expect Aristotle to say that, in the case of the practical syllogism, the drawing of the conclusion, 'here is something to be done', is necessary, and is necessarily followed by the action or the decision to act. But he does not in fact say that the conclusion and the action are distinct and inseparable; he does not distinguish them. It is natural to take Aristotle's insistence here on the necessity or inevitability of the conclusion as clinching the suggestion he has made already that the incontinent man does not know, in the sense of actively contemplating, both premisses. If he did have such knowledge he would not fail, as he does fail, to act. But this is a point on which we should still, at this stage, keep an open mind in view of two phrases in the sentences rendered in our preceding paragraph: 'When a single judgement results' (1147 a26–7) and 'not prevented' (1147 a30–1). Take the second phrase first. It is natural, and probably right, to take 'prevention' as referring only to external and physical interference: a man might not taste if his hand were seized or the cup dashed from his lips. But, if it could be said that an incontinent man might be 'prevented' from acting by his desire or passion, then it might be the case that he had fully grasped both premisses. But I can see nothing in the text to show that 'not prevented' is to be understood in so wide a sense. The reservation indicated by the other phrase, 'when a single judgement results', must, as we shall see shortly, be taken more seriously. What it suggests is that a man might have actual knowledge of both premisses and yet fail to draw the conclusion, theoretical or practical, because he did not 'put two and two together'. Some commentators, Joachim in particular,[12] have thought that this is what happens, according to

Aristotle, in *akrasia*. We shall have to say more about this interpretation in connection with the immediately following stage in
Aristotle's exposition.

'When, then, the universal judgement is present in us forbidding
us to taste, and there is also the judgement that everything sweet
is pleasant, and that this is sweet, and the latter opinion is active,
and when appetite happens to be present in us, the one judgement
bids us to avoid the object, but appetite leads us towards it; for it
can move each of our bodily parts' (1147 a31–5). The first difficulty
raised by this passage is that the last two lines, taken by themselves,
would suggest that the *akratēs* succumbs to passion with his eyes
open, knowing that the moral rule applies to the present situation.
Thus Burnet takes the phrase 'bids us avoid the object' to imply
that the moral syllogism 'may even be completed; but, in the
absence of *orexis* to which it can present itself, nothing happens.
For *dianoia* (thought) alone moves nothing.' A more adequate
statement of this interpretation would be that the moral motive,
even if present, is overcome by the greater strength of passion
(*epithumia*). The objection to this interpretation is that it attributes
to Aristotle a view which flatly contradicts the view stated in the
context, both before and after this passage, that the *akratēs* does not
actually know that what he is doing is wrong. A few lines later
he speaks of the *akratēs* 'regaining his knowledge' (1147 b6–7).
Burnet's interpretation would also involve us in understanding
'prevent' in 1147 a31 as covering the intervention of passion, and
this we have seen to be questionable. These considerations make it
difficult, perhaps impossible, to accept Burnet's view. We must,
therefore, follow other commentators in taking Aristotle's reference
to the moral rule as 'telling' us 'to avoid this' as meaning that the
rule implies this, or at least as meaning something less than the
explicit application of the rule to the present case.

The second difficulty to be noticed in this passage is connected
with Aristotle's omission to formulate determinately the principle
which 'forbids us to taste'. It is natural to take as implied, as do
Burnet and Gauthier–Jolif, the formula 'sweet things should not
be tasted'. This principle will be in incidental conflict (1147 b2)
with the major premiss, everything sweet is pleasant, of the syllogism
of appetite. But then the two syllogisms have the same minor
premiss, this is sweet. This proposition must be actually known if
the incontinent man is to be led astray by appetite. But it seems to
be Aristotle's doctrine in the rest of the chapter that the minor
premiss of the moral syllogism is not actually known. Commentators
offer two different possible solutions of this difficulty. The first

solution is to suppose, with Ross, that the conflicting syllogisms have different subject-terms in their major premisses and hence different minor premisses. The second solution is to suppose that there is indeed only one minor premiss, and that the *akratēs* goes wrong by connecting it with the major premiss of the appetitive syllogism and failing to connect it with the major premiss of the moral syllogism. This is on the whole the interpretation of Joachim. We mentioned it earlier (pp. 87–8 above) in our discussion of the phrase 'when a single judgement results' in 1147 a26–7.

Ross, in his brief paraphrase of the passage (*Aristotle*, p. 223), formulates the moral rule as 'nothing that is X should be tasted'. X presumably represents a word like 'indigestible' or 'harmful'. Ross assumes that the minor premiss will be known only in the remote sense, as a drunken man may know the verses of Empedocles. The merit of this interpretation is that it agrees with the doctrine which we have found in 1146 b35–1147 a24, and which seems to be repeated in the concluding section (1147 b9–17), still to be considered, of the chapter. The demerit of the interpretation is that 'X' is not in the text but is only assumed by Ross. It is, therefore, worth while to consider whether the passage can be understood without the assumption of a second minor premiss.

Joachim maintains that Aristotle's solution of the problem of *akrasia* 'follows his treatment of error' in the *Prior Analytics*, ii. 21 (p. 226). 'Nothing prevents a man who knows both that A belongs to the whole of B, and that B again belongs to C, thinking that A does not belong to C, e.g. knowing that every mule is sterile and that this is a mule, and thinking that this animal is with foal: for he does not know that A belongs to C, unless he considers the two propositions together' (67 a33–7). Aristotle explains that there are three senses in which one can 'know' a sensible thing: knowledge of a universal under which it falls, the knowledge proper to it, and the exercise of such knowledge (67 b3–5). Lacking the third kind of knowledge, a man may be deceived about the particular although he knows a major premiss which contradicts his erroneous belief, and does not affirm any opposing major premiss which would contradict the premiss he knows.

Nothing then prevents a man both knowing and being mistaken about the same thing, provided that his knowledge and his error are not contrary. And this happens also to the man whose knowledge is limited to each of the premisses and has not previously considered the particular question. For when he thinks that the mule is with foal he has not the knowledge in the sense of its actual exercise (*to energein*), nor on the other hand has his thought caused an error contrary to his knowledge: for the error contrary to the knowledge of the universal would be a syllogism (67 b5–11).

This treatment of error in the *Prior Analytics*, ii. 21, seems to resemble in a number of respects Aristotle's account of the failure of knowledge in *akrasia*. In both analyses there is a known rule and a failure to subsume a sensible particular under the rule. In the mistake about the mule there is no acceptance of a general proposition inconsistent with the proposition that mules are sterile. Similarly the *akratēs* does not accept a general principle which contradicts the rule that sweet things should not be tasted. This is stated in the passage we are considering: 'so it happens that a man behaves incontinently under the influence, in a sense, of a rule and an opinion, and of one not contrary in itself, but only incidentally – for the appetite is contrary, not the opinion – to the right rule' (1147 a35–b3). That sweet things are pleasant does not contradict the right rule although it leads to an action contrary to it. Again in the case of the mule there is no failure to know the minor premiss, this is a mule. Because the premisses are not viewed together there is a failure to know the conclusion which they entail, that this animal is not with foal. Similarly the *akratēs*, while he knows that this is sweet, fails to combine the premisses and conclude that to taste it is wrong. The interpretation is attractive and neatly overcomes the difficulty that the two general premisses seem to require the same particular premiss. But, as we shall see, to accept the interpretation would involve us in the supposition that there is a confusion, in the final section of the chapter, between the minor premiss and the conclusion of the practical syllogism.

I have said above that Joachim 'on the whole', basing his interpretation on the *Prior Analytics*, locates the 'ignorance' of the *akratēs* in a failure to think the premisses together. The qualification is required by the fact that Joachim, following the ambiguities of the text, fails to distinguish this solution sharply from a solution in terms of the suppression of the minor premiss. Thus in the following passage the two solutions are run together. 'He will know that the piece of cake is sweet but will not fully see the implications of its sweetness: i.e. his knowledge of the minor will be a mere piece of information in his mind, not in vital connection with his main thinking – he will not use his knowledge, or his knowledge will not be *theōria* but merely *hexis*' (p. 224). In a later passage Joachim formulates the knowledge which the *akratēs* fails to realise as 'this is sweet and therefore comes under the principle' (p. 228). There is thus in Joachim a slide from non-realisation of the minor premiss to non-realisation of the conclusion. It is not clear whether he is indicating a confusion in Aristotle or merely reproducing it.

Aristotle's discussion in vii. 3 of knowledge and ignorance in *akrasia* concludes as follows. I quote the Oxford Translation by Ross. The interpretation of 'last premiss' (*teleutaia protasis*) in 1147 b9 is doubtful and in 1147 b16 the homoeoteleuton (*dokousēs parousēs*) is almost certainly a corrupt reading.

> Now, the last premiss both being an opinion about a perceptible object, and being what determines our actions (*kuria*), this a man either has not when he is in the state of passion, or has it in the sense in which having knowledge did not mean knowing but only talking, as a drunken man may utter the verses of Empedocles (cf. a20). And because the last term (*horos*) is not universal nor equally an object of scientific knowledge with the universal term, the position that Socrates sought to establish (cf. 1145 b22–4) actually seems to result; for it is not in the presence of what is thought to be knowledge proper that the affection (*to pathos*) of incontinence arises nor is it this that is 'dragged about' as a result of the state of passion (*dia to pathos*), but in that of perceptual knowledge (1147 b9–17).

A case has been stated in our preceding discussion for the view that, according to the solution offered by Aristotle in this chapter, what the *akratēs* fails to know effectively, in the sense of actual contemplation, is a prescriptive conclusion rather than a merely factual premiss: 'avoid this' or 'this is sweet and to be avoided' rather than 'this is sweet'. Can the 'last premiss' (1147 b9) be a proposition of this kind? A protasis is a proposition which is 'put forward' for acceptance, offered as a basis for argument. In the *Prior Analytics* (42 a32) we are told that a syllogism is composed of two protases. Thus, even if *protasis* has uses which suggest 'proposition' rather than 'premiss', it is not possible, in a context where syllogisms are being considered, to defend any *translation* except 'premiss'.

Could the minor premiss of a 'practical syllogism' be an assertion which contained a moral term, an assertion which was prescriptive or evaluative and not merely factual? Takatura Ando maintains that in the practical syllogism the minor premiss 'recognises the presence of a value in a particular case'.[13] He finds fault with Teichmüller and other scholars for failing to see that the ignorance in *akrasia* is ignorance of value and not, as in action which is involuntary, ignorance of fact (pp. 300 ff.). But, although Ando's

contention may represent what we are sometimes inclined to expect
Aristotle to say, he makes no attempt to justify it by the detailed
interpretation of what Aristotle says in vii. 3. It would be difficult
for him to do so since, as Walsh remarks, 'the text of book vii offers
no clear examples of a minor premiss which is itself moral and not
factual' (p. 109) This is an understatement of the difficulty. For the
text does offer examples of minor premisses which are factual.
Ando admits (p. 280) that the fullest statement in Aristotle of the
scheme of a practical syllogism is that given in the *De Anima*, Γ
11, 434 a16–21, and here the minor premiss is of the form, 'this is
such and such an action and I am such and such a man', the major
premiss being 'such and such a man should (*dei*) do such and such
an action'. The syllogism in 1147 a5–7 conforms to this pattern and
this is the pattern also of the syllogisms referred to in 1147 a29–34.
So far, then, the evidence seems clear that the 'last premiss' must
be factual and not evaluative. We may be reminded at this point
of the suggestion in 1147 a28 that, in the case of the practical
syllogism, the conclusion is not an assertion at all but an action.
But, even if action follows immediately, a conclusion which can be
expressed in words is entailed by the assertions which are the
premisses; the assertion that I ought to do this. If so, and if all
the assertions which lead to the action as conclusion were called
premisses, then the last premiss would be evaluative and not merely
factual. But I do not think that there is any substance in this line of
interpretation.[14]

If protasis means premiss and the minor premiss must be factual
we are driven to fall back on the suggestion made earlier that, in
the chapter as it stands, there is a slide, along the route indicated
by Joachim, from factual premiss to moral conclusion; that Aristotle
sometimes speaks of the minor premiss when he also has in mind
what should properly be called the conclusion. We have seen that
the treatment of mistakes concerning perceptible individuals in
the *Prior Analytics*, ii. 21, supports this suggestion. There is further
evidence in the way in which Aristotle speaks of the 'last premiss'.
It is described as 'determining our actions', and this phrase is
appropriate to a proposition containing a word like 'right', or
'expedient' and not purely factual. Similarly in vi. 2, 1143 b2–5, it
is difficult to take 'the other premiss' as a bare statement of fact,
since it is described as 'the starting-point for the apprehension of
the end' and as apprehended by practical reason (*nous*). Again in the
Magna Moralia B6 (1201 b24–39), we find an apparently confused
transition from ignorance of a particular fact to ignorance of the
application of a rule to the fact: 'for it is possible for the incontinent

man to possess the knowledge of the universal, that such and such things are bad and hurtful, but yet not to know that these particular things are bad, so that while possessing knowledge in this way he will go wrong; for he has the universal knowledge but not the particular' (1201 b35–9).

Commentators are divided on the interpretation of the contrast between 'knowledge proper' and 'perceptual knowledge' (1147 b15–17). I think that the prevalent, and certainly a natural, view is that knowledge proper is knowledge of a universal rule or major premiss and perceptual knowledge is knowledge of a proposition with a singular term as its subject, whether a minor premiss or a moral conclusion. The difficulty which this view has to deal with is that the text as it stands appears to be inconsistent with what Aristotle has been saying, viz. that the knowledge which fails, and is in a sense absent, is knowledge not of the general rule but of the particular fact. But Burnet takes 'knowledge in the proper sense' to be not knowledge of the general rule but scientific knowledge in which 'all the terms are universal'. The contrast then is between the scientific syllogism and the practical syllogism, not between the two premisses of the practical syllogism. This interpretation is implied by the footnote to 1147 b17 in the Oxford Translation: 'Even before the minor premiss of the practical syllogism has been obscured by passion, the incontinent man has not scientific knowledge in the strict sense, since his minor premiss is not universal but has for its subject a sensible particular, e.g. "this glass of wine".' The interpretation is supported by the treatment of error (*apatē*) in the *Prior Analytics*, ii. 21; the mistake there analysed is similar to the mistake of the *akratēs* and is conditioned by the fact that the relevant knowledge involves the application of a universal principle to a singular term, i.e. it is perceptual knowledge and not scientific knowledge in the full sense.

If 'knowledge proper' is understood as knowledge of the major premiss of a practical syllogism, the text as it stands can be defended only by giving a Pickwickian meaning to the statement that this knowledge is not 'present' when *akrasia* occurs. The knowledge, Stewart suggests, is not 'immediately present', not 'near enough to the passion to be suppressed by it'. 'The true *epistēmē* which he has, and has consciously, is not in a position to be affected by *pathos*, because it is universal, and does not enter the arena of particular action.' But Stewart feels the strain of this explanation.

'On the questions whether knowledge is or is not present when *akrasia* occurs, and what kind of knowledge it is that is involved, this answer must suffice' (1147 b17–19). To Cook Wilson it seemed that the answer is 'worse than no answer': 'a mental struggle is impossible, since there is no actual knowledge for appetite to struggle with' (p. 49). Somewhat similarly Ross says that Aristotle's answer is 'inadequate to his own real view of the problem' (p. 224). Aristotle should recognise that 'incontinence is due not to failure of knowledge but to weakness of will'.

In the preceding discussion I have tried to do two things. First, following in detail what Aristotle says in vii. 3, I have tried, where the text is ambiguous, to make clear what interpretations are possible. Secondly, I have tried to explain Aristotle's formulation of the question and to exhibit the merits of his method. Is incontinence due to failure of knowledge or to weakness of will? We find the question difficult partly because the facts are complicated, but partly because the question has a definiteness which is delusive. Immersing ourselves in the facts, and in what we say about the facts, we become aware of a new dimension of doubt. What is to count as knowing or not knowing, accepting or not accepting, a moral principle? What are we asking when we ask whether the incontinent man has knowledge? Philosophers sometimes speak as if, once a question has been clarified, there is no longer in philosophy a question to be answered. But, if this were so, every question would be dissolved in turn into a question of higher order. And so, when we have decided what we mean or should mean by knowledge and ignorance, strength and weakness, we have still to say what descriptions match best the facts of experience. We may well doubt whether Aristotle's patterns of analysis cover all the facts. It is pertinent, for example, to ask, as Ross does, how, if the wrong act is done in the absence of knowledge, the knowledge has come to be absent (p. 224). Perhaps, if we tried harder, we could grasp our knowledge more firmly, keep a grip on ourselves. The explanation of incontinence in terms of ignorance would be unhelpful if we had to admit that, unless we had been incontinent, we would not be ignorant. But, if we say this, we may still be puzzled by the coming to be absent of knowledge. Is it like being hit on the head and passing out? Is it like relaxing one's grip on a golf club when told to do so by an instructor? Sometimes it is not like either. For neither is like what happens when we go to sleep or fall asleep. And Aristotle has indicated that coming to be in a state in which we act incontinently is like falling asleep (1147 a17). We shall have learned something from Aristotle if, on this issue, we come to distrust, even if we must continue to seek, sharply demarcated alternatives, apparently unambiguous questions and crisply decisive answers. Any answer which is short and simple will, in Aristotle's phrase, be true perhaps, but not clear.

PART TWO

Hare's Paradox

V Assenting to a value-judgement

R. M. Hare

EDITOR'S NOTE

The first of these two extracts from The Language of Morals *comes from ch. 2 of pt i. In pt i, Professor Hare divides what he calls 'prescriptive language' (language whose central function is to guide conduct) into two categories: imperatives and value-judgements. He begins with the former, and discusses the logical character of commands – using 'command' to cover all the 'sorts of things that sentences in the imperative mood express'. In the first extract below, Hare outlines what he takes to be 'the essential difference between statements and commands', a difference in what is involved in 'assenting' to them.*

In pt ii of The Language of Morals, *Hare turns to consider the 'logical behaviour of value-words, the other main instrument for prescribing with which our language provides us'. His main emphasis is on the action-guiding function of such words, and it is on the ground that this is their* central *function that he argues, against naturalism, that words like 'good' cannot be defined or analysed in terms of any set of factual characteristics. In ch. 11 (from which the second extract comes) it becomes clear that Hare thinks that if value-judgements are action-guiding in a* distinctive *way, and not just 'in the sense in which even plain judgements of fact may be action-guiding', they must entail imperatives. In the end he so defines 'value-judgement' that a judgement does not count as such unless it entails an imperative. The second extract is a statement of the definition and its implications.*

1. If we assent to a statement we are said to be sincere in our assent if and only if we believe that it is true (believe what the speaker has said). If, on the other hand, we assent to a second-person command addressed to ourselves, we are said to be sincere in

our assent if and only if we do or resolve to do what the speaker has told us to do; if we do not do it but only resolve to do it later, then if, when the occasion arises for doing it, we do not do it, we are said to have changed our mind; we are no longer sticking to the assent which we previously expressed. It is a tautology to say that we cannot sincerely assent to a second-person command addressed to ourselves, and *at the same time* not perform it, if now is the occasion for performing it and it is in our (physical and psychological) power to do so. Similarly, it is a tautology to say that we cannot sincerely assent to a statement, and *at the same time* not believe it. Thus we may characterise provisionally the difference between statements and commands by saying that, whereas sincerely assenting to the former involves *believing* something, sincerely assenting to the latter involves (on the appropriate occasion and if it is within our power) *doing* something. But this statement is oversimplified, and will require qualification later.

2.   I propose to say that the test, whether someone is using the judgement 'I ought to do X' as a value-judgment or not is, 'Does he or does he not recognise that if he assents to the judgement, he must also assent to the command "Let me do X"?' Thus I am not here claiming to prove anything substantial about the way in which we use language; I am merely suggesting a terminology which, if applied to the study of moral language, will, I am satisfied, prove illuminating. The substantial part of what I am trying to show is this, that, in the sense of 'value-judgement' just defined, we do make value-judgements, and that they are the class of sentences containing value-words which is of primary interest to the logician who studies moral language. Since what we are discussing is the logic of moral language and not that tangled subject known as moral psychology, I shall not here inquire farther into the fascinating problem, discussed by Aristotle, of *akrasia* or 'weakness of will' – the problem presented by the person who thinks, or professes to think, that he ought to do something, but does not do it. The logical distinctions which I have been making shed considerable light on this question: but much more needs to be said, chiefly by way of a more thorough analysis of the phrase 'thinks that he ought'. For if we interpret my definition strictly, and take it in conjunction with what was said earlier about the criteria for 'sincerely assenting to a command', the familiar 'Socratic paradox' arises, in that it becomes analytic to say that everyone always[1] does what he thinks he ought to (in the evaluative sense). And this, to put Aristotle's objection

in modern dress, is not how we use the word 'think'. The trouble arises because our criteria, in ordinary speech, for saying 'He thinks he ought' are exceedingly elastic. If a person does not do something, but the omission is accompanied by feelings of guilt, etc., we normally say that he has not done what he thinks he ought. It is therefore necessary to qualify the criterion given above for 'sincerely assenting to a command', and to admit that there are degrees of sincere assent, not all of which involve actually obeying the command. But the detailed analysis of this problem requires much more space than I can give it here, and must wait for another occasion.

VI On assenting to a moral principle

P. L. Gardiner

It has, at various times and in different ways, been suggested by some philosophers that a person cannot be said sincerely to think that he ought to do something and not do it, or, again, sincerely to think that he ought not to do something and do it. Although this suggestion has an air of paradox, it is not easy to locate precisely what, if anything, is wrong with it, one of the principal difficulties being the lack of clarity that characterises the way in which it is formulated. The suggestion concerned is to be found in certain passages of Professor R. M. Hare's book, *The Language of Morals* (although in a very compressed form, *en passant*, and with explicit qualifications), and, as it has been expressed by him in a precise and intelligible way, I shall consider it in the context of what he says. And, to do this, I must begin by considering his statements concerning what is involved in the notion of 'sincerely assenting to a command', since these turn out to have a considerable bearing upon his later remarks about the problem with which I am dealing.

I

On the first point, here are the relevant passages as they occur in his book:

> If . . . we assent to a second-person command addressed to ourselves, we are said to be sincere in our assent if and only if we do or resolve to do what the speaker has told us to do; if we do not do it but only resolve to do it later, then if, when the occasion arises for doing it, we do not do it, we are said to have changed our mind; we are no longer sticking to the assent which we previously expressed. It is a tautology to say that we cannot sincerely assent to a second-person command addressed to our-

selves and *at the same time* not perform it, if now is the occasion for performing it and it is in our (physical and psychological) power to do so. Similarly it is a tautology to say that we cannot sincerely assent to a statement and *at the same time* not believe it. Thus we may characterise provisionally the difference between statements and commands by saying that, whereas sincerely assenting to the former involves *believing* something, sincerely assenting to the latter involves (on the appropriate occasion and if it is within our power), *doing* something (Chapter V, 1).

Later on, Hare qualifies his statement by saying it is necessary to admit that there are 'degrees of sincere assent' to a command, although he does not specify what these are (Chapter V, 2).

I am puzzled by the passage quoted for the following reasons. To begin with, the expression 'assent to a command', even when such assent is described as being given to second-person commands, is not one with a common use. We ordinarily speak of obeying commands, of intending to obey commands, of giving it to be understood that we will obey commands, and (perhaps) of giving it to be understood that we intend to obey commands. But 'assenting to commands' seems to me to be peculiar. Hare, however, elucidates his usage. Thus he indicates what he means by giving a 'sign of assent' to a command: '. . . . if I said "Shut the door" and you answered "Aye, aye, sir", this . . . would be a sign or assent, if we wished to express what it is equivalent to, we might say "Let me shut the door" or "I will shut the door" (where "I will" is not a prediction but the expression of a resolve or a promise).' Elsewhere, 'Let me shut the door' is described as a 'first-person command' addressed to the speaker; as I do not find this clear, I will concentrate on the other explanation of what is meant by 'sign of assent', namely, where such a sign is interpreted as being equivalent to the expression of a resolve or a promise. On this interpretation it appears that, for a person to be sincere in his assent to a second-person command, he must be sincere in the resolve or promise he makes to obey that command.

It is here that my real difficulties begin. For Hare makes it a condition of such sincerity that the man who thus gives his assent must either do what the command orders him to do, or, if he does not do it but 'only resolves to do it later', then 'if, when the occasion arises for doing it (he) does not do it, (he) is said to have changed (his) mind . . .'. What this seems to imply (when taken in conjunction with the statement a few lines further on to the effect that sincerely assenting to a command involves carrying the command out on the appropriate occasion) is that a man is not sincere in his resolve (or promise) if he does not do what he has resolved (or promised) to do. If I interpret what is being said correctly, it is not possible for a man not to carry out his resolve or promise and still be called 'sincere' in giving that promise or making that resolve, unless we have reasons of supposing him to have changed his mind. Now it is, of course, true that people often explain why they have not done something on the grounds that they have changed their minds, e.g. 'I resolved that I would give up smoking altogether, but I subsequently came to the conclusion that I had set myself too high a standard, and I decided instead to limit myself to five cigarettes a day'. To say things of this kind is to imply (sometimes, not always) that non-compliance with the original resolution was in some way deliberate, or undertaken after careful reflection; and it may be that when such things are said, they are said in order to forestall a possible imputation of weakness of will or failure to live up to the standards one has set oneself. Or again, while no implication of deliberate alteration of purpose or intent may be involved (people are often said to have *realised* that they have changed their minds without their being able to identify any particular occasion on which this happened), it will at any rate be implied that a person described as having changed his mind can no longer be expected to do what he previously said he would do in a certain situation or set of situations, and it will not (ordinarily) be in place to ask whether he felt compunction in not doing as he originally intended or determined. On the other hand, it seems to me clear that we often do say that a person has failed in his expressed resolve or promise without wishing to imply that he has changed his mind and at the same time without wishing to suggest that the person was not sincere in giving that promise or making that resolve. If a person says that he will do something and then does not do it, he has put himself in a position where he has something to answer for; for he has given it to be understood that he will do something which he has not carried out. And in such circumstances we may say that the question of his sincerity is raised; it is not, however, answered. As Hare says, something may have physically prevented him from doing what he has said he will do, and this is sufficient conclusively to rebut the imputation of insincerity. But there are, of course, other considerations which might exculpate him from the charge of being insincere, although they would not necessarily exculpate him from other charges, e.g. fecklessness, irresponsibility, forgetfulness. Consider what might be said in answer to the question: 'He said he would do it – what happened?' Possible answers are: 'He tried but gave up after one or two attempts', 'He got panicky when the time came', 'There was something else he very much wanted to do, and as a result he put off doing it until it was too late', 'By some sort of Freudian slip he got the terms of the promise mixed up', etc., etc. All these answers may, in one way or another, remove the suggestion that the man was *insincere* in his resolve or promise, whatever else they may imply concerning his character. One might say that, if a man does not do what he states that he will do, this is a prima facie reason for doubting his sincerity, and in certain circumstances it may be a conclusive reason, depending upon such factors as, for example, the length of the time-interval between the moment when the verbal assent is given and the moment when it is appropriate to act: although in this connection one must not forget those cases where questions of sincerity or insincerity simply do not arise. For where there is no possibility of deception or misunderstanding, it is out of place to speak of sincerity. If someone orders me to shut the door immediately and I say 'All right' but don't move, I might be said either to have misunderstood the order, or, if I have not misunderstood it, to be deliberately provocative. What I could not, in such circumstances, be described as being is *insincere*. Often the expression 'sign of assent', where giving such a sign is giving it to be understood that the person to whom the order is addressed will carry out the order, is not appropriate as a way of referring to the use we sometimes make of phrases like 'Very well', 'I'll do it', etc.: in many contexts they are employed simply in conformity with certain conventions of manners, and their occurrence partly characterises the way in which an action was done, e.g. 'he did it politely, courteously'. On the whole, however, we are less inclined to regard a person as having been necessarily insincere in his professed intentions when the occasion for doing what he has said he will do and does not do is separated by a fair interval of time from the time at which he said he would do it.

The criteria for deciding, in a particular case, whether a man was sincere in his stated resolve or intention vary according to the circumstances. At times we may be inclined to say that only the man himself really knows, and even for him there may be difficulties. It may be a question of the qualifications he inwardly makes to himself; again, it may be one of his taking, or of his not taking, certain steps which would be relevant towards achieving what he has said he will do. But here again it may be necessary to ask in what manner these steps were taken; were they, for instance, taken half-heartedly, as a mere gesture? In general, questions of the form 'Was he in earnest?' or 'Did he mean what he said?' seem to involve some appeal to what the man did if they are to be decided; but (and this is really my only point) it is not necessary if we are to be justified in answering them in the affirmative, that what the man did should be such as to make the statements 'He complied with the order' or 'He acted in accordance with his resolve' true. The only circumstances in which we might insist upon such a requirement are those where there is no obvious source of resistance to his doing what he has said he will do (and in using the phrase 'source of resistance' I do not have in mind physical prevention merely, but, for example, counteracting interests, desires or fears which would make conforming to the command or resolve in question difficult). For charges of insincerity arising out of the non-performance of an action may be, and often are, met by saying, e.g., 'I fully intended to do it, but I was cowardly, yielded to an incompatible desire, etc.' with perhaps additional pleas to the effect that the person struggled with himself or did not fail in his resolve without compunction or remorse.

It might be replied that the expression 'sincerely assenting to a command' is being used in a special sense, and that in this sense there is no question of a person's being sincere in his assent and not carrying out the order. And, of course, it is always legitimate to use an expression in a special way, provided that this way is not confused with the ordinary way. I have already suggested that the expression 'assenting to a command' is in any case unusual, and it might therefore be held that no mistake of this sort can arise. Hare, however, defines his usage of the phrase in terms of giving a promise or making a resolve, and, in so far as this is how he *is* using it, then it seems to me that his criteria for 'sincere assent' are not the *ordinary* criteria by which we determine whether or not a man is sincere in the resolves or promises he makes. And I think that this is important in view of the subsequent use which Hare makes of the notion of sincerely assenting to a command when he comes to discuss the criteria for saying that somebody is sincere in his assent to a moral judgement concerning what he should do in a particular situation. For, in so far as he makes it a necessary condition of a person's sincerely assenting to a judgement of the form 'I ought to do X' (where this is interpreted as a 'value-judgement') that he should sincerely resolve to do X, it follows that a person can only be sincere in his assent to such a judgement if he actually does what the judgement says that he should do. And this, as he recognises, is paradoxical, for it makes it self-contradictory to say of someone that he has acted as he sincerely thought he ought not to act. Moreover, in so far as assenting to a moral principle entails assenting to particular moral judgements concerning what the person who assents to the principle should do in specific cases, it would appear that, on this definition, if a man recognises himself to be in a situation to which the principle applies, he cannot be said to be sincere in his assent to that principle if he does not act in the situation as the principle requires him to act. And this seems odd. For it appears curious to suppose that we must choose between saying that a man has changed his mind about a principle he previously claimed to acknowledge and saying that he was insincere when he claimed to acknowledge it, if, on a particular occasion, he does not do as the principle prescribes that he should. We have a use for expressions like 'doing what I believed to be wrong' or 'acting contrary to my principles' where there is no obvious implication of insincerity or of change of mind. In what follows I shall examine a number of widely varying cases in which a man would be said to have acted contrary to his professed moral beliefs, in an attempt to throw some light on the question of the conditions under which we are inclined (or disinclined) to say that someone has forfeited his right to hold that he did in fact sincerely assent to the beliefs in question. How far what I have to say bears upon Hare's analysis of the notion of sincerely assenting to a moral judgement of the form 'I ought to do X' will be left to the end.

II

We sometimes say that a man has acted as he does not think that he should, although he was not aware of doing so at the time. We sometimes say that a man has acted as he does not think that he should, although at the time he may have believed, or persuaded himself into thinking, that he was not acting wrongly. And, again, we sometimes say that a man has acted as he does not think that he should, and that he was clear at the time that what he was doing was wrong.

(1) There are many cases where a person might be described as not being aware at the time that what he was doing was wrong. Sometimes the description is used where we wish to imply that the agent 'knew no better', that he had not been told (and therefore could not be expected to realise) that actions of a certain type are morally reprehensible; the boy who has been strictly brought up to believe that he should always tell the truth may not, for example, know that the application of this precept is bounded in various ways, and that it is not always obligatory upon him to say what happened in circumstances where, for instance, he is not asked and where saying will involve disagreeable consequences for somebody else.

There are, however, other cases where this is not so; in such circumstances there is no question of a person's not being aware of a certain moral rule – indeed it is presupposed that he claims to assent to it – but it is suggested, on the other hand, that for some reason he did not recognise the situation in which he found himself to be a situation to which the moral rule 'applied'. For example, he may have forgotten some relevant circumstance, e.g. that he had given his word that he would do something, and hence does not act as, if he had remembered, he would have thought that he should. Again, he may have acted without thinking of the likely consequences of his action, and it may be said that, had he foreseen them, he would not have done what he did. In such cases as these we should not, generally, be inclined to say that what the man had done indicated that he was insincere in the principle he professed to hold, simply on the grounds that he was not aware of what he was doing.

There is, however, another type of case. For example, a man may be asked why, in view of his repeated professions of principles of loyalty, he has repeated something discreditable about a friend, and may claim in reply that the idea that what he was doing was wrong did not occur to him at the time, that he acted 'unthinkingly', and that it was only afterwards that he realised that he had not done as he should. And, if we accept the man's story, it would (I think) be seriously misleading to describe a situation of this type as being one in which a man has done what he thought *he ought not to be doing*. For to say of a man that he is doing something which he thinks he ought not to be doing, as opposed to saying that he is doing something which he thinks he ought not to do, is to imply that he is aware that what he is doing is wrong, either immediately before, or while, he does it – although it does not, of course, follow that the principle which he believes himself to be infringing is hovering before his eyes or beating in his ears. And in the case in question, it is suggested that, had the agent been aware, or had he been reminded by somebody else, that what he was doing was an infringement of the principle of loyalty, he would not have done what he did: although to say this is perhaps, even so, to describe the situation in over-theoretical terms, for it implies once again that a man's thinking that he ought to be doing something in a particular situation is a matter of his formulating moral judgements to himself or of his carefully subsuming what he is doing under principles. The position is better illustrated by considering situations where a man is said to have awakened (or to have been awakened by somebody else) to the moral character of what he has done, after he has done it; where he; for example, asks himself how he conceivably came to do what he did, in view of the facts that there were no material circumstances relevant to the action unknown to him, and that in retrospect he found himself disapproving so strongly of what he had done. Tolstoy, for instance, describes Anna Karenina as being suddenly appalled while she is waiting for the train to run over her, although it is worth noting that he does not put into her mouth words expressing a formal subsumption of her action under a principle, but makes her ask instead 'What am I doing?'

It has been suggested by some philosophers, e.g. Sidgwick, that cases like this may be cases where we should explain what has happened by saying that the agent had 'temporarily forgotten' a principle. But the notion of 'temporary forgetfulness of principles' in such contexts as these is surely very odd. For what is the criterion of the person's having forgotten, apart from the fact that he has not realised that what he is doing is not in accordance with the principle involved? And how, therefore, can his having forgotten *explain* what he is doing? In the case of some of the rules we learn, e.g. rules for using certain instruments or the rules of games, we sometimes forget, in the sense of not being able to describe or do what the rule prescribes without refreshing our memories. But it would be strange to speak of someone's refreshing his memory about rules against cheating or blackmail; and it is clearly not in this sense that we should wish to speak of a person's forgetting a moral principle in the present instance. What would seem to be meant, if the notion of 'forgetfulness' were applied here at all (and not in irony), would be that he has not seen that what he is doing is something of which he would ordinarily disapprove. And bringing home to him what has happened, if he has not realised it already, might be a question of characterising his action in a certain fashion – e.g. 'That's blackmail' – so as to draw his attention to an aspect of his conduct which is presumed to have escaped him, perhaps in his anxiety to further some purpose of his own or because he is 'carried away'. For coming to see that a certain description 'fits' an action *is*, in many cases, coming to see that it is wrong: there is no question of first pinning on the label and then seeing whether there is a principle which applies to actions with this name.

When and how far we should be prepared to accept explanations of this kind when they are offered to us, as opposed to explanations in which the person claims not to have known of the existence of certain relevant facts or to have momentarily forgotten them, depends upon the circumstances. There are occasions when it is plainly absurd to talk of 'slips' of this sort being conceivable. In other cases it may be a question of observing a person's subsequent reactions, of considering how far it was in character for him to have behaved as he did, of taking into account the circumstances and context. If a man made a habit of passing off his violations of the principles he professed in this manner, we should quickly become suspicious; the type of plea in question loses all point when it is continually repeated, and the fact of a man's consistently failing to realise, until it was too late, the moral implications of what he was doing would be sufficient to confirm the judgement that he attached very little weight to what he professed. 'He is careless about principles' would be, at best, only a polite, or ironical, way of saying that he had no principles at all. But, in so far as we do accept the man's explanation, we should not be inclined to regard his behaviour on the occasion in question as casting suspicion upon his sincerity, provided that we had evidence that he was genuinely sorry and that he took steps to prevent a recurrence of the situation.

(2) There are, however, other, more interesting, cases in which a man might be said to have acted against the principles he professes without being wholly aware that he is doing so. Such cases are distinguishable from those just mentioned in that a man in such a condition could not be inhibited from action by having his attention drawn to the fact that what he was doing was not in accordance with a rule to which he claimed to assent: for he would be ready to produce arguments to show that he was not infringing it. It might be said that he was 'reinterpreting' a prin-

ciple he claimed to hold in order to suit his convenience. The ways in which such 'interested reinterpetations' may be carried out are various. Frequently it may be a matter of describing what is being done so as to make it appear that it does not fall within the scope of the principle in question. On the other hand, a different line may be adopted, according to which it may be claimed that, although the agent holds the type of action contemplated to be wrong in certain circumstances, there are cases where there is some overriding obligation, and that this is so in the present instance. Thus when Karenin wondered whether it was his duty to fight a duel with Vronsky about his wife, he found little difficulty in persuading himself that he was under no such obligation; and his reasoning is a paradigm of self-justification. By arguing that the action contemplated would be one of 'killing a man in order to define one's relations with one's wife' and, further, of 'challenging a man in order to cover myself with false glamour', he implied (*a*) that the words 'fighting a duel' were inappropriate to describe what he would be doing and (*b*) that, in any case, the conditions under which duelling is justified, namely, when it is a question of satisfying honour and not one of covering oneself with bogus glory, were absent. Again, he argued that he had an obligation of a stronger kind – to give his wife an opportunity to repent, which was to 'conform with religion'. Thus three different types of consideration are introduced:

I. What he would have been doing could not properly be described as 'duelling', and hence did not fall within the terms of a principle he claimed to accept.

II. Even if it had been so describable, it would not have been justified under the circumstances.

III. There was in any case an overriding obligation towards his wife, and to fight a duel in the face of this obligation would have been wrong.

By describing what he would be doing as 'killing a man in order to define his relations with his wife', Karenin could, of course, be interpreted as implying something else, namely, his rejection of the entire principle of fighting duels under any circumstances. And frequently a man, confronted with a situation to which he recognises that a principle he would ordinarily claim to accept applies, may call in question the principle itself, by, e.g., formulating it in terms that make it appear unacceptable and in conflict with other principles whose validity he recognises. The reformulation of the principle will thus blur the dividing line which he has previously believed to separate the type of action it describes from other sorts of action of which he disapproves.

If a man acts on a particular occasion in a way that is not consonant with the principles to which he would ordinarily claim to assent, and justifies his behaviour to himself in such ways as those outlined, should we say that this showed that he did not really assent to the principles he professed? There seem to be various possibilities. One is to say that the man was in fact aware that what he was doing was contrary to the principles he professed, that, in spite of his arguments, he did not in fact believe that they justified him in avoiding a duel, and that his dissent from the judgement 'I ought to do X' was 'apparent', not 'real'. How would this interpretation be supported? One method would consist in showing how the person subsequently viewed his action; thus he might, if he were honest, admit that, in his anxiety to avoid physical harm to himself, he had presented the case to himself in a false light, that he could not, now that the danger was past, continue to accept the arguments which he had previously used in order to dissuade himself from acting as his principles demanded that he should act. Again, it would be in point to see whether he felt shame at what he had done, whether, e.g., he refused to discuss it. And cases of self-deception of this type would, it seems to me, count *for* rather than *against* the sincerity of the agent's professed moral beliefs; for it might be held that the very fact that the man found himself obliged to justify himself in this way was evidence that it was difficult for him to act in opposition to the principles he claimed to uphold. What in such a case it might be hard (for somebody else) to determine would be whether the man's protestations that he did not recognise what he was doing to be an infringement of a moral principle were an instance of genuine self-deception or whether they were merely intended to deceive others, although this difficulty need not arise so acutely for the man himself. And deciding this (in so far as it is decidable) would be, partly, a matter of observing the way in which the protestations were made, how the man reacted under the pressure of certain arguments, even the tone of voice used. On the other hand, in the case of a man who in some sense seems to 'accept his own excuses', who appears, moreover, to show no regret for what he has done, and does not seem to be under any misapprehension concerning the *meaning* of the principle he claims to hold, **since** he continues to exhibit disapproval of others who behave similarly to himself in the same circumstances, it might be difficult to know precisely what to say. It might be suggested that he regarded the principle as applying to others and yet not to himself, in the sense that excuses which he allowed himself he was not prepared to admit in the case of others. And there would then be grounds for saying that, if this were so, the principle to which he claimed to assent was not a *moral* one. But, if this were indeed the case, what would be the sense of talking of the man's 'excusing' his action? And could one speak of 'sincerity' in connection with a man's assent to such a principle? – even if we had evidence of the man's earnestness in exhorting others to behave in the ways he claimed that they should behave. Nevertheless we might, under such peculiar circumstances, be diffident about calling the man an unqualified hypocrite. The difficulty here seems to centre round what, if anything, could be meant by saying that the man 'accepted his own excuses'.

There is, finally, another possibility. For it might be suggested that, when the person was actually confronted by a situation in which he had previously stated that he believed a certain type of action to be obligatory, he recognised, or came to the conclusion, that what he had previously, in all sincerity, thought to be right conduct was in fact wrong, or at least not morally obligatory, and that he could not regard himself as being bound to act in the way he had previously maintained to be correct. It might occur to him that his standards had been too stringent, and that his disapproval of others for not complying with them had been unjustified. And, if this were so, he would have to be described as having changed his mind; although, again, the criterion of his having genuinely modified his moral beliefs, as opposed to merely modifying them to suit his own case, would involve a changed attitude on his part towards the conduct of others. But, if such a change of moral principles were to occur as a result of personal experience, it does not seem possible to say that the man was insincere in the principles he previously professed, in spite of the fact that when they were put to the test in his own experience he found himself rejecting them.

(3) So far I have been describing cases where there are, or might be, grounds for saying that *in some sense* what a man has done has been done without his being fully aware at the time that he is acting contrarily to his own professed principles, while nevertheless suggesting that, in some cases at least, we might say that he has done what he does not really think that he should

have done. But there are other cases where there seems to have been no doubt in the man's own mind that what he did offended against a moral principle which he professed to believe, and that he sincerely thought that what he was doing was wrong. It is in such cases as these that the statement that every man always does what he thinks that he ought to do (or that no man ever does what he thinks he ought not to do) appears most obviously paradoxical. And I am not sure that this can be accounted for by saying, as Hare seems to suggest, that the expression 'He thinks that he ought' is 'elastic', for this gives the impression, to my mind at least, that it is in some *stretched* sense that we speak of a person's doing as he thinks he ought not. I should want to say, on the contrary, that this usage is normal, and that a usage which makes the statement 'He (sincerely) thinks that he ought to do X' entail the prediction 'He will do X' is abnormal. That is to say, there are cases where we might say of a man with perfect propriety that he not merely acted in a way which he realised *in retrospect* to be against his true principles, but that he believed *at the time* that he was doing as he should not. What do seem to me to be elastic are the criteria according to which he, or others, would decide that he had acted with a bad conscience. It might be, for example, that he had certain uneasy feelings, or that he manifested physical symptoms, e.g. that he hesitated, blushed or muttered, or even that what he did was done with a particular bravado or abandon; and if such things happened the man would have to be in some way dishonest or misleading if he were to claim after the event that he did not in any way think that what he was doing was wrong. What we have here are a host of possible variations, and it becomes a question of modifying and qualifying our terminology in order to describe the case accurately. Under circumstances like these we should, I think, be prepared *in general* to accept such feelings and behaviour as justifying the statement that the man recognised that he was acting as he should not be acting (as contrasted with realising that what he was doing conflicted with some 'conventional' rule which he did not accept), although it might be said that it would not *always* be sufficient to justify such a statement. For if, in spite of these manifestations, he was observed to experience no subsequent regret or remorse, and to show no signs of trying to alter his behaviour, we might be inclined to regard him as someone who, for all his hesitations and manifestations of guilt at the time, at most only *partly* believed that he was acting wrongly, who might even be regarded as a kind of 'moral masochist' in that he derived enjoyment from the thought that what he was doing conflicted with established morality. Again, it might be said that he was still under the spell of the moral code in which he had been brought up, to which he no longer gave conscious assent but which still influenced him in various respects. (Consider the remark: 'I felt that in some way I was acting wrongly, *although I could not have said why.*' This distinguishes it from more usual cases, where recognising something as being wrong implies being able to say, if asked, *why* it is wrong.)

There are certainly cases where a conflict may exist in a man's mind as to whether or not he holds a certain moral belief, and this may be reflected in the genuine difficulty we find – because of the presence of conflicting criteria – in deciding whether he regards the things he does and the choices he makes as being right or wrong. An obvious case is that of the man who 'reacts' against the moral ideas in which he has been brought up, e.g. the Communist with the bourgeois background. Such a man may be asked, and may feel himself obliged, to do things towards which he feels at the same time a strong moral repugnance. Sometimes it may be possible to explain repugnance of this kind by saying that it is a question of the man's having to allow one moral obligation which he accepts to be overridden by another one of greater weight – for example, the obligation to aid the Party may be considered to be of greater weight than the obligation to be loyal to one's friends. But in other cases a man may feel genuine doubt about the morality of his actions, in spite of the fact that at other times, and when he reflects, he believes them to be right. Communists sometimes speak of being worried by 'bourgeois scruples' and of questioning themselves about their sincerity. And such self-questioning may be prompted by what the Communist feels on occasions when he is serving the Party interest, and in spite of the fact that his actions rigidly conform to the Party line. It is by no means always *what is done*, but *the frame of mind in which it is done*, that causes anxiety. Thus the Communist might, at crucial moments of action, find himself criticising, from a non-Communist angle, what he was undertaking. One method of reassuring himself would be to put his doubts down to some other motive, e.g. cowardice, or sentiments of friendship which must be disregarded when the Party interest is at stake: in this manner the doubts might be explained away as mere rationalisations of some disreputable, or at least irrelevant, motive. And to do this is to treat doubts about a certain principle of action as apparent only, and as unrepresentative of the man's true convictions, provided that they are belied by what he in fact does and provided that satisfactory explanations can be found. On the other hand, such doubts may, in the light of the subsequent development of the man's career, be seen to have an immense significance. It may be, for example, that they are symptomatic of a general change of attitude and of conversion to a different stand-point.[1] And during such a period it may be incorrect to say that he is either sincere or insincere in his assent to either of two opposed principles – this is part of what is meant by saying that a person is undergoing a change of this sort – although we may want to say that he is 'sincerely undecided' or 'seriously torn' between two different sets of beliefs. Situations of this sort have been described by an ex-Communist as being ones in which two sets of opposed reactions were operating: 'Sometimes one seemed in the ascendancy, sometimes the other. . . . At any moment, after having quite serious doubts about some aspects of Soviet or Party policy, I might still react violently in defence of the Party, especially if I heard it attacked by someone outside its ranks, etc., etc.'[2] Of such a pre-dicament it would obviously be misleading to say that the man was insincere in the beliefs he publicly professed and proclaimed, although it would be equally misleading to say that he was sincere: what *could* be said was that he *both* believed *and* disbelieved his professed principles, or (less paradoxically) that he was in the process of coming to disbelieve them while continuing to some extent to support them, where saying that 'he continued to some extent to support them' is not to be construed as meaning that he continued to support them in a modified form. There is no question of compromise.

In general, the demand for precise and simple criteria in terms of which it can be determined whether or not a man genuinely believes that he ought to do a certain thing, or whether or not he genuinely believes that he ought to behave in a certain way whenever he finds himself in a particular type of situation, seems to be mistaken. There are occasions when we might wish to affirm that a man had done what he thought he ought not to have done owing to his not having recognised, for one reason or another, the nature of the situation in which he acted; in such cases as these we have seen that we should not want to say that the man acted deliberately against his (real or professed) moral beliefs, and we should not therefore wish to say that in such a situation what he had done gave us a prima facie reason for thinking that he might not sincerely hold those beliefs. On the other hand, his subsequent behaviour, e.g. his showing surprise (and regret), together with his conduct on other occasions when similar conditions held, might support the supposition that, had he been aware of what he was doing, he would have thought that it was wrong, and would not have done it. And it would be natural to say, in this case, that even if there was no question of the man assenting to (or dissenting from) the judgement 'I ought not to do this' *at the time*, since he did not recognise the situation to be one in which moral considerations were involved, he nevertheless assented to the statement that he should not have done it, this being determinable in the types of ways outlined. Again, in the case of the man who justifies what he is doing to himself (and to others) by claiming that his action is not of a certain kind, does not fall within the scope of a certain principle, and so forth, and thus excuses himself from moral blame, there are ways of deciding or judging whether what he is doing is really something he regards himself as being morally at liberty to do in spite of his apparent failure to recognise its nature. Finally, in cases of wrongdoing in the absence of such attendant circumstances as these there is a very complex and intricate variety of considerations which, depending upon the nature of the case, would be relevant towards reaching a conclusion about a person's sincerity or lack of sincerity, or even towards reaching the conclusion that no conclusion could be reached, at any rate in such simple terms.

The suggestion that what a person thinks he ought to do he does is tempting because, in the first place, it has a hard-headed ring which accords well with realistic maxims that bid us judge a person by his deeds, not his words; in the second place, because it provides an unambiguous verificatory criterion for concepts whose use is liable to become obscured by unrewarding speculation concerning 'mental processes'; and in the third place, because it seems to solve in a neat and tidy fashion some of the problems that arise about the differences in function of evaluative and non-evaluative expressions. But such tidiness is bought at a price, the price of (to some extent at least) misrepresenting ordinary usage. For what are relevant in determining the sincerity of a person's moral beliefs are a host of considerations, behavioural and non-behavioural according to the circumstances and according to who is trying to discover the truth. To take an extreme example, even a person who consistently acted in ways contrary to principles which he claimed to accept might conceivably be regarded as in some sense believing in those principles: he may not be sincere, but then neither perhaps is he wholly insincere. It could, for instance, be said that lying about what one has actually done, as well as lying about the considerations that moved one do to do it, may (in some cases) be interpreted as counting against the total insincerity of one's professions, although here it is difficult to discount the operation of motives like vanity. But it is possible for a person to lie out of shame, out of a sense that he has not lived, and is not living, up to a conception of what his life should be, and the extent to which a person lies from this motive is relevant to questions about his sincerity. Thus Proust wrote (*La Prisonnière*, ii, p. 246): 'I do not know whether this was the case with her, but it is a strange thing, and so to speak a testimony by the most incredulous to their belief in good, this perseverance in falsehood shown by all those who deceive us.'

III

In what has been said I have deliberately avoided the trying problem of how moral judgements are to be analysed. I shall not enter upon this question now; in particular, I do not wish to discuss Hare's proposal that we should make it a test of 'whether someone is using the judgement "I ought to do X" as a value-judgement' that he should 'recognise that if he assents to the judgement, he must also assent to the command "Let me do X"' (Chapter V, 2 above). It does, however, seem to me that, whatever may be the advantages or disadvantages of adopting a terminology which makes 'I ought to do X' (interpreted as a value-judgement') entail 'Let me do X' (interpreted as an expression of a resolve or promise), there are analogies (although I suspect these should not be pressed too far) between the ways whereby we decide whether a person is sincere or insincere in the promise he gives us or the resolve he expresses in our presence and the ways whereby we decide whether a person is sincere or insincere in the things he tells us about his moral beliefs. Certain of these analogies have been sufficiently exhibited in what has already been said about the criteria we are accustomed to use in the respective cases. But, in particular, I should like to repeat something I said earlier concerning the keeping of resolves and promises. For I then said that, if a person says that he will do something and does not do it, the question of his sincerity is raised, though it is not answered. And in the same way, if a man tells us that he feels that he is morally obliged to do something and does not do it, the question of his sincerity is raised, although it is again not answered. What has happened is that he has put himself in a position that requires accounting for. The form this account may take varies in the kinds of ways I have tried to describe. Thus it may take the form of justification; the man may not have been in a position to do what he said he should do, or he may have changed his mind after realising that he was under a more pressing obligation. It may take the form of explanation; he was hypnotised or forgot, or, again, he was carried away by temptation, grew panicky when the time came, etc. And if considerations of this description are not forthcoming, and if certain other factors are absent, e.g. signs of compunction or remorse, or resolutions to mend his ways, we may, with more or less confidence as the case may be, reach the conclusion that the man was insincere. And the same type of considerations apply when it is a question of assessing a man's professed acceptance of a moral principle or viewpoint: his not doing what the principle requires him to do in a given situation presents him with something to answer for. This seems to me to be the truth behind such *dicta* as 'Everyone does what he thinks he ought to do' and 'A man cannot sincerely assent to a moral principle and not do as that principle prescribes'. We might put this by saying that 'assenting to a moral principle P' excludes 'not doing as P requires', *in the absence of a wide and variegated range of circumstances and factors.* And it is these that so often count.

I should like to add that, in what I have been saying, I have been conscious of using expressions like 'assenting to principles', 'recognising situations to be ones to which a principle applies' and 'assenting to moral judgements'. I think that this can be a misleading way of referring to people's normal reactions to situations which call for some kind of moral decision or choice; but as I have largely been concerned with discussing professions and claims, and with methods of testing these, such a terminology has been difficult on occasions to avoid. On the whole, however, I prefer, and have tried for the most part to use, less intimidating locutions, like 'thinking that one ought' and 'coming to the conclusion that one should'.

VII The criteria of assent to a moral rule

H. J. N. Horsburgh

I

In his book, *The Language of Morals*, Professor Hare emphasises anew the problem of *akrasia*, which has been a recognised source of difficulty to philosophers since the time of Plato. Part of the problem is how to escape between the horns of opposing absurdities. On the one hand, one must avoid the Socratic paradox of maintaining that everyone always does what he thinks he ought; and, on the other hand, one must discountenance the devil's paradox according to which a man may be held to assent to a moral rule to which he only pays the courtesy of verbal acceptance. According to Hare the trouble arises because our criteria in ordinary speech for saying 'he thinks he ought...' are very elastic. Thus, even if a person fails to fulfil an obligation we are normally prepared to say that he has not done what he thinks he ought if the omission is accompanied by remorse or feelings of guilt. It is therefore necessary to admit that there are degrees of assent not all of which involve the actual fulfilment of an obligation.

I agree with Hare that the elasticity of our criteria is a source of difficulty, and part of what I wish to do in this paper is to justify Hare's use of the word 'elasticity' in this connection. But there is also a tendency for us to be misled by language into the adoption of unsatisfactory views with regard to the nature and interrelations of our criteria; and therefore, I shall begin by examining a group of theories which seem to illustrate this tendency. (It is not implied that any of these theories is held by a reputable philosopher.) The conclusions of this section will be largely negative. It should serve to clarify the requirements of a satisfactory theory, however. I shall then consider what is the criterion of full acceptance. Next I shall attempt to justify the view that our less exacting criteria are derived from this strict criterion by a process of stretching or dilution. I shall then inquire whether the theory that I have been developing is able to cope with various difficulties that emerge in section II. And finally, I shall try to relate what I have said to the question of weakness of the will.

II

Hare's account of the matter suggests, although this may not be his view, that obedience to a moral rule and feeling remorse when one has failed to conform with it are both criteria of assent to the moral rule. There may also be other criteria; e.g. having feelings of guilt when one has broken a moral rule and being tempted to break a moral rule (for temptation implies resistance to breaking the rule, though not necessarily sufficient resistance to refrain from breaking it). This seems a plausible view. After all, if one were asked what leads one to suppose that A assents to a moral rule, on one occasion one might say, 'Because he conforms with it', and on another, 'Because he's remorseful when he fails to conform with it'. This suggests that one uses conformity as a standard at one time and remorse as a standard at another.

It seems that a similar multiplicity of criteria can be detected with regard to some of our uses of the verb 'to know'. Suppose that A asks B whether he knows the more celebrated of Eisenhower's Christian names. B says that he does but that he cannot at the moment recall what it is. 'I know it,' he declares, 'but for the time it escapes me. But if you presented me with a list of names which included it I'd be able to pick it out at once.' A now recites a list of names: 'Franklin, Elmer, Willard, Dwight – .' 'Yes,' B interrupts him, 'that's right, it's Dwight.' In such a case, although B has failed to recall the name he claims to know we should certainly accept his claim on the ground that he instantly recognised it when he heard it spoken.

The cases in which we say that a man accepts a moral rule to which, on some particular occasion, he fails to conform, may be thought to be similar to the cases in which we allow that someone knows a certain name, although, on some particular occasion, he is unable to recall it. In both sorts of situation, it might be said, failure to satisfy one criterion is offset by the capacity to satisfy another. Thus, in the cases of failure to conform with a moral rule, although the obedience criterion of assent is unsatisfied, the criteria of remorse, feelings of guilt and repentance may all be satisfied – and the satisfaction of these criteria is sufficient to dispose us to say that we are concerned with a case of assent to a moral rule.

But if we have several independent criteria for saying 'he thinks he ought...' surely that phrase must be exceedingly ambiguous? Yet, although we are prepared to concede that it is vague, I think that on reflection we are disposed to deny that it is ambiguous in the sense implied by the alleged plurality of independent criteria. It would seem, therefore, that our criteria do not operate with the independence attributed to them on this view.

An alternative theory can be conveniently considered by first returning to the criteria of recognition and recall. Suppose that B is never able to recall Eisenhower's Christian name although he invariably recognises the name 'Dwight' when he is presented with it, would we still say that he knows Eisenhower's Christian name? I think we might because of the triviality of the claim. On the other hand, if B claimed that he knew the correct translations into French of a number of English words but was unable to do more than recognise the correct translations when presented with them, we should be more grudging. We might say, 'You don't really know the French for these words,' or, 'You only half-know these French words.' By these qualifications we signify that while we are sometimes prepared to regard recognition as a sufficient criterion of knowledge, this is in the nature of a concession which we are not prepared to make when faced with important claims to knowledge. Such claims can be made good only by satisfying both criteria. Now, it should be noted that these criteria are logically independent in the sense that there is no logical connection between the satisfaction or non-satisfaction of one criterion and the satisfaction or non-satisfaction of the other. In view of this it might seem strange that the fact that there are two criteria for the use of the verb 'to know' does not give rise to ambiguity. The most vital protection against ambiguity has already been mentioned, namely, that the verb 'to know' is not countenanced in any important context unless both criteria can be satisfied. But the verb 'to know' is protected in two further ways. The first of these is that the combined criterion can always be insisted upon because it is always possible to apply both criteria. This also potentially reduces the different kinds of cases that have to be allowed for to those in which both criteria are satisfied, those in which one criterion is satisfied, and those in which neither criterion is satisfied. A fortunate empirical consideration simplifies the situation further. I have in mind the fact that those who are able to satisfy the criterion of recall can almost invariably satisfy the criterion of recognition. Satisfying the former criterion, therefore, is like passing one part of an examination with such high honours that one secures exemption from the rest of the examination. The cases in which one criterion is satisfied are therefore all of one sort, namely, cases in which the criterion of recall is unsatisfied. For all these reasons, then, the multiplicity of criteria for the use of the verb 'to know' very seldom gives rise to ambiguity even when trivial matters are under discussion.

Perhaps we avoid ambiguity analogously in our use of the phrase 'he thinks he ought...'. In other words, may we not say that on important occasions we insist on the satisfaction of all our criteria of assent to a moral rule? But such insistence is only possible if our criteria are logically independent in the sense explained above. Unfortunately this is not the case. Thus, when the criterion of obedience is satisfied it is impossible for us to apply the criteria of remorse, feelings of guilt, and repentance; and, on the other hand, when the latter criteria are applicable the criterion of obedience is at least partially unsatisfied. It follows that the threatened ambiguity of the phrase 'he thinks he ought...' cannot be overcome in this fashion.

Suppose, then, that we say it is the total patterns of results that emerge from the application of as many criteria as possible that determine our judgements of assent to a moral rule. Such an interpretation is suggested by the fact that we do appear to collate the evidence for remorse, feelings of guilt, temptation and repentance. Furthermore, the partial logical independence of our criteria does not seem so fatal to this view as it was to the first that I considered. For we might claim that although our patterns of results are not always the products of applying the same criteria, they have a certain common membership, e.g. the criteria of obedience and temptation which are always applicable, and this saves the notion of assent from extreme ambiguity. But this claim is a dubious one. Worse, the vagueness implied by the present interpretation does not seem of the kind that we would attribute to our uses of the expression 'he thinks he ought...'. But a more fatal objection is that the theory seems unable to accommodate the fact that it is always possible to make rational comparisons of degree of assent when people claim to accept the same moral rule. For how are such judgements to be rationally formed when A satisfies the criteria p and q and cannot have the other criteria applied to him, and B fails to satisfy the criteria p and q but satisfies the criteria r, s and t? The problem in such a case is not like that in which a teacher has to estimate the relative scholastic achievements of A and B who have each surpassed the other in some answers to questions of the same examination paper; it is more like attempting to estimate the relative merits of A and B when they have sat examinations in different subjects.

The superior status of the criterion of recall may be thought to suggest a way out of this difficulty. May we not hold that when the criterion of obedience is fully satisfied we are, as it were, exempted from the application of the other criteria? Such a view seems reasonable since it is precisely the fact that the criterion of obedience has been fully satisfied which prevents the other criteria from being applicable. Its acceptance also equips us with a priority rule for dealing with awkward comparisons; for it enables us to say that the satisfaction of the criterion of conformity is to count for more than the satisfaction of all the other criteria and the partial satisfaction of the criterion of conformity. Awkward cases can still be imagined, of course; but the problems which they present seem to be analogous to those which are successfully handled by teachers when marking examinations. Unfortunately, not all our judgements of relative completeness of assent are consistent with the operation of so simple a priority rule. Thus, it sometimes happens that we attribute a higher degree of assent to a person after he has violated a moral rule than we did before. Suppose that A, who has always acted honestly, loses his money and commits a theft, afterwards suffering from intense remorse. Might we not estimate the degree of his acceptance of the moral rule proscribing theft more highly than we did before, especially if, on independent grounds, we had doubted the worth of his character? If we might, surely we sometimes attach more weight to remorse than we do to conformity? 'No,' it might be objected, 'all we do is to hold our previous estimate of A's character more confidently than we did before.' But whether this is so or not, cases of the kind that I am envisaging show that our judgements do not conform with the simple priority rule in question; for clearly, if they did, any failure to conform with a moral rule would be bound to lower our estimate of the agent's degree of assent – and that is not always the case.

None of these views, therefore, can be regarded as satisfactory. What is required is a quite different approach to the problem.

III

Before we can speak of assenting in some not quite rigorous sense it seems necessary to be clear about what we mean by a full or unreserved acceptance of a moral rule. That is the question to which I shall now proceed.

It seems to be generally admitted that A cannot be said to accept a moral rule unreservedly if he sometimes transgresses it – unless, of course, his violation of the rule is due to its having come into conflict with another moral rule which he also accepts.

Conformity is therefore part of what we mean when we say that someone unreservedly assents to a moral rule. But, as I have already shown, this is not all that we mean; for sometimes we conform with the moral rule for unacceptable reasons. Mere conformity, then, is not enough; the conformity must be attributable to the operation of the right motive.

Suppose that we wish to determine whether A assents to the moral rule, 'One ought to return what one borrows'. We examine A's conduct and find that he always conforms with the rule. It does not follow that he accepts it, for his reason for obeying it may be a desire to establish a reputation for honesty that will enable him to perpetrate a greater fraud than would otherwise be possible. When, then, should we be satisfied that he does accept it? The answer one feels inclined to make is: when we are satisfied that he conforms with the moral rule because he accepts it. But clearly, we cannot say that by fully assenting to the moral rule, 'One ought to do x', one means (i) that the person in question does x, and (ii) that he does x because he assents to the rule enjoining it; for the criterion governing the use of a word can never legitimately contain the word whose use it governs. Although this information is unacceptable, however, we may very well feel that it is a defective expression of the answer that we wish to give.

Consider the conduct of A who does x in accordance with the moral rule, 'One ought to do x'. If A does x because it pays, he is making it a rule to do what pays him, and therefore his allegiance is to the rule, 'Do what pays you'; if, on the other hand, he does x because he has made it a rule to do x, then he is doing x because he accepts the moral rule, 'One ought to do x', and his allegiance is to this moral rule. In the former case his conformity with the moral rule is conditional. If x pays he does x; if x does not pay he does something else which either pays or is expected to pay. The link between the two rules is empirical, not logical; the moral rule is not subsumed under the rule of self-interest; it is simply regarded as a more or less reliable means to conformity with it. We do not require the moral rule to explain what A does; what we require is the rule, 'Do what pays you'. If, on the other hand, A does x because he has made it a rule, we do indispensably require the moral rule to explain what A does. When this is the case, and A conforms with the moral rule, the conformity can be spoken of as unconditional. We may say, then, that A accepts the moral rule enjoining x without reserve if he makes it a rule to do x and always does x in the appropriate circumstances unless the moral rule is overridden by another rule with which it comes into conflict.

But this statement of the criterion, while it avoids the difficulty which the previous formulation ran foul of, may not seem in harmony with what was said earlier about the necessity of having the right motive. I shall therefore conclude this section with a few remarks about our use of the word 'motive'.

Suppose A is asked, 'Why do you do x?' He replies, 'Because it pays me'. Here we have his motive: self-interest. We also have a reference to an explanatory maxim or rule of conduct, namely, 'Do what pays you'. At least part of the point of A's answer is that it puts us in possession of a predictively reliable rule. If A does x because it pays him, the moral rule, 'One ought to do x', is a less reliable guide to his future conduct than the rule, 'Do what pays you'. We imply this by saying that doing x is a means to doing what pays. When we say that one is a means to the other we have sketched in the conditions under which the moral rule will be observed. When a rule is not observed simply on certain conditions, when there is no more predictively reliable rule to which reference can be made, it is pointless to ask a man for his motive. Thus, if A is asked, 'Why do you do what pays you?' all he can say is, 'Well, I'm just like that', or 'I just do', or 'I make it a rule to do so' – unless, of course, he offers us an unhelpful dispositional translation, e.g. 'Because I'm selfish'. Similarly, if B is asked, 'Why do you do x?' he may reply, 'Because it's right'. This formula has the same force as, 'I make it a rule to do so' – though that by no means exhausts its significance. It points out that conformity is unconditional, and therefore, that it is pointless to look for a further motive.

It must be admitted, however, that whereas we are satisfied with the answer, 'Because it pays', and do not press for more fundamental motives, we tend not to be satisfied with the answer, 'Because I make it a rule'. There seem to be two reasons for this. In the first place, when we are using the language of motives the most satisfactory answer to reach in the end is, 'Because I'm like that'. It satisfies us because it suggests that we are dealing with a rule of conduct which has the law-like character of being descriptive. It is not regarded as exclusively descriptive, however, for we should want to maintain that the individual concerned may properly be held responsible for acting conformably with the rule. Thus, although we should deny that he has made it a rule, we should insist that he is not compelled to conform with it. It is therefore negatively prescriptive. We prefer law-like to clearly prescriptive rules, provided they are fundamental, because they are thought to govern the conduct of a larger number of human beings, and hence, to possess greater explanatory value. But this preference is sometimes irrational. If A always observes a rule which is not a means to conformity with some other rule, this rule is no less indispensably required to understand A's conduct for its being true that it is prescriptive or that it is not required to explain the conduct of the majority of human beings.

In the second place, while there is clearly a limit to the number of questions which one can answer by referring to more and more fundamental law-like rules, it is much less clear that there is a limit to the number of questions one can answer by reference to prescriptive rules. The ground of this difference is that there is a tendency to think of moral and other prescriptive rules as forming systems in a way in which psychological laws do not. Sometimes these systems are conceived of as roughly analogous to logical calculi, of which it can be said that although they must contain axioms and postulates which cannot be questioned, substantially the same calculi can be developed on the basis of different sets of axioms and postulates; hence, they open up the possibility of endless manipulation and re-organisation – endless questioning. At other times these systems are thought of as possessing the kind of coherence which allows us to proceed indefinitely, by questions and answers, in a virtuous circle of mutually reinforcing prescriptions. Now, I think it is sound to attribute some kind of coherence to moral and other prescriptive rules which does not belong to laws of nature (including psychological generalisations, different as these are in some respects from the laws which a physicist attempts to formulate); and hence, I consider it quite proper to ask, 'Why do you make it a rule to do x?' and thereby to explore the interconnections of a moral agent's decisions. But once A has accepted a moral rule he can be said to act as he does because he has accepted that moral rule; for, although his decision to conform with it may not have been made if he had

not previously arrived at certain other moral decisions, he now
regards it as an independent source of obligations. This is to say that
our reasons for assenting to a moral rule are related to our acceptance of it more nearly in the way in which the reasons for a piece of
legislation are related to its enactment than in the way our reasons
for catching a train are related to our decision to catch it. If I decide
to catch a train I may refer to this decision rather than to its grounds
if asked why I am unable to meet a friend at a certain time, my
reasons being either that this is the simpler explanation or that I
am unwilling to review the connections between my decision and its
grounds. Such a decision remains wholly dependent on its grounds,
however; for if these grounds were to shift, the decision would be
automatically affected. Thus, if I am catching a train to London to
meet a friend, this decision is automatically annulled by his un-
expected arrival at the door of my house. The case of an Act of
Parliament is very different. The Act can be justified in the sense
that reasons can always be given for enforcing actions of the sorts
which it prescribes; nevertheless, once it has been enacted it is true
to say not only that the actions which it prescribes are enforced
because it prescribes them but that they will continue to be enforced
for as long as the Act remains an Act even if its effects are not those
which were anticipated so that it can no longer be justified in the
original way. Thus, in becoming a source of legal obligations the
Act has acquired a certain independence of the reasons for its enactment. Moral rules, once they have been accepted, are recognised
sources of obligations, and have a similar independence in that the
reversal of the moral decisions most closely connected with them
does not entail their automatic cancellation. When a moral rule is
accepted, therefore, there is a sense in which one cannot get beyond
it. In such cases the only motive which can be given for actions
conforming with it is the existence of the rule itself. That is what is
meant by having the right motive.

IV

When I say that A accepts the moral rule, 'One ought to do x',
without reserve, I mean (i) that he always obeys this moral rule, and
(ii) that his obedience is unconditional in the sense that it is to be
explained by reference to the rule. In my view, the weaker criteria
are derived from this strict criterion by a process of stretching or of
dilution of meaning. These criteria shade into one another forming

a descending scale of strictness. There are only two additional formulations, however. These are: (1) A accepts a moral rule if (*a*) he intends to obey it, and (*b*) his intention to obey it is unconditional. (2) A accepts a moral rule if (*a*) he wishes to obey it, and (*b*) his wish to obey it is unconditional.

There are three preliminary points which I wish to make with regard to these formulations. First, it is easy to see that they are derived from the criterion of full assent by means of a process of stretching, leading to the thinning-out of meaning. Obedience includes both the intention and the wish to obey; and the intention to obey includes the wish to obey. Secondly, these words, 'obey', 'intention to obey', and 'wish to obey' operate in such a manner as to give rise to a continuous scale of weakening criteria such as is implied by such terms as 'stretching' and 'elasticity'. Thirdly, there is something unconditional about each of these formulations; for without some kind of unconditionality one cannot speak of assenting in any degree whatsoever, since without unconditionality of obedience, or intention, or wish, no reference need be made to the relevant moral rule to explain how the agent behaves, in which case it becomes meaningless to speak of his having made it a rule to act in a certain way.

(1) is the formulation of that part of the scale of criteria we most commonly employ. It is suitable for application to people who normally, but not invariably, measure up to their standards. If they did not normally conform with the moral rules they claim to accept, we should not be prepared to speak of them as intending to conform with them. Their lapses can be held not to involve any change of intention if they are unpremeditated and are followed by signs of remorse, feelings of guilt and repentance.

(2) formulates that part of the scale of criteria which we use to speak of the incontinent, as Aristotle calls them, e.g. of alcoholics. An alcoholic may seldom resist the temptation to drink to excess, yet we may be prepared to grant that he assents to the moral rule, 'One ought to be temperate in one's consumption of alcohol', if he invariably struggles before succumbing to temptation and feels remorse, etc., when he is sufficiently recovered from his lapses to know that it was he who hit the bottle and not the bottle which hit him. These signs of remorse, struggle, etc., are interpreted as proceeding from an unconditional wish to obey the moral rule which he so frequently transgresses.

The more exacting the criterion which a moral agent can satisfy, the higher the degree of assent we attribute to him.

V

I shall now briefly consider whether the view that I have outlined is able to cope with the difficulties that emerged in section II. These difficulties point to five requirements of an adequate theory, namely: (i) that it accounts for the vagueness of 'he thinks he ought...' without implying that that phrase is grossly ambiguous; (ii) that the relations which it holds to obtain between the criteria should involve no logical difficulties; (iii) that it should account for the special importance that we attach to conformity without implying an untenably simple priority rule; (iv) that it should be consistent with rational comparisons of degrees of assent; and (v) that it should be able to explain certain anomalous judgements of relative fullness of assent. As far as I can see at present these five requirements are satisfied by the above theory.

Although I assert a multiplicity of criteria, my view does not imply that 'he thinks he ought...' is ambiguous; first, because the criteria form a scale and are derived from a single strict criterion, and secondly, because there are no discontinuities in the scale which they form. The proper word to apply to a phrase whose use is governed by such a scale of weakening criteria is not 'ambiguous' but 'vague'; and it has already been admitted that 'he thinks he ought...' is a vague phrase.

It can also be claimed that the theory does not give rise to logical difficulties of the kind which proved fatal to several of the views which I examined in section II.

Again, the theory seems consistent with rational comparisons of degree of assent. These can be made by comparing the relative rigorousness of the criteria which are satisfied by different individuals or by the same individual at different times. One cannot be said to assent unless one satisfies some criterion; and all the criteria which one might satisfy belong to a single scale. It follows that it is always possible to compare the criteria which different individuals satisfy.

It seems equally successful in accounting for the special importance of conformity without implying a simple priority rule. Conformity is an essential part of the criterion of full assent. Remorse, on the other hand, is only evidence for either the wish or the intention to conform, both of which are clearly less satisfactory than conformity itself. But one can conform from the wrong motives.

Hence there are times when we attach more weight to remorse than we do to conformity in our judgements of relative fullness of assent; that is to say, those judgements in which we appear to up-grade individuals after they have failed to conform with a moral rule they claim to accept. These judgements may be interpreted in two ways: (i) as the attribution of a higher degree of assent to individuals; and (ii) as an accession of confidence with regard to the rightness of previous estimates of their degree of assent. The theory has room for both interpretations. Suppose A, once rich and seemingly honest, loses his money and resorts to fraud on a single occasion. If he feels remorseful and makes reparation (as is required by our criteria of repentance), we may up-grade him. At first sight this is hard to explain, for his failure to conform necessitates his being judged by a lower criterion than might previously have been applied to him. But on grounds of his general character as this was revealed to us outside the sphere of business relationships, together with the absence of temptation to transgress the rules of honesty, we may have previously supposed, in spite of his conformity, that these moral rules meant little or nothing to him. Now we do repose some confidence in his claims to accept them. He therefore rises in our estimation in spite of his moral lapse. The theory accommodates the second interpretation still more easily; for it is obvious that there is often little evidence to go upon till after a man has transgressed the moral rules to which he claims to assent.

VI

By way of conclusion I shall now attempt to relate what I have said to the question of weakness of the will.

It seems that we place men high or low upon the scale of strength of will or character according as we estimate their actions, intentions and wishes to be relatively united or disunited. But the nature of this scale is not immediately clear. For while we may feel some hesitation in saying that a weak man does what he intends, we feel no hesitation in saying that, in some sense, he does what he wishes. Of the three words 'action', 'intention' and 'wish' it is therefore the word 'intention' that tends to disappear when we are talking about extreme weakness of will. This may be attributed to the fact that 'intention' suggests premeditated behaviour, and part of what we want to say is that the extremely weak-willed are largely at the mercy of their impulses, and hence, that they seldom pursue a settled plan of action.

But this can easily be exaggerated. Even alcoholics are sometimes capable of premeditated behaviour; indeed, they tend to follow settled plans of action because of the unbalanced nature of their desires. Hence, it is not the difference between premeditated and unpremeditated behaviour which most needs to be stressed; a more important distinction is that between behaviour which conforms with law-like rules and behaviour which conforms with clearly prescriptive rules. Alcoholics and other weak-willed people are often painfully predictable; but the maxims of their conduct (in Kant's sense) have power in their lives without possessing authority; and the rules which they attempt to impose on themselves have authority without possessing power. And herein lies their weakness – their failure to translate this authority into power. In people of strong character these rules hold dominion so that their actions are relatively predictable like those of the extremely weak-willed; the difference is that whereas the weak-willed man's actions only conform with law-like rules, the strong-willed man's actions conform with clearly prescriptive rules, moral or otherwise. The moral rules which a strong-willed man accepts invade his life and totally subdue it; the moral rules which a less strong-willed man accepts only control his intentions so that some of his actions escape their dictation; and finally, the moral rules which a weak-willed man accepts do not permeate his life beyond the level of idle wishing, so that its course proceeds almost entirely outside the pale of the rules to which he assents. It is the actions, intentions, and wishes, then, which have a bearing upon the dominion of prescriptive rules that we examine when estimating weakness of will. In the strongest men these are, as it were, united; in the weakest men they fall utterly apart.

The scales of fullness of assent and strength of character are therefore closely connected. Those who fully assent to moral rules are persons of strong character; those who only partially assent to moral rules are persons of weak character. But the scales are nevertheless distinct, the latter being used for a more comprehensive set of judgements. Thus, it does not follow from a person's having either a strong or a weak character that he accepts any moral rules, although it does follow from his having a strong character that he fully accepts some prescriptive rules, e.g. those of self-interest, and from his having a weak character that he does not fully assent to any prescriptive rules.

But is this a satisfactory view of the relations of the two scales?

Are there not occasions when we wish to say that a strong man accepts a moral rule with a low degree of assent? Although at first sight there do seem to be such occasions, I think they are mainly to be explained by the ambiguity of the phrase, 'a strong man', which sometimes means 'a person of strong character' and sometimes 'a man whom other men readily fear or obey'. It seems to me that when men of strong character claim to accept a moral rule with which they seldom conform, we normally maintain that they are lying, hoping to deceive us for some purpose of their own. Occasionally, however, we seem to accept their claims. But when we do so we no longer regard them as men of strong character. Instead of interpreting their conduct as the expression of a strong will, we now view it as obsessive in character, arising out of uncontrollable urges which, unlike those of the alcoholic, can be mistaken for the operation of fully accepted rules of a non-moral nature. Thus, we rapidly turn from one idiom to another, the adjustment being necessitated by our acceptance of the claims that have been made. I think, therefore, that the modes of speech that we employ in connection with the men whom we call strong, far from being a source of difficulty, actually confirm the rightness of the view that I have adopted with regard to the relations of the scales of fullness of assent and strength of will.

VIII Backsliding

R. M. Hare

EDITOR'S NOTE

In Freedom and Reason *(from which the following extract is taken) Professor Hare further develops the ethical theory argued for in* The Language of Morals. *The central tenets of this theory are that moral judgements are universalisable and prescriptive. They are universalisable because 'when we make a moral judgement about something we make it* because *of the possession by it of certain non-moral properties'. We are, therefore, logically committed to make the same judgement about anything else which is relevantly similar in respect of its properties. They are prescriptive in that 'they are typically intended as guides to conduct'.*

In the fourth chapter of the work Hare advances the view that it is the prescriptivity of 'ought' that accounts for 'the commonly accepted notion that "ought" implies "can".' When 'ought' has its full force its function is to offer guidance to someone asking the practical question, 'What shall I do?' So 'if we say that someone ought to do a certain thing, and "ought" has its full ... force, then we give our listeners to understand that the question arises to which this is a possible answer ...'. However, it is an important feature of 'ought' that we can say 'I ought but I can't'; but, as according to Hare, in this use the 'ought' is 'weakened', and 'is not (fully) prescriptive in meaning at all'.

In the following extract (ch. 5 of Freedom and Reason*), Hare goes on to discuss an objection to the view that moral judgements are prescriptive.*

1.   The ethical theory which I have set out is a type of prescriptivism, in that it maintains that it is one of the characteristics of moral terms, and one which is a sufficiently essential characteristic for us to call it part of the meaning of these terms, that judgements containing them are, as typically used, intended as guides to conduct. Now there is one objection to all kinds of prescriptivism

which is so commonly made, and is of such intrinsic interest, that it requires separate consideration. This is the objection that, if moral judgements were prescriptive, then it would be impossible to accept some moral judgement and yet act contrary to it. But, it is maintained (in Hume's words), "'tis one thing to know virtue, and another to conform the will to it';[1] people are constantly doing what they think they ought not to be doing; therefore prescriptivism must be wrong.

There are two points from the discussion of 'ought' and 'can' which are relevant to a consideration of this objection. The first is that, there too, there was a problem raised by our feeling that 'ought' implies 'can'. If 'ought' were always, as it is sometimes, purely descriptive, there would be no question of 'ought' implying 'can', and therefore no problem: the problem arises because of the fact that in some, and those the typical and central, of their uses moral judgements have that affinity with imperatives which makes me call both prescriptive. To this extent, the very existence of the problem – the fact that ordinary people feel that 'ought' implies 'can' and that this creates philosophical difficulties – is prima facie evidence against descriptivism. If a descriptivist were to argue that moral judgements are purely descriptive, and thus do not imply 'can', and that therefore a moralist can happily accept the extremest form of determinism, his argument would not be plausible. Now it must be pointed out that the same sort of manoeuvre is possible here: if moral judgements were not prescriptive, there would be no problem about moral weakness; but there is a problem; therefore they are prescriptive. In fact, the argument from moral weakness is very much of a two-edged weapon in the hands of the descriptivist.

The second point to be remembered from the discussion of 'ought' and 'can' is that not all moral judgements have the full, universally prescriptive force that the perfect specimen has. There are a great many kinds of 'off-colour' moral judgement which do not, like the perfect specimen, 'imply "can"'. Thus the man who says 'I ought but I can't' is not necessarily saying anything absurd; all that he is doing is to use 'ought' in one of the many off-colour ways that are possible. Some of these we listed.

Now we shall see that typical cases of 'moral weakness' are cases where a man *cannot* do what he thinks he ought; but the 'cannot' here requires very careful examination, since in other senses such a man very well can do what he ought. Nevertheless, in discussing moral weakness we have to deal with a special case of 'ought but

can't'; and what was said earlier about 'ought but can't' in general
will be relevant.

2. The view that there is no problem (that is to say no *philosophical* problem) about moral weakness rests in the main on an
analogy between the moral words and other common predicates of
our language. Since in the case of 'ought' the analogy is not so
plausible, let us for a moment take one of the moral *adjectives*,
namely 'best'. On the view that we are considering, there is nothing odder about thinking something the best thing to do in the
circumstances , but not doing it, than there is about thinking a stone
the roundest stone in the vicinity and not picking it up, but picking
up some other stone instead. If I am not looking for a round stone,
but just for a stone, there will be nothing which requires explanation if I leave the round stone and pick up, say, a jagged one; and
if I am not seeking to do the best thing in the circumstances, but
just wondering what to do, there will be nothing that requires
explanation if I choose to do what I think to be, say, the worst
possible thing to do and leave undone what I think the best thing
to do.

One will be likely, that is to say, to think that there is no problem (given that one has considered the matter at all), if one assimi-
lates moral predicates to ordinary descriptive predicates, and
ignores their differences. To think that there is no problem is, as
we have seen, the mark of a descriptivist. This is a matter of
degree. Only the most out-and-out descriptivist will be completely
unworried by the possibility of there being a problem; most descriptivists are prepared to admit that if someone does what he says is
the worst possible thing to do, an explanation is called for. But
nevertheless the attitude of a moral philosopher to this question
puts him, as I have already implied, on one side or the other of one
of the deepest cleavages in ethics – that between descriptivists and
prescriptivists.

For a certain kind of descriptivist, indeed, the existence of 'moral
weakness' will still present a problem – namely any descriptivist
who approaches these questions in a way which goes back to
Aristotle and beyond, but has been associated especially (how
justly, I do not know) with the name of Aquinas. This is to say
there is a 'law of nature' (a true but synthetic universal proposition)
that all things do, as a matter of fact, seek the good and eschew
the evil. The logical properties of this proposition would be like
those of the proposition that silkmoths lay their eggs in mulberry-

trees – except that the latter is more restricted in scope. Only silk-moths seek mulberry-trees to lay their eggs in, but *everything* seeks the good. Naturally it will not do to say that everything just *happens* to seek the good; this must therefore be some sort of synthetic necessary truth – but perhaps the same would be said about the proposition that silkmoths lay their eggs in mulberry-trees – they do not just happen to lay their eggs there; they do it because that is their *nature*. The concept of 'natural necessity' that is here said to be involved is exceedingly obscure and elusive. I find it much more credible to say that the only kind of necessity here is a logical necessity; in so far as, and in the sense that, it is true at all that everything seeks the good, it is true in virtue of the meanings of 'good' and 'seek'. And this should teach us something about the meaning of the word 'good', and of other such words – namely that they are not purely descriptive. In any case, since this kind of descriptivist will have the same problem on his hands as the pre-scriptivist, no separate treatment is perhaps necessary.

3. Nevertheless it is incumbent on the prescriptivist to say why there is a problem, and to do something about elucidating it. The problem is posed by the fact that moral judgements, in their central use, have it as their function to guide conduct. If this is their func-tion, how can we think, for example, that we ought not to be doing a certain thing (i.e. accept the view that we ought not to be doing it as a guide to our conduct) and then not be guided by it? No one can say that there is no problem here, unless he denies that it is the function of moral judgements to guide conduct.

There are analogies here between expressions like 'think good' and 'think that I ought', on the one hand, and the word 'want' on the other. These analogies are what give force to the old maxim referred to in the previous section, that everything seeks the good. For the Greek and Latin words for 'to seek' (*ephiesthai, appetere*) mean also 'to want'. It has rightly been said that 'the primitive sign of wanting is trying to get',[2] and this should warn us that to want something, and especially to want something more than any-thing else (where this is the genuine active kind of want and not mere 'idle wishing') is to have a very different kind of thing going on in our minds from what we have when we think that some descriptive proposition is true (for example that a certain cloud is shaped like a duck). To speak very crudely, the kind of thought that we have when we want something belongs with the kinds of thought that are expressed in prescriptive language, such as choices, resolves, requests, prayers, and, lastly, moral and other evaluative judgements. To draw attention to the close logical relations, on the one hand between wanting and thinking good, and on the other between wanting and doing something about getting what one wants, is to play into the hands of the prescriptivist; for it is to provide yet another link between thinking good and action.

4. We must not, however, become so obsessed by the analogies between wanting and making value-judgements that we ignore their differences. Doing just this, perhaps, led Socrates into his famous troubles over the question of moral weakness. It is in their universalisability that value-judgements differ from desires;[3] and nearly all the difficulties of Socrates stem from failing to notice this. In this respect wanting is like assenting to a singular imperative, not to a moral or other value-judgement. If I am trying to make up my mind what to do, I may simply ask myself what I most want to do; or I may ask myself what I ought to do. If I want to do A in these circumstances, I am not committed to wanting anyone else placed in exactly or relevantly similar circumstances to do likewise. But if I think that I ought to do A in these circumstances, I am committed to thinking that anyone else similarly placed ought to do the same. This means that making up my mind what I ought to do is a much more difficult and complex matter than making up my mind what I want to do; and it is these complexities that lead to the problem of moral weakness, and their unravelling to its solution. In making up my mind what I most want to do I have to consult only my own desires. But in making up my mind what I ought to do I have to consider more than this; I have to ask myself 'What maxim (to use Kant's term) can I accept as of *universal* application in cases like this, whether or not *I* play the part in the situation which I am playing now?'

Are we not all, frequently, in circumstances in which we should most like to do A, but should very much dislike it if someone did A in similar circumstances when we were the victims of his act? I mention this case as an example only, not meaning to imply that all cases of moral weakness are cases where it leads us to harm other people's interests. Indeed, moral weakness is most typically exhibited in falling short of our *ideals*, which need not, as I shall later show, have anything to do with other people's interests.[4] But in all cases moral weakness is the tendency not to do ourselves something which *in general* we commend, or to do something which *in general* we condemn. This is perhaps the central difficulty of the moral life; and it is no accident that this moral difficulty is reflected in a similarly central difficulty in theoretical ethics. Some moral philosophers speak as if it were easy to make up one's mind what one ought to do. It would indeed be easy, if either of two one-sided ethical theories were a full account of the matter. If deciding what we ought to do were a mere matter of our own desires – like deciding what we most want to do – then it would be a relatively easy task. We should decide what we most wanted to do, and, if it were in our power, do it. To put the same point in a more technical way: if moral judgements were *singular* prescriptives of some sort, then there would be less difficulty in deciding which of them to accept, and acceptance of them would lead to action; there could be no question of weakness of will. That was why Socrates, who paid insufficient attention to the universalisability of moral judgements, found himself saying that there was no such thing as weakness of will.

5.   That is one spurious way of easing our moral difficulties. The other way consists in accepting the universalisability of moral judgements, and the descriptive meaning that goes with it, and forgetting the universal *prescriptiveness* of moral principles. Then it again becomes easier to make up one's mind what one ought to do, because one is no longer, in saying that one ought to do A, prescribing to oneself. If this view were correct, I could decide that I, and that anyone in like circumstances, ought to do A, and then, without any hint of going back on what I had decided, not do A. There are a great many things which we should be perfectly prepared to say that we ought to do if we did not think that, in saying this, we were committing ourselves to any prescription, and thus action. The real difficulty of making a moral decision is, as I have said before, that of finding some action to which one is prepared to commit oneself, and which at the same time one is prepared to accept as exemplifying a principle of action binding on anyone in like circumstances. This is what makes the moral life, for one who takes it seriously, so appallingly difficult.

So difficult is it, in fact – so great is the strain between prescriptivity and universalisability in certain situations – that something has to give; and this is the explanation of the phenomenon of moral weakness. Not only do *we* give, because we are morally weak; we have found for ourselves a language which shares our weakness, and gives just where we do. For moral language is a human institution. It is the business of the moral philosopher to say, not what the logical behaviour of moral terms *would* be like, if they were devised by and for the use of angels, but what it actually is like.[5] To use another of Kant's expressions, a 'holy' moral language would be a very simple one; it would consist of universalisable prescriptive judgements without any way of escaping from either their prescriptivity or their universality. It would, in fact, be like the evaluative language described in the last chapter of *The Language of Morals* (which was, it will be remembered, a simplified artificial model) without any of the escape-routes for backsliders which are so amply provided in our actual moral language, and which were, some of them, described in the body of that book (e.g. 7.5, 9.4, 11.2). No shift of ground from the viewpoint of that book *is* implied in saying that human moral language, unlike a holy or angelic moral language, has, built into its logic, all manners of ways of evading the rigour of pure prescriptive universality. These we shall have to chart in more detail. But nevertheless it would be a slander upon human moral language and on its users to claim that they do not even *aspire* to have universal prescriptive principles; not all who speak morally have already given up the struggle in one of the two ways just referred to, by reconciling themselves to a moral language that is either not prescriptive or not fully universal.

An angel, in making up his mind about a moral question concerning his own conduct, might proceed as follows. He might ask himself to what action he was prepared to commit himself, and at the same time prepared to accept as exemplifying a principle of action binding on anyone in like circumstances. As we have seen, this question is an appallingly difficult one in many situations – the source of the difficulty, we might say, is that in setting out to live morally we are aspiring to be like angels, which is a formidable undertaking. But angels, unlike human beings, do not find any difficulty in answering such questions, because, having holy wills and no selfish inclinations, they do not ever want to do actions whose maxims they cannot universalise. But we are not angels; and therefore, although the *simplest* logic for a moral language would be that of the universalisable prescriptive, we shy at this rigorous and austere simplicity, and, in our vain struggles to find a more comfortable way of speaking, have introduced complexities into the logic of our moral language – vain struggles, because the ideal of pure universal prescriptive moral principles obstinately remains with us, and we are not in the end satisfied with anything which falls short of it.

The complexities are very great, and it will be impossible to mention all of them.[6] The inquiry into them will be, as are most philosophical inquiries, at one and the same time about language and about what happens; for to ask about different senses of 'ought' and of 'think that one ought', in the way that the philosopher asks this, is at the same time to ask about different possible states of mind; the two inquiries are inseparable. One cannot study language, in a philosophical way, without studying the world that we are talking about.[7]

6. Here, however, it is necessary to qualify somewhat the expression 'different senses of "ought"'. The impression may have been given by certain passages in *The Language of Morals* that moral words are somehow ambiguous, in that they have a series of distinct senses, so that one could ask a man in which sense he was using them – for example the 'inverted commas', the 'ironic', the 'conventional', and so on (ibid., 7.5). It is wrong to say this. Fortunately Professor Nowell-Smith has now provided us with a terminology for saying much better what I was trying to say. He has invented the expression 'Janus-word' to describe words of the sort we are considering, which have two or more aspects to their meaning, one of which may on occasion be emphasised to the neglect of the others.[8] We cannot say that such a word is ambiguous; it is indeed an inseparable element in its meaning that it can shift in this way. The human word 'ought', unlike its counterpart in an angelic moral language, not only faces both ways in the sense of having both descriptive and prescriptive meaning – for the angelic word does that – but can sometimes look in the direction that suits its user's interests, and bury its other face in the sand. Even if we are at our most moral when we say that we ought to be doing such and such a thing (getting up, for example), and fully intend to set about doing it there and then, we know only too well that if our moral strength were to fail us at the last moment, and we did not get up, we could still go on saying that we thought that we ought to be getting up – and saying it, though in a way in an attenuated sense, without in another way departing from the meaning of the word as we were using it all along: for all along the meaning of the word was such that we *could* backslide in this way.

There are many different methods of backsliding without appearing to. The commonest, perhaps, of these subterfuges is that known as special pleading. We start off as it were prepared to accept a certain moral principle as binding on everybody; and we start off by accepting it as prescriptive, and therefore as committing *us* in particular to acting in accordance with the principle. But when we consider how contrary to our own interests it is for us to act in accordance with the principle, we weaken. While continuing to prescribe that everyone *else* (or at any rate everyone whose interests do not especially concern us) should act in accordance with the principle, we do not so prescribe to ourselves (for to do this fully and in earnest would commit us to acting). The word 'ought' can remain universal in that it retains all the descriptive meaning that it ever had; but it ceases to express a universal prescription – the prescription is not universal and the universality is only descriptive. To restore the appearance of prescriptive universality, we substitute, in our own case, for genuine prescriptiveness, a mere *feeling*, varying in strength, that we are not playing our part in the scheme which we claim to be accepting (that we are, as it were, leading our regiment from behind). This feeling is called a guilty conscience. It is essential to the success of this manoeuvre that the feeling should not, at the time, be too strong. The man who wishes to act against his conscience must make sure that his conscience is less powerful than the desires which oppose it; for if conscience pricks us too hard it will prick us into doing the action, and genuine prescriptive universality will be restored.

Suppose, however, that this does not happen, and that we fail to do the required action, and merely feel uncomfortable about it. Has the expression 'think that I ought' changed its meaning for us? We have, indeed, accepted, as exemplifying the state of mind called 'thinking that I ought', something less robust than formerly; but then from the start the expression 'think that I ought' had the potentiality of such a decline – it is an expression of human language, and humans are always doing this sort of thing. There are, indeed, many ways in which it can lose its robustness without, in a sense, departing from its original meaning; we shall notice some others later.

7.   I have been speaking as if we were extremely self-conscious and purposive about adopting such a device as I have described. Now there are indeed people who know what they are going about when they do this; such are the real hypocrites. But this is not the state of most of us. Far from it being a matter of freely chosen policy to think in this way, most of us find it impossibly hard, not being angels, to think in any other. Our morality is formed of principles and ideals which we do not succeed in persuading ourselves to ful-

fil. And this *inability* to realise our ideals is well reflected in the
highly significant names given in both Greek and English to this
condition: Greek calls it *akrasia* – literally 'not being strong
enough (sc. to control oneself)'; and English calls it 'moral weakness' or 'weakness of will'. Nor is this the only evidence that the
state of mind that most people are thinking of when they speak of
weakness of will involves an inability, in some sense, to do what
we think we ought. There are two extremely well-worn passages in
literature which are constantly quoted in this controversy, usually
against the prescriptive position. Since those who quote them
frequently show themselves unaware of the contexts in which
they occur, I shall quote them at length, in order to show how
many references there are to the powerlessness of the speakers. The
first describes Medea, trying to resist the onset of love for Jason:

> Meanwhile, Aeetes' daughter's heart took fire;
> Her struggling Reason could not quell Desire.
> 'This madness how can I resist?', she cried;
> 'No use to fight; some God is on its side . . .
> Dash from your maiden breast these flames it feels!
> Ah, if I could, the less would be my ills.
> Alas I cannot quench them; an unknown
> Compulsion bears me, all reluctant, down.
> Urged this – that – on Love's or Reason's course,
> I see and praise the better: do the worse.'[9]

Ovid here again and again stresses the helplessness of Medea;
and so does St Paul stress his own helplessness in the famous passage
from Romans vii:

We know that the law is spiritual; but I am not: I am unspiritual,
the purchased slave of sin. I do not even acknowledge my own
actions as mine, for what I do is not what I want to do, but what
I detest. But if what I do is against my will, it means that I agree
with the law and hold it to be admirable. But as things are, it is
no longer I who perform the action, but sin that lodges in me.
For I know that nothing good lodges in me – in my unspiritual
nature, I mean – for though the will to do good is there, the deed
is not. The good which I want to do, I fail to do; but what I do
is the wrong which is against my will; and if what I do is against
my will, clearly it is no longer I who am the agent, but sin that
has its lodging in me. I discover this principle, then: that when I

want to do the right, only the wrong is within my reach. In my inmost self I delight in the law of God, but I perceive that there is in my bodily members a different law, fighting against the law that my reason approves and making me a prisoner under the law that is in my members, the law of sin. Miserable creature that I am, who is there to rescue me out of this body doomed to death? God alone, through Jesus Christ our Lord! Thanks be to God! In a word, then, I myself, subject to God's law as a rational being, am yet, in my unspiritual nature, a slave to the law of sin.[10]

The impression given by these two passages is very different from that conveyed by descriptivist philosophers who quote scraps from them out of context. Taken as a whole, these passages do not even run counter to the summary view which I put forward in *The Language of Morals*. For I said there that I proposed to use the word 'value-judgement' in such a way that 'the test, whether someone is using the judgement "I ought to do X" as a value-judgement or not, is "Does he or does he not recognise that if he assents to the judgement, he must also assent to the command "Let me do X"?' And earlier I said 'It is a tautology to say that we cannot sincerely assent to a command addressed to ourselves, and *at the same time* not perform it, if now is the occasion for performing it, and it is in our (physical and psychological) power to do so'.[11] The purpose of putting in the words 'physical and psychological power' was precisely to meet the possible objection which we are considering. Nobody in his senses would maintain that a person who assents to an imperative must (analytically) act on it even when he is unable to do so. But this is what I should have to have been maintaining, if these quotations from Ovid and St Paul were to serve as counter-examples to my view. It is not in Medea's or St Paul's psychological power to act on the imperatives that are entailed by the moral judgements which they are making.

8.   We see, therefore, that the typical case of moral weakness, as opposed to that of hypocrisy, is a case of 'ought but can't'. We have therefore to put it in its place within the general account of 'ought but can't'.[12] What is it that distinguishes 'psychological' impossibility from 'physical', and this kind of 'psychological' impossibility from others? And what happens to 'ought' in all these cases? We saw that 'physical' impossibility (and also such allied cases as impossibility due to lack of knowledge or skill) causes an

imperative to be withdrawn altogether, as inconsistent with the admission of impossibility; but that in a similar case an 'ought' does not have to be withdrawn but only down-graded. It no longer carries prescriptive force in the particular case, though it may continue to do so with regard to actions in similar circumstances (similar, except that the action is possible). I referred to this pheno-menon as 'a lifting of a corner of the net'. We are now, perhaps, in a better position to understand it. We also saw that, although the prescription for the particular case has to be withdrawn, this does not prevent agony of mind, or even, in some cases, social reprobation. Jocasta was the victim of destiny, and knew it; but she hanged herself, and people no doubt called her incestuous, which is a term of disapproval.

In cases of moral weakness, where the impossibility is psycho-logical, remorse and disapproval are even more in place; for, though unable to overcome this temptation, they keep alive the will-power which may overcome lesser ones. It is therefore not a consequence of our account of the matter, which stresses the im-possibility of resisting the temptation, that the morally weak man is exempt from adverse moral judgements. In terms of the pre-ceding chapter, the question 'What shall I do?' arises for him (as it does in cases of physical impossibility); and even if we can be sure that he will answer it in a certain way, it may nevertheless be of value to say that he ought not to act so, in order to reassert the general prescriptive principle. St Paul gives plenty of evidence of remorse, and Medea was no doubt subject to parental disapproval. St Paul, we may be sure, did not want himself to sin likewise on future occasions; and Aeetes did not want his other daughters to go falling for foreign adventurers. To this extent their remarks were prescriptive. But it was clearly of no immediate use for either St Paul or Medea or Aeetes to prescribe for the particular cases. Sometimes, by uttering a prescription, another person may help a morally weak agent to overcome his moral weakness – the actual utterance, by reinforcing the will of the agent, alters the situation, so that what was impossible becomes possible. But the cases we have been considering may be supposed to lie beyond the reach of such help on the part of fellow humans – though the divine help which St Paul invokes is partly of this kind.

The form of prescription is preserved, however (and this shows how reluctant we are to suppress it), in the curious metaphor of divided personality which, ever since this subject was first discussed, has seemed so natural. One part of the personality is made to issue commands to the other, and to be angry or grieved when they are disobeyed; but the other part is said either to be unable to obey, or to be so depraved as not to want to, and to be stronger than the part which commands. Medea actually uses the imperative; and St Paul speaks of a 'law' which he 'agrees with' or 'consents unto' (*Rev. Version*). And so two interpretations of this phenomenon become possible, both of them metaphorical, and both consistent with prescriptivism. The first is that the person who accepts some moral judgement but does not act on it is actually giving commands to himself, but unable to obey them because of a recalcitrant lower nature or 'flesh'; the other is that he is, in his whole personality or real self, ceasing to prescribe to himself (though there may be a part of him that goes on prescribing, and though he may be quite ready to prescribe to others). These two metaphors are so natural and so deeply imprinted in our common speech that the philosopher who wishes to abandon them in pursuit of literalness will have to invent his own language. Cases differ, and possibly one metaphor is sometimes more appropriate and sometimes another.

9. We may conclude, at any rate, that typical cases of moral weakness do not constitute a counter-example to prescriptivism, as I have been maintaining it. But, since it may be objected that there are other cases which do provide counter-examples, it will be helpful to approach the problem from the other end, and ask what sort of case would provide a counter-example to prescriptivism, and whether it exists.

As we have seen, it will not do to quote cases in which people *cannot* bring themselves to do what they think they ought to do. The fact that in such cases it is often true that a man is *physically* in a position, and strong, knowledgeable, and skilful enough, etc., to do what he thinks he ought, is irrelevant. For, whether or not the psychological inability down-grades the 'ought', as I have suggested, it certainly makes it impossible to act on any prescription that may survive, and so explains how prescriptivity, if it survives, is still compatible with disobedience. We may remark that the fact that 'physical' possibility may be unimpaired is the cause of a common initial reluctance to accept the account of the matter which I have given. It cannot be said, it is objected, that the morally weak person *cannot* do what he thinks he ought, because he is obviously as able as the rest of us. But 'able' here refers only to 'physical' ability. In a deeper sense the man cannot do the act. This is clearest in cases of compulsive neuroses in which 'psychological' impossibility comes close to 'physical'; but it holds also in more normal cases of weakness of will, as the very word 'weakness' indicates.

Nor will it do to quote cases in which a man goes on saying that he ought, but fails to act, even though he can act, in every sense of 'can'. For this is the case of what I called purposive backsliding, or hypocrisy; and these are allowed for. If a man does what he says he ought not to, though perfectly able to resist the temptation to do it, then there is something wrong with what he says, as well as with what he does. In the simplest case it is insincerity; he is not saying what he really thinks. In other cases it is self-deception; he thinks that he thinks he ought, but he has escaped his own notice using 'ought' in an off-colour way. The residual feelings of guilt have supplied the place of real prescriptiveness. There are endless possible variations upon this theme; but until one is produced which really does run counter to prescriptivism, the prescriptivist need not be concerned.

Equally irrelevant is the case of the man who *thought* that he ought to do something, but, now that the time has come to do it, has let pass from his mind either the thought that he ought, or the thought that now is the time. And so is that of the man who thinks that in general *one ought*, but has not got as far as realising that *his* present case falls under this principle. These cases can be ruled out by confining our attention to cases in which a man does not do what he thinks (now) that *he* ought *to be* doing.[18]

Then there are the cases of people who *think* that they ought, but lack complete moral conviction. They may be using the word 'ought' in the most full-blooded possible way; but they are not so *sure* that they ought as to commit themselves to action. These cases, likewise, present no difficulty.

Then there is the case, mentioned already above and in *The Language of Morals* (11.2), in which a man, in saying that he ought, means no more than that the action in question is required by the accepted morality of his society, or that it is the sort of action, the thought of whose omission induces in him certain feelings. Since such a man is not using the word 'ought' prescriptively, and since I have allowed for such uses, this case needs no further discussion.

In all this, we find no case that provides a true counter-example. And since I myself am unable even to describe such a case, let alone to find one in real life, I am content to leave the search to critics of prescriptivism.

Lastly, it may be objected that I have been altogether too elusive – a common fault in philosophy at the present time. In *The*

Language of Morals I performed what some have thought an evasive manoeuvre by *defining* 'value-judgement' in such a way that if a man did not do what he thought he ought, he could not be using the word evaluatively. I have in this book done something similar with the word 'prescriptive' – only with the qualifications made above. The purpose of both manoeuvres was, however, not to evade objections but to clarify the problem by locating it where it can be seen. The problem exists for evaluative or prescriptive uses of moral words; and it is therefore necessary to know which these are. Therefore we have to exclude from the category 'evaluative' or 'universally prescriptive' such uses as do not belong to it. This I tried to do in *The Language of Morals*, and have tried to do in greater detail in this chapter. This is clarification only. The substantive part of the prescriptivist thesis is *that there are* prescriptive uses of these words, and that these uses are important and central to the words' meaning. That they are important and central is shown by the fact that the problems which notoriously arise concerning moral language would not arise unless there were these uses. Such problems are: the impossibility of defining moral words naturalistically (ibid., 11.3); the problems raised by ' "ought" ' implies "can" ' (4.1 ff.); the problem discussed in this chapter; and others besides. All these problems are indications that moral language is stronger meat than the bellies of descriptivists are accustomed to.

But that prescriptive uses of moral language *exist*, at any rate, cannot be doubted. Prescriptivism would be refuted if it could be shown that we do not ever use moral words in the way that I have characterised as prescriptive. To counter this attack, it is only necessary to produce examples of such a use, and to ask the reader whether he finds them at all untypical. I will produce just one. If a man is faced with a difficult moral choice, and asks a friend or adviser 'What do you think I ought to do?', is it not sometimes the case that if he says 'You ought to do A', and if the man then proceeds not to do A, he will be said to have rejected the advice?

IX Moral weakness

Steven Lukes

What is at issue in a discussion of weakness of the will? In the philosophical history of the problem there seems to have been little disagreement over the facts, either of language or of moral psychology, nor has there simply been a conflict of first-order moral views. The problem has, I suggest, arisen primarily as a result of a divergence over the extent to which an ideal should determine the description of the facts.

In the classical dispute between Socrates and Plato, on the one hand, and Aristotle, on the other, the divergence was fundamentally of this nature.[1] Plato was primarily concerned with discovering and inculcating that moral knowledge which, once it was attained, was final and irresistible. Aristotle was more concerned with the facts of moral psychology and language. Of Socrates' view he says, 'this theory is manifestly at variance with plain facts', the view being 'that there is no such thing as Unrestraint (*akrasia*), since no one, he said, acts contrary to what is best, believing what he does to be bad, but only through ignorance'. (p. 64 above). What Plato and Socrates were doing was to offer a tacit persuasive definition of 'knowledge' so that a man cannot, by definition, know what is right and good if his actions are wrong and bad. Part of the background to this is the familiar Platonic doctrine that virtue is knowledge, an ability, or technique, or 'knowing-how', which is the necessary pre-condition of acting rightly, and it is only for the lack of this that a man acts wrongly (or does not act rightly), not because of a failure of will. There is, in the Socratic–Platonic doctrine, a solid basis of moral certainty such that if a man is said to make a judgement or believe in a principle, it is only *knowledge*, according to the doctrine, if the judgement or principle is the true or right one – and the assumption is that there is a final test to establish whether this is so or not. Further, it is only knowledge, as opposed to 'right opinion', if one is sufficiently acquainted with that which is to be known.[2] Thus there is a double claim: that a man only knows what is right when his knowledge is, so to speak, irresistible, that is, when he acts rightly; and that he only knows what is right when he has an acquaintance with the truth, as opposed to a mere 'right opinion'. Thus it can plausibly be argued that Plato, at times at least, wanted to make a qualitative distinction between moral knowledge and moral belief, whether the latter is right or wrong. But, as Aristotle pointed out, some men are as convinced of their beliefs and opinions as they are of their knowledge, so that right opinion would presumably be as irresistible as knowledge. However this may be, in Plato, cases of wrong-doing are persuasively redefined as the products of ignorance. What Aristotle did was to take this view literally and to insist that men do in fact act inconsistently with both their knowledge and their beliefs, though his own explanation of these cases is far from complete and satisfactory. He is interested in describing the facts as accurately as possible. As he says:

> We must, as in all other cases, set the various views about this subject before us and, after first discussing the difficulties, go on to prove, if possible, the truth of all the common opinions of these affections of the mind, or, failing this, of the greater and most authoritative; for if we both refute the objections and leave the common opinions undisturbed, we shall have proved the case sufficiently (pp. 63–4 above).

So, to sum up, what I am suggesting is that, so far as Plato, Socrates and Aristotle were concerned, the dispute seems now to have been mainly of terminology, of how to describe the facts. The former were concerned to present them in a certain light, to describe them in an unusual and paradoxical way, which encapsulates a philosophical and moral view (i.e. the description of wrongdoing as ignorance),[3] the latter was more concerned to look carefully at the facts and describe them faithfully, accurately and consistently, keeping as closely as possible to what we ordinarily say and think.

The problem of moral weakness has reappeared in recent moral philosophy in a markedly different but no less puzzling form. The question is asked 'Can a man consciously do what he sincerely believes to be wrong or fail to do what he sincerely believes to be right?' One kind of answer given is that, broadly speaking, he cannot. Of this kind of answer two forms may be distinguished, a stronger and a weaker. The stronger answer, which is very implausible, is that a man always does what he thinks he ought to, so that a failure to act is a knock-down criterion of a failure to believe – unless he is physically prevented from acting as he thinks he ought.

In other words the criterion of a man's holding a moral belief, making a moral judgement, assenting to a moral principle or rule is, on this view, to be restricted to acting rightly on the appropriate occasion – making the obvious assumption that there is no physical impossibility and that the occasion is recognised as appropriate. This implausible view has been (falsely) attributed to Professor Hare, on the basis of a few remarks in *The Language of Morals*, by e.g., Dr Ewing.[4] It is also the view attributed by Hare to Socrates. Socrates, he says, failed to notice an important distinction between value judgements and desires, namely that the former are universalisable, and for this reason found himself saying that there was no such thing as weakness of the will. In other words, Socrates assimilated moral judgements to wanting, or, in Hare's terms, 'assenting to a singular imperative', and thus denied that one could at the same time make them and fail to act on them. But if what I have said above is right, this is not an accurate account of Socrates' view, since he was concerned to narrow the class of moral judgements, not to widen it.

The weaker form of the view that a man cannot consciously act against or fail to act up to his moral beliefs, judgements or principles is that which is adopted by Hare in his book, *Freedom and Reason*, and it is this view that I propose to consider, at some length, sticking as closely as possible to Hare's own formulation.

In general the argument is that when a man makes a moral judgement or assents to a moral principle, and is using the relevant moral words in their full sense and therefore prescriptively, he thereby, by definition, assents to a self-addressed imperative of the form 'Let me do X'. But, importantly, he also assents to a universal rule, which is universal because of the meaning of moral words, and which is accepted as a principle of action binding on anyone in like circumstances. If he then acts wrongly or fails to act rightly when the occasion is suitable and he recognises that this case falls under his principle, we are to explain the matter by any one (or a combination of) the following possible reasons:

1. 'Purposive backsliding, or hypocrisy', which seems to be subdivided into insincerity and self-deception (pp. 144–5 above) – e.g. in the latter case 'ought' is being used in an 'off-colour way'.
2. The assent or belief was not real because the man thinks he ought but lacks complete moral conviction. People of this kind 'are not so *sure* that they ought, as to commit themselves to action'.
3. Physical impossibility: he *cannot* act as he thinks he ought.

4. Psychological impossibility: likewise, but in 'another sense' of 'cannot'.

Thus, if the moral words are being used in a fully evaluative, i.e. universally prescriptive way, the explanation of moral weakness boils down to either insincerity, lack of conviction, physical impossibility or psychological impossibility.

It is, in passing, worth noting how this differs from the Socratic doctrine. The classical dispute, as I have tried to show, turned upon knowledge, so that wrongdoing was claimed to be the product of ignorance; whereas the dispute between Hare and those who would disagree with his views on moral weakness turns upon belief and assent, so that conscious wrongdoing (if one can act otherwise) is claimed to be the result of a lack of full belief or sincere assent. I shall suggest that the latter dispute arises from the same cause as the former, namely, a divergence over how to describe familiar facts. I suspect that this divergence may have wider moral and philosophical implications.

Let us characterise the present dispute more clearly. Suppose a man claims fully to assent to the moral principle 'One ought to do X', the question of doing X arises and he fails to act. (For the sake of clarity we can ignore the cases where he fails to recognise the situation as covered by the principle, as well as the cases where some other overriding moral principle is adopted, e.g. lying to save a friend.) According to Hare, the man is either lacking in full and sincere assent to the principle or else it is not in his physical or psychological power to perform the action. Whereas the opponent of the Hare view will argue that a man can consciously fail to do what he fully believes he ought to be doing and that this is not to be explained in terms of either a failure of belief or an inability to act. People, he will insist, are pretty imperfect on the whole, and sincerely as they hold their moral beliefs, principles and ideals, many is the time that they have failed to live up to them and could have done so if only they had tried harder; he will argue further that it is perfectly possible for a man consciously to do what is incompatible with his moral beliefs.

The crucial feature of the Hare doctrine is a tautology at its very heart, namely, the definition of a value-judgement as entailing imperatives, such that to assent to the judgement 'I ought to do X' is also to assent to the self-addressed command 'Let me do X'. He writes, 'It is a tautology to say that we cannot sincerely assent to a second-person command ... and *at the same time* not perform it, if now is the occasion for performing it and it is in our (physical and psychological) power to do so' (Chapter V, 1, above). There are, however, 'degrees of sincere assent, not all of which involve actually obeying the command' (Chapter V, 2). We are here being presented with an ideal limit, peculiar to angels, which is both psychological and linguistic, to which all other states of affairs are inferior. At the limit there is (1) full and sincere assent and (2) universality and prescriptivity: here action follows by definition. At a position less than the limit, i.e. where there is a failure to act rightly, there are two possibilities: (a) less than full and sincere assent but full universal prescriptivity; and (b) full and sincere assent but less than full universal prescriptivity. In case (b), where a man is aware that he is doing what he sincerely believes he ought not to be doing or that he is not doing what he sincerely believes he ought to be doing, Hare says that it is *impossible* for him to act otherwise. This, he says, is the typical case of moral weakness.

Failure to act on one's moral beliefs is a situation that occurs frequently enough. Hare recognises this: 'Our morality', he says, 'is formed of principles and ideals which we do not succeed in persuading ourselves to fulfil' (p. 140 above).[5] Yet his description of this situation is in terms of the *inability* to realise our ideals, and indeed he writes that 'the typical case of moral weakness, as opposed to that of hypocrisy, is a case of "ought but can't"' (p. 142). In particular, he takes the familiar cases of Medea trying and failing to resist her love for Jason, and St Paul battling against the flesh, in order to point to the powerlessness of the speakers. Finally, he argues that this account of moral weakness in terms of psychological impossibility (plus remorse and a failure of universal prescriptiveness) is borne out by the English phrase 'weakness of will' and the Greek *akrasia*.

I do not think it is possible to dispute the Hare doctrine on its own terms, for it is curiously self-protecting. Hare himself says that he is unable even to describe a counter-example to his view (p. 145). I am not interested in either producing a 'true counter-example' or 'refuting prescriptivism'. The question is whether the Hare doctrine is right and compelling and, more generally, what its nature and status is.

First of all, what is one to make of psychological impossibility? In cases of moral weakness we are told that a man may be physically able to do the act but 'in a deeper sense the man cannot do the act'. And 'the state of mind that most people are thinking of when they speak of weakness of will involves an inability, in some sense, to do

what we think we ought' (pp. 140–1). As well as being somewhat
obscure, this is not plausible as an explanation of a large class of
cases where a man does what he believes to be wrong or fails to do
what he believes to be right. Given his sincere moral beliefs, we do
not have to accept his excuses ('I knew it was wrong but I could not
help doing it', 'I knew I shouldn't have done it but I just had to',
'I knew I should do it, but I just couldn't'). Of course, there are
cases, too familiar to describe, where a person's character or situation really puts the action beyond possibility for him, but there are
also many cases where we would normally say that a man failed to
live up to his principles, though he could have done, meaning that
it was in his power. It is very difficult to see what Hare's 'deeper
sense of inability' is, nor how it is distinguished from the everyday
superficial sense, nor is the distinction between physical and psychological impossibility clear. If psychological impossibility is meant
to account for all cases of failing to act upon sincerely-held beliefs
and principles, it would seem to entail a crude psychological determinism, which would make Hare's use of the phrase 'in X's psychological power' look very Pickwickian, and which he elsewhere dis-
owns (*Freedom and Reason*, p. 63). There is a difference, after all,
between the compulsive neurotic or even the man overcome by
passion or emotion, on the one hand, and the average backslider
on the other.

One can only here appeal to an intuitive understanding of the
phenomenology of moral action (and inaction) and doubtless all
the cases I will adduce can be described in Hare's terms, that is to
say, in a way which only recognises as a sincerely-held moral principle or belief one which is action-compelling in situations which are
relevant and '*optional*' (to coin a term). A relevant situation is one
which a person sees as appropriate and falling under the belief or
principle: he has 'got as far as realising that *his* present case falls
under this principle' (p. 145). An optional situation is one where
the required action or inaction is in fact possible: the question arises
of a choice between alternatives and these alternatives are genuine
ones (this would, of course, sometimes be very difficult to ascertain,
but not impossible in principle). These situations are those in which
the agent has the freedom which engenders moral thought. In them
'Shall I?' and 'Ought I?' questions arise, as genuine practical
questions, with alternative genuine practical solutions. Hare's account of beliefs and principles is thus definitely linked to the
paradigm of the relevant and optional situation, for here the required action must occur.

It is my argument that Hare's descriptions of the cases in dispute always embody one particular interpretation of them, which we may not wish to accept, and which does violence to our natural understanding of the facts.

First, it seems evident that Hare's quotations of and comments upon the passages from Ovid and St Paul are particularly favourable to his views, although these passages are usually quoted against them, since these cases are described in terms of the will battling against fearful odds and being *overpowered*, as by physical force. But it is not obvious that these and other, perhaps less heroic, cases of temptation are cases of quasi-compulsive behaviour. Take the following example, that comes from Tolstoy's biographer, Aylmer Maude:

> When he was nearly seventy he one day expressed to me his conviction that, despite all difficulties and despite repeated failures, one should never cease to aim at chastity; and he added: 'I was myself a husband last night, but that is no reason for abandoning the struggle; God may grant me not to be so again.'

I suggest that one reason for which one finds this story amusing is precisely the reason that would lead one to reject Hare's account of moral weakness. Apart from Tolstoy's age, it is the appeal to God that makes one smile, as though it were only by God's determining will that the lapse has occurred. In general, the Hare doctrine is saying that when sincere men are faced by temptation, if they resist it they act freely, but if they do not, they are unable (in a deeper sense) to do so.

It is interesting to compare Hare's position with what Professor Nowell-Smith calls the 'theory of the self-propelling conscience', in which 'moral conflict is represented as a battle between "me" (or my "self" or "my conscience") and "my desires" '.[6] Nowell-Smith points out that this theory is often found in conjunction with the view that conscientiousness is the only virtue and acting against one's conscience the only vice. He goes on:

> it is this combination that is paradoxical, since on this theory a conscientious action is the only type of free action, all actions being prompted by desire being unfree. If conscience wins the day, I act freely and am good; if desire wins the day, I am bad but *I* do not choose to do what I do. Now all this may be true; but, if so, ordinary men have for centuries been labouring under a profound delusion. For nothing is more certain than that they

believe that a man can choose to do what is wrong and that he chooses in exactly the same sense of 'choose' as he does when he chooses to do what is right.

Hare seems at least to condone this theory *in cases of moral weakness.*

It is evident that our standards are far more flexible and most situations far more complicated than Hare's account allows. Take Sartre's cases of *mauvaise foi* (e.g. the girl who leaves her hand in that of her seducer),[7] which Hare seems to want to take as a case of purposive backsliding or hypocrisy (p. 144 above); for here we do not accept her excuses, though we may not doubt her sincerity – one can blame her and she is to blame, but precisely for the failure to connect her thought with her action. It is not simply to be dismissed as 'self-deception' – itself a very difficult notion requiring extended treatment: she has not just 'escaped (her) own notice using "ought" in an off-colour way' (ibid.), although a failure of attention *is* involved here. There is, in brief, a large class of cases (that is, the normal and standard cases of moral weakness) where we would refuse Hare's dichotomy of hypocrisy and psychological impossibility. Of course (to borrow Gardiner's formulation), the question of sincerity is always *raised* by cases of conscious wrongdoing, and in some cases (e.g. where there is a long-term or systematic divergence between a man's professions or beliefs and his actions, though not even always here) we would answer that the man is insincere. However, we would, and often do, say of people that they voluntarily and consciously behave as they genuinely feel they should not. Yet Hare wishes to force us intò saying that *either* they do not really hold their ideals or assent to their moral principles *or* that their actions are in some sense compelled or compulsive.

Let us examine some of these cases. Take the case of a man A who sincerely believes in happy marriage as an ideal and is faced with the situation of a friend B who is about to lose his wife, because of his (B's) adultery; and let us suppose that B had left his first wife and had been the cause of the first marriage breaking up. A's problem is that his own moral ideal disposes him to want to heal the breach if he can. Let us suppose a situation in which A could act in order to do this, e.g. B comes to him for advice, and he fails to act. Now, there are a number of possible explanations here, of which I shall select four. In the first place, it may be that A's ideal (the picture of married bliss) is not connected in any clear-cut way with principles of action, for himself or others: it is a norm by which he judges the world of personal relationships or a vision with which he compares it, but he has not got so far as being clear how to realise it in action. He has no cut-and-dried principle to which he can appeal, such as 'One ought to help mend breaking marriages'. He is an impractical idealist and he does not act, though he senses he should be doing something. In the second place, it may be the case that he does actually subscribe to the principle, 'One ought to help mend breaking marriages', and yet he fails to tell himself to do this at what he knows to be the appropriate time – he suddenly decides not to bother, that he is too busy, that he won't take on the responsibility (this must be distinguished from his acting on another, overriding, moral principle). At the crucial point he fails to tell himself to apply the principle, probably with a bad conscience. Or, thirdly, he may actually tell himself to act, but at the crucial moment he falters and lets the chance slip by. He just does not act, though he meant to and could have done, and afterwards perhaps feels great remorse. In Hare's terms, these three cases are respectively cases of (1) sincerely holding the ideal but not connecting it with a principle of action, and therefore failing to act; (2) sincerely assenting to a principle but not in fact assenting to an imperative it may be said logically to entail, and therefore failing to act; (3) sincerely assenting to an imperative (making a resolve – see Chapter V, 1 above) and yet not acting. There is also a fourth possibility which is worth noticing: he may believe in the critical situation that he cannot do anything about the matter, that his friend is beyond salvation, and yet be wrong. Here he believes, wrongly, that acting as he thinks he should will, so far as he can see, be unavailing, so he fails to act (though let us assume that in fact he could save the marriage –say, someone else acts and the marriage is saved).

What do these cases show? First, that people can fail to connect in a number of interesting ways that are not allowed for in Hare's picture. In the first three cases, would we not say that there was a (probably culpable) failure to connect ideals with principles, principles with resolves, resolves with actions – though these connections could have been made, had only the man been, e.g., more rational, attentive, conscientious, etc.? There are logical or quasi-logical connections between these, which, if a person does not draw them, give rise to questions of a psychological nature about him. He may have failed clearly to see that he was being inconsistent or he may have seen this but failed to care. We generally assume, in a rationalist manner, that such deviation from a rational norm requires explanation, as well as castigation. There is an analogy here with the man who sincerely holds, at the same time, beliefs which are incompatible or logically inconsistent with one another. With further effort, involving an attempt at, so to speak, 'integrating his consciousness', he could make the required connections, and for his failure to do so we blame him and perhaps he is to blame.

Now, Hare may describe these cases in terms of either not really holding the ideals and/or principles and not really believing, or else being unable (in a deeper sense) to act suitably. But this must assume a degree of conscious integration that only the most rational possess. Hare can always *say* that if a man does not do what he purports to think he ought to be doing, the choice is between less than full and sincere belief and impossibility, yet to say this is to presuppose a certain psychological doctrine about the practicality of belief, i.e. that really believing something involves or perhaps even just is a disposition to act in certain specified ways.[8] This doctrine, if applied to particular cases, can be denied, without denying the complex logical connections between belief and action in general: what is true in general need not be true of any given case. In those cases which we have taken, a possible and, I think, more accurate description would be in terms of (possibly) culpable disconnectedness. Connections that are there to be drawn are not. The reason is that either they are seen clearly or, more importantly, that they are ignored. Furthermore, the fourth case (where A only believes that the thing cannot be done) is interesting, since here a man sincerely believes he ought to do something, recognises that this is a situation covered by the principle (i.e. it is relevant) and as a matter of fact the situation is one in which the action is possible (i.e. it is optional). Yet, because he believes he cannot succeed, he does not even try. But this is a case where he could have tried and succeeded yet did not, though he really believed he ought to. (This is to use 'ought' in a way which does not imply 'thinks one can succeed' – for we can say that he ought at least to try even though he believes it to be impossible that he could succeed.) It seems necessary to draw a distinction between various cases of 'believing something to be impossible'. A man cannot think he ought to make two and two equal five or jump over the moon. But there are other cases where the grounds for the belief in impossibility are not sufficient to annihilate the obligation to attempt the action, however strong the belief itself may be. If a man persuades himself that he cannot succeed and thus does not act, this may be a case of neither purposive backsliding nor impossibility, physical or any other, but simply conscious and culpable failure to try harder.

The question arises, what is the nature and status of Hare's whole theory? First and foremost, the theory is an 'account of moral reasoning' with the aim of 'helping us to think better about moral questions by exposing the logical structure of the language in which this thought is expressed' (*Freedom and Reason,* p. *v*). It is clearly a *theory* of moral reasoning and the logic of moral language; he admits that he has adopted a 'certain conceptual apparatus' (ibid., p. 187) and that he is recommending a type of moral reasoning (ibid., p. 193), though he rightly claims that this does not necessarily commit him to any particular first-order moral views. My suggestion is that this theory cannot be refuted, just as an axiomatic system cannot be refuted, that it is a system abstracted from our language. (Hare may not mind this suggestion. He asks, 'If a man wants to escape from my concepts, where is he going to flee to?') He constructs an ideal language of universal prescriptivity, allowing evaluative words different mixtures of prescriptiveness and descriptiveness, a holy moral language for the use of angels. Yet this, he sees, is not our language, for 'we are not angels; and, therefore, although the *simplified* logic for a moral language would be that of the universalisable prescriptive, we shy at this rigorous and austere simplicity, and, in our vain struggles to find a more comfortable way of speaking, have introduced complexities into the logic of our moral language – vain struggles, because the ideal of pure universal prescriptive moral principles obstinately remains with us, and we are not in the end satisfied with anything which falls short of it' (p. 138). The result, he says, is that we 'stretch' the ideal language to accommodate our ordinary unholy lives; for instance, we use the word 'ought' in an 'off-colour way' that does not imply 'can', as it does when used in the 'full sense'. In other words, in the case of moral weakness, we cannot act and the 'ought' is 'down-graded' and 'we lift a corner of the net' (p. 142). But the net is, I suggest, Hare's, not ours.

The issue may be expressed as follows. What Hare has done is to build a model of moral reasoning, based on certain selected features of ordinary language, built with a view to austerity, maximum simplicity and internal consistency. It is an impressive model and it is highly illuminating in many cases. Yet the theory, embodying this model, is used in other ways: that is, partly, as an explication of the language of morals and, partly, and importantly, as a set of concepts used to describe the facts – i.e. as a tacit theory of moral psychology.[9] He sees our actual language as an aspiring angelic language, which is a common procedure of logicians faced with natural languages. But he also often speaks of moral agents as though they in fact reasoned in the way he recommends – i.e. as though all cases of people making moral judgements, coming to decisions, even just acting, are to be described in his terms, that is to say, as consulting universal and prescriptive principles of action (of varying degrees of generality) in determinate situations and then acting (e.g. see, *Freedom and Reason*, pp. 40–1). The Hare theory of the angelic moral language presupposes his theory of the rational man (angels), with self-executing beliefs, and his account of the unholy language of ordinary men presupposes the psychology and circumstances of fallen angels, that is, angels capable of hypocrisy and subject to conditions which render certain things impossible, whether physically or psychologically, but not being capable of irrationality: fallen angels who, when they are sincere, have self-propelling consciences. Hare is, in fact, on the side of the angels. His logical-cum-psychological ideal of rational language-cum-behaviour leads him to give one particular, and I think often misleading, account of what ordinarily happens when sincere people do what they believe they should not be doing or do not do what they believe they should be doing. (Compare the use in classical and neo-classical economics of models assuming ideally rational behaviour to explain situations in the real world, where all awkward facts have to be explained away as frictions). Indeed, moral weakness only appears as a problem for Hare because of his conceptual apparatus. For him there are tight logical connections between (*a*) the statement of an ideal, (*b*) the statement of a principle, (*c*) a self-addressed imperative, and (*d*) the action. Further, (*d*), in an appropriate and optional situation, is entailed by (*a*) (*b*) and (*c*). My argument is that the psychological connections between (*a*) holding ideals, (*b*) assenting to principles, (*c*) making resolves, and (*d*) performing actions are, for most of us, for most of the time, by no means so tight.

In conclusion, a parallel with Plato and Socrates suggests itself. For now, just as then, we are being offered one particular and seemingly paradoxical way of describing what ordinarily happens and a tacit proposal to see morality and use language in a certain way, in the interests of wider moral and philosophical preoccupations. Plato was deeply concerned about knowledge, because he firmly believed in the possibility of a final and rational moral science, a sort of unity of theory and practice, such that, if men really did have true knowledge, there could be no wrongdoing: his moral theory has the aim of getting people to seek this knowledge. Hare is,

I venture to suggest, primarily concerned about moral principles and the conscience that assents to them and he sees morality as a system of principles compelling deliberate actions in determinate situations. Further, he shows a philosophical-cum-moral desire for clear, public criteria of the 'inner life' (by their deeds ye shall know them). For these reasons he sees morality also as a kind of unity of theory and practice, such that, if we really believe in our ideals and principles, our actions will inevitably be the 'right' ones, unless we are overcome by irresistible temptations. Just as with Plato, reality is described in terms of the ideal (conscious wrongdoing is hypo-critical or compulsive), an ideal that is, among other things, distinctly Protestant and Kantian. And perhaps it is essential to an ideal that it be, in Aristotle's phrase, 'manifestly at variance with plain facts'.

X Weakness of will

Gwynneth Matthews

I

'Backsliding', 'weakness of will', 'moral weakness', 'lack of self-restraint', 'lack of self-control'. Do all these have the same meaning? Is there a philosophical problem here, and if so, what precisely is it? How is an account of what happens in cases to which these terms apply related to the meaning of the words, and to the philosophical problem? These are the question which I shall try to discuss in this paper.

There is, in many discussions of this subject, a marked tendency to let 'the problem' dominate the whole. The way in which this is envisaged by any particular philosopher largely determines his answers to the other two questions. One example of this is Aristotle's treatment of *akrasia*.[1] Here, although there is a considerable amount of discussion to delimit the meaning of this concept by contrasts and incompatibilities, and an attempt to distinguish two different kinds of *akrasia*, the whole argument centres round the Socratic problem 'How can one know what is right and yet do what is wrong?' We find that the meaning of *akrasia* is given in these terms: the *akratēs is* one who, knowing that certain things are wrong, does them on account of desire. We find also that the account of what happens in such cases is geared to this problem.

Another example is Hare's discussion of 'Backsliding' (Chapter VIII above). Hare is here supplementing suggestions made in *The Language of Morals*, and defending his prescriptive analysis of moral judgements against the objection that the fact of weakness of will makes this analysis unplausible. The philosophical problem as Hare sees it is 'posed by the fact that moral judgements, in their central use, have it as their function to guide conduct. If this is their function, how can we think, e.g., that we ought not to be doing a certain thing (i.e. accept the view that we ought not to be doing it as a guide to our conduct) and then not be guided by it?' (p. 135 above). Here too we find the meaning of words like 'weakness of will' set out in the terms in which the problem is posed; e.g.

(p. 136) 'In all cases moral weakness is the tendency not to do ourselves something which *in general* we commend, or to do something which *in general* we condemn' (commending and condemning being two concepts which play an important part in Hare's prescriptive analysis in *The Language of Morals*). We also find that any account of what happens in cases of weakness of will is given as part of an answer to the question of how, in terms of the problem, it *can* happen.

There are recurring features in these discussions. There are also differences. Taking these together it becomes evident (1) that in setting out the problem Aristotle and Hare are concentrating on different concepts. While there are, no doubt, similarities between the Socratic problem about knowledge and that posed by Hare about the use of 'ought', it is not immediately obvious that these similarities amount to identity, and that we have here precisely the same problem; (2) that to give the meaning of 'weakness of will', etc., in the terms in which the problem is posed (whichever these may be) may well be leading to oversimplifications, and different oversimplifications in each case; (3) that to give an account of what happens in cases of weakness of will by referring simply to the terms of the problem is too much of an *a priori* procedure. If this whole method is unsatisfactory, it would seem advisable to take and discuss separately questions about the meaning, and questions about the problem, without prejudging the issue.

II

Let us start with the question 'What do we mean by "weakness of will", "backsliding", etc.? How do we use these terms, and with what contrasts?'

Much use is made, in discussions of this topic, of the terms 'moral principles' or 'moral judgements', and 'desires' or 'inclinations', and also of the contrast between moral weakness and moral wickedness. Aristotle is complimented for having recognised both the case where a man cheerfully accepts bad principles and acts in accordance with them without compunction, and the case where he follows his desires against his moral principles and feels contrition and remorse. Despite this appeal to authority, however, this scheme is too oversimplified, if it is intended to cover the facts without distortion of the concepts involved. On the one hand it makes 'moral weakness' cover too much. To preserve the dichotomy, all cases in which principles are not being impugned but in which people blame themselves for not having thought of the situation in a particular way, or not having thought of doing certain things, or not having realised how someone else was feeling, must be classified as cases of weakness of will (and are, at least, often discussed under this rubric), however different they may be from cases of succumbing to temptation. On the other hand, some cases which would usually be regarded as cases of weakness of will do not seem to be covered at all, e.g. while I have no rule or moral principle about getting up early, I may decide to get up early on a particular day, and then, when the time comes, although awake remain comfortably and indolently in bed. It will not save an analysis given in terms of principles and desires if one says that here too one is acting against a principle that one accepts, the principle of always doing what one has decided to do provided that one is not prevented and has not changed one's mind. This would be to say, in effect, that one ought not to be weak-willed. It gives no moral principle in terms of which this instance of weak will is to be analysed.

Making a fresh start, I would suggest that all of the following cases, except the last, would usually be regarded as cases of weakness of will, and that all of them, except again the last and perhaps the first, could be regarded as cases of moral weakness.

1. *Putting off the evil moment*
Knowing that one must go to the dentist, that one must tackle a batch of marking, or that one must break a piece of bad news, and knowing too that eventually one will, one may yet keep putting it off. Here one is aware at the time that one is being weak and also perhaps cowardly, and feels dissatisfaction because of this. It is not that failure to go to the dentist is itself so wrong, though it may be foolish. It is that having decided that one must go, and having unquestioned reasons for this, one still does not go. One is irritated at oneself for not being the sort of person who, having decided to do something, just goes ahead and does it.

2. *Backsliding*
The first case was concerned with some particular action. One may also make resolutions, in fairly general terms, about one's future course of behaviour in some respect or towards certain people, fully intending to implement them, and one may succeed for a time. But then gradually one slips, allowing an exception here, forgetting

about the resolutions there, until one finds oneself back where one started, and feels thoroughly ashamed.

It is to this particular form of weakness of will that the term 'backsliding' is usually applied; and much of Hare's discussion under this title does seem to fit this rather better than some other forms, for here moral principles and moral judgements are clearly involved, and the actions one does against one's resolutions are regarded as in themselves wrong. The kind of analysis given by St Paul in *Romans* vii (quoted by Hare) does seem to make some sense here.

3. *Irresolution*

One may decide to do a certain thing, or make a resolution to do certain kinds of things, and then start looking at the situation again from a different angle, considering counter-reasons and aims and principles which militate against the original decision or resolve. If one then thinks that one was right in the first place, one may blame oneself for weakness and vacillation even if one has not done anything contrary to the decision or resolution, nor even delayed doing something in accordance with it.

4. *Being persuaded against one's better judgement*

Other people may lead one to consider the whole situation differently, and in consequence to do something which one later considers wrong, or not as beneficial, profitable, or pleasurable as what one would otherwise have done. One may then blame oneself for one's weakness in having been overpersuaded in this way, and for being influenced by insufficient reasons, which only seemed sufficient at the time.

In both this and the previous case, the conflict, whether felt as a conflict or not, may not be a simple one between desires and principles. It may be the conflict between one whole way of looking at a situation, complete with aims, desires, reasons, principles and emotions, and some other complete way of looking at it. A possible example here is the conflict in *Macbeth* before the murder of Duncan, in which at one moment he is influenced by moral scruples, gratitude, and fear of failure, and the next by ambition, belief in prophesy and the moral censure of his wife.

5. *Being too easily discouraged*

One may decide to do something, or adopt a certain resolution, and even embark on the course of action, and then be put off by thoughts of how hard it is, and how unlikely one is to succeed, and by feelings of self-pity, and later realise that one might well have succeeded if only one had not been so defeatist. In such a case one might well blame oneself for lack of will-power.

6. *Being unable to bring oneself to do something*

One may decide on a whole course of action which involves doing some particular thing, and when the time comes be unable to bring oneself to do it, as Macbeth, filled with revulsion, was unable to return to the scene of the murder and place the daggers beside the grooms. If one blames oneself, at the time or afterwards, it may well be on the score of weakness.

7. *Being overcome with desire, or being unable to resist the temptation*

Through lack of self-control, or lack of self-restraint, one may succumb to temptation or be overwhelmed by desire so that one does something which, at the time or later, one admits is wrong. There are in fact many different kinds of cases here, and we may use different words in speaking of them, but in all the reason given for the action, which is admitted to be wrong, is passion, or desire, or pleasure, or inclination.

This is the kind of case with which Aristotle is most concerned, and in his discussion we have the further restriction to pleasures of a certain sort, namely those of the profligate and intemperate. Many seem to follow Aristotle's lead here, and to take this as the paradigm or indeed the only case of weakness of will. Aristotle may have been justified in the restricted meaning he gives to '*akrasia*'. It may have been in accordance with current Greek usage. But the English terms 'weakness of will' and 'moral weakness' do not seem to be so restricted. The nearest English equivalents to Aristotle's '*akrasia*' are 'lack of self-control' and 'lack of self-restraint' (inability to resist temptation not being restricted to certain pleasures).

8. *Failure to control one's anger*

This is classified by Aristotle as a type of *akrasia*, and we too apply some of the same terms to this and the previous case. We blame ourselves for not being in better control of our tempers as well as our desires, and for not showing more restraint in our outbursts of anger as well as in our manifestations of passion. Despite these similarities, however, it would seem odd to suggest that failure to

control one's temper was a form of weakness of will. If one resolved
not to lose one's temper, then losing it might be a case of weakness
of will, but only because one had resolved not to.

This list is certainly incomplete, and some of the cases could, for
some purposes, be further sorted out. It is perhaps a sufficient basis,
however, for a discussion of the correct analysis of the concepts
involved. With the exception of the last, they are all cases of weakness of will, and, although this term seems sometimes overweighty,
of moral weakness. They are not all cases of backsliding, although,
against a background of resolutions and resolves, all the others
could be ways in which backsliding occurs. They are not all cases
of lack of self-control or lack of self-restraint. These do not seem
to be the generic concepts, but rather species of weakness of will.
The traditional analysis in terms of desires or inclinations versus
moral principles or moral judgements is, in fact, taking part for
whole.

This would be relatively unimportant if the traditional analysis
delimited the only cases in which moral censure is applied, but this
is obviously not true. To classify any of the above cases as cases of
weakness of will or moral weakness is to imply that moral censure is
appropriate. The blame may vary in amount, but the grounds for
it are sufficiently similar in all cases to warrant the use of the same
word. We blame ourselves and others for not sticking to our
decisions, acting in accordance with our principles, carrying out
resolutions, doing what we said we would do, and this sometimes
out of all proportion to the importance of the particular decisions,
principles or resolves in question, or the seriousness of their non-
fulfilment. The traditional analysis oversimplifies the whole praise/
blame situation. It suggests that that there three simple alternatives:
(1) we can stick to the right principles or moral judgements even
against contrary desires, which is praiseworthy; (2) we can subscribe to the wrong principles and act accordingly, which is
blameworthy; (3) we can subscribe to the right principles and make
the right judgements but, on occasions, act contrary to them because of desire, which is also blameworthy. But in fact we both
praise and blame people much more widely than this; and one of
the things for which we praise people is their carrying out of
decisions, fulfilling resolutions, and doing what they said they
would do, and we blame people for not doing these things.

Sometimes, however, we praise the man who changes his mind,
and blame the obstinate, pig-headed individual who refuses to

budge. Those complications show that we use 'weakness of will' as a form of blame when a person's reasons for havering or for not doing what he decided, resolved, or thought he ought to do are regarded as insufficient to justify a change of mind. Furthermore here, as in many other places in morals (see, e.g., Hare on 'happiness', *Freedom and Reason*, p. 126), there is the complication of different points of view. The judgements of agent and observer may coincide. They may both regard a particular action as a case of weakness of will, or both regard it as the outcome of a perfectly justified change of mind. What happens, however, if they disagree? Nowell Smith, among others, seems to suggest that we should take the agent's point of view ('The morally weak man condemns himself'), but we do not always do this. As observers we may blame him when he himself does not; as agents we may deny that we deserve this form of blame, whatever someone else may say. An example of this is the difference of opinion between Odysseus and Neoptolemus in Sophocles' *Philoctetes*. Neoptolemus has promised to tell a lie for the good of the state, but then, filled with compassion and thoughts of honour, refuses to lie, and thinks he is perfectly right to change his mind. Odysseus, however, is absolutely furious. He does not accept Neoptolemus' view of the case, but condemns this 'weakness' in no uncertain terms. Aristotle maintains that this is not *akrasia* because Neoptolemus is motivated by noble pleasure, and we applaud him. Maybe we do and, if so, we do not blame him for weakness of will; but Odysseus certainly did not. Conversely, we may refuse to blame a man for weakness even when he himself is filled with remorse, or insist on blaming ourselves when others do not. In such conflicts of assessments we find bandied about such remarks as these (in support of exculpation): 'It was the original decision that was wrong, and only a fool refuses to admit a mistake.' 'Once I realised that such and such was the case, a change of mind seemed perfectly reasonable.' 'No one could possibly have done anything else in the circumstances.' 'In cases of obsessive disorders blame is out of place, so it is absurd for him to blame himself', and (in support of blame) 'Yes, but he (I) said that he (I) would do such and such.' 'He admits that he does not think (I do not think) that one ought to do things like that.' 'These are just excuses. Of course he (I) *could* have acted otherwise.'

Disputes of this kind, sometimes acrimonious, if they are settled at all, may be settled one way or the other. Perhaps the bias is on the side of the agent, but his first view does not always win.

As regards the meaning of 'weakness of will', it seems therefore

(1) that the main function of this and similar terms is moral appraisal. They are used to give blame-type judgements about a situation rather than either descriptions or explanations of a phenomenon or range of phenomena. We do not use them to describe what happened, and then blame the man for it. We use them to express blame or self-criticism, at the same time indicating the kind of grounds we have for this disapproval; (2) that this 'descriptive' part of the meaning is oversimplified in the traditional analysis. It can, in fact, be set out only in the form of alternatives. A man is said to do something from weakness of will when, for whatever reason, he fails to act in accordance with some previous resolution or decision, or acts against his moral principles and what he thinks is right, or puts off doing something he knows he must do, provided that, in the view of the person judging, he could have acted otherwise, and his reasons for acting as he did, or for delaying action, do not seem to justify a change of mind or a reassessment of the situation. He need not have done something which is regarded as wrong in itself; he need not blame himself or feel remorse; and it may not be a case of a simple conflict between inclinations and moral judgements. These more restricted criteria, which philosophers following Aristotle tend to insist on, apply to some cases but not to all.

Here I shall leave the discussion of the meaning of these terms, and turn to 'the problem' of weakness of will.

III

'How can you do that, when you know it's wrong?' 'Given your expressed opinions, I don't know how you could do such a thing.' Such expostulations (cf. 'How could you be so cruel?') have their place in actual moral conversations. They do indeed express puzzlement about the person concerned, his character and his motives; but they do not express philosophical puzzlement, and cannot therefore lend respectability or force to the philosophical problem. This arises because the analysis given to one concept is found to be incompatible with its application to certain sorts of situation, to which it nevertheless seems to apply. The solution then takes the form of replacing the original analysis, at least in some cases, by a more complex and sophisticated scheme. The concept is allowed to 'give' in certain ways, and it is found that ordinary language permits this to happen. Thus the original incompatibility is avoided. We have, in fact, the pattern: If all xs are ϕ, then no x can be not-ϕ. But some xs could be sort of ϕish, and at the same time sort of not-ϕ; or there could be some things which are $x$ish, but not genuine xs, and which are not-ϕ.

Although Hare talks of *the* problem of weakness of will, it is not always precisely the same concept that gives rise to this trouble. For Socrates it was the concept of 'knowledge', and the problem which so greatly influenced Aristotle's discussion of *akrasia* was the apparent impossibility of reconciling the Socratic view of knowledge with the apparent facts. How can a man know what is right and yet do what is wrong, if no one can wittingly go for the worse, and there is nothing stronger than knowledge? If knowing what is good entails doing what is good, then *akrasia* is impossible. Aristotle's solution is worked out in terms of this concept of knowledge. It is this that 'gives' under the influence of desire so that in at least two types of case, 'knowing' and 'not doing' are perfectly compatible. The two cases Aristotle seems to give us are (*a*) that of the man who knows, in the sense that he accepts the principle, that he ought not to do something or other (e.g. eat sweet things), but in the particular instance does not apply this principle. He does not think of the sweet things in front of him as things which he ought not to eat. So, in a sense he knows that he ought not to eat them; but there is no conceptual difficulty about his knowing, in this sense, and his eating. (*b*) The case of the man who applies the principle in the particular instance and knows that he ought not to do certain things, but has a passionate desire to do them; and the effect of this desire is that his 'knowledge' becomes like the knowledge of a drunken man. He may say 'I know I ought not to do this', but the knowledge has lost its force. He is doing little more than repeating the words. So here again it is possible to know what is wrong, in a sense, and yet to do it.

In this way Aristotle resolves the paradox, and delineates cases which a follower of Socrates might be led to accept. It would indeed be difficult not to accept them and to allow this much complexity in the concept of knowledge, since they are real-life cases of mitigating excuses. The sentence-form 'I know that what I did was wrong, and that I ought to have done such and such, but . . .' can certainly be completed by 'I didn't think of it in this way at the time', and by 'I was so overwhelmed by passion that I couldn't see straight. Everything seemed different somehow.' Whether these are the only possible mitigating or semi-mitigating excuses here is another question; and whether a semi-mitigating excuse of any kind is always possible is a further question again, which Aristotle does not raise. Having broken the conceptual block felt by Socrates by means of his distinctions between different kinds of knowledge, he leaves the following propositions standing:

(1) Desire, passion and anger cannot enslave and drag about the knowledge of the major premiss, the judgement that such and such sorts of things are wrong.

(2) If one knows the major premiss, and applies it in the particular instance with all one's wits about one, then one *must* act in accordance with it.

In Hare's discussion of 'Backsliding' there are parallel features, but also differences, owing to the fact that the problem arises with a different concept. Here it is not the issuing-in-action concepts of knowledge, but the concept of ought, and other moral concepts, interpreted in accordance with Hare's prescriptive analysis. The problem is: How can a man accept some moral judgement and yet act contrary to it, seeing that 'moral judgements, in their central use, have it as their function to guide conduct'?

The solution is that in some cases, and backsliding in particular, the moral judgement is 'off-colour' and despite appearances not really intended to serve as a guide to action, or not really intended to serve as a guide to everyone's action. It is not, Hare says, that there are different senses of 'ought'. It is rather that 'ought' is a Janus-faced word, having both descriptive and prescriptive meaning, and it can sometimes bury one of its faces in the sand. Language 'gives' just where we do to allow for human frailty.

The typical cases of moral weakness, we are told, are cases where a man *cannot* do what he thinks he ought. The inability here is a psychological inability which Hare illustrates with quotations from Ovid (Medea's speech when trying to resist the onset of love for Jason) and from St Paul. In both these cases the speaker claims to be powerless, and it is this powerlessness which renders null and void the prescriptivity of the 'ought' judgement in the particular instance. 'Nobody in his senses would maintain that a person who assents to an imperative must (analytically) act on it even when he is unable to do so.' One may feel that there is a difficulty here. How can a person assent to an imperative if he knows he is unable to carry it out? But Hare defends this on the grounds that the moral judgement has also the feature of universality, and the prescription is still regarded as holding in other instances, where the fulfilment is not impossible, and so may guide others and strengthen one's own resistance to lesser temptations. For the same reasons, remorse and reproof are not out of place. They may be pragmatically useful.

In this discussion Hare is making the same methodological move as Aristotle in allowing the recalcitrant concept to 'give' in certain ways in certain cases, and he too could appeal to real life cases and the would-be mitigating plea of 'I know I ought not to do that sort of thing, but I couldn't help it'. It may be doubted, however, whether the move is here successful, since if in such a case the plea is accepted and interpreted at its face value, which seems to be necessary for Hare's analysis, then we would not judge this to be a case of weakness of will at all. If it is literally true that the agent was powerless, could not help himself, could not do anything else, then, however much he blames himself, we would be as little inclined to reproach and reprove as we would in a clear case of kleptomania. From the point of view of the agent, if he is still claiming some responsibility for his action, as he must be if he is blaming himself for weakness of will, the plea of 'I couldn't help it' must be interpreted as a mitigating excuse rather than as an exoneration. Hare's solution to the paradox in terms of the lifting of the prescription from this particular instance seems to be removing too much from this use of 'ought'. Medea, for instance, is saying that she ought to resist this onslaught of love for Jason. She is indeed saying that, in a sense, she cannot; but she still continues to say that she ought to, and that what she ought to do is precisely resist this onslaught of love for Jason. She does not think merely that other people similarly situated should resist such onslaughts, nor merely that she herself should resist some lesser onslaught of love for someone else who may turn up on some other occasion. It seems, indeed, very strange to suggest that it is not with the intention of guiding her own immediate action that Medea makes all the moral judgements she does make in the course of this seventy-line speech with herself, of which Hare quotes the first nine lines.[2] While considering reasons, motives and consequences on both sides, and seeing the whole situation now this way, now that, she is all the time desperately trying to persuade herself not to fall in love with Jason, and by the end of the speech is completely confident that she has her feelings under control. When by mischance she meets Jason again, this confidence is proved to be misplaced; but this does not alter the fact that the point of her making these ought-judgements is to guide, and mainly to guide conduct, whether or not the guidance has much hope of success. Even if in a particular case a moral judgement containing 'ought' does not succeed in fulfilling the function of guiding action, it does not follow that its function in this case is not to guide action here and now. Even if this function is not fulfilled, it does not follow that the person is (absolutely) prevented from doing what he thinks he ought. In fact Hare's resolution of the paradox here seems to rest on an unsatisfactory analysis of 'I couldn't help it', since the nearer this approaches to real impossibility the less it seems like a case of weakness of will.

The other main kind of case that Hare mentions is that of insincerity of some sort, varying from self-deception to hypocrisy. A man may say that he ought to do something and yet not do it, when he is fully aware that he does not really think that he ought; or when at the time he is making a special exception in his own favour, so that his judgement could be put in the form 'I think that everyone ought to do this sort of thing, but in this particular instance I don't really think this applies to me, although I feel rather uncomfortable about it'; or when he is deceiving himself, and only thinks that he thinks he ought, but does not really think so. In all these cases, which seem to be taken from life, both the prescriptive analysis of 'ought' and the fact of human frailty are saved by saying, in effect, that these uses of 'ought' are really misuses, or at any rate a fall from the ideal standards, because universal prescriptivity is missing.

One similarity, then, between Hare's and Aristotle's treatment lies in the way in which the problem arises, and the kind of solution offered. Another is that no argument is given to show that the cases mentioned in the solution exhaust the field. The only other kinds of case that Hare mentions, as also being reconcilable with the prescriptivist thesis, are that of the man who fails to apply the general principle which he holds (cf. Aristotle); that of the man who is not really convinced that such and such ought to be done; and that of the man who is making a conventional moral judgement which he does not endorse. A third similarity is that, the reconciliation having been propounded for some cases, a considerable amount is left standing. In Hare's account it is the view that if one really and sincerely judges that one ought to do something, and is not physically or psychologically prevented, then one will inevitably do it.

Perhaps the same pattern of argument could be constructed with some other concept, e.g. 'decide' or 'resolve', which would reveal the same features, uncover some 'off-colour' uses of these concepts, and leave standing the original thesis which tied these concepts quasi-analytically to actions. In any case it is clear that the problem can be posed with different concepts; and, depending on which concept is selected, different cases of weakness of will are highlighted, and ordinary language is found to be flexible in rather different ways. These different discussions may supplement each other as regards the facts, but they undermine each other's claims to be dealing with *the* problem of weakness of will.

There is, indeed, another way into the problem, and one which may lend illusory support to any discussion of it. In answer to the question 'Why did you do that?' we very often accept one of the following as a sufficient explanation: 'Because I knew that it was the right thing to do', 'Because I thought I ought to', 'Because I had decided that it was the best thing to do'. The puzzle then arises about weakness of will, where this explanation no longer applies. 'I knew that it was the right thing, but I didn't do it.' How can this possibly happen? The posing of this question may suggest what it is that has gone wrong here. What is, *ceteris paribus*, a sufficient explanation, if what one is interested in is the agent's motives and the way in which he was looking at the situation, is wrongly taken to be a causally sufficient condition for his performing the action. One is then puzzled about how this sufficient condition can suddenly cease to be operative. The solution to this puzzle clearly lies in the sorting-out of different types of explanation.

A similar puzzle can arise in the case of 'wants'. How can it happen that the explanation 'Because I wanted to', which is often accepted as a sufficient explanation, suddenly ceases to hold? How can one possibly do anything that one really does not want to do? One finds the counter-Socrates maintaining that this is indeed impossible, and that whatever one does, one does because one wants to; and one finds other philosophers drawing a distinction between different uses of 'want'.

IV

The question 'How can it happen?' links up pretty closely with the question 'What actually does happen in these cases?' The answers given by philosophers to this question tend to fall into two groups, depending on whether the problem is due primarily to trouble with such concepts as 'know' and 'ought', or primarily to a failure to distinguish different kinds of explanation. The latter kind of answer is that the contrary desires are so strong that they overcome the will or the reason. This semi-causal account, which is encouraged by metaphors of struggling against desires, being overwhelmed by passion, etc., suggests some sort of mechanism made up of weights and pulleys and floodgates and opposing forces, but as an explanation of what happens has little informative value. If one accepts the implied restriction of the term 'weakness of will' to cases where a man knows what is right but does what is wrong because of desire, then this account does nothing more than repeat this restricted definition in a causal tone of voice. It is an oversimplified account of the meaning dressed up as an account of what happens, and misleadingly suggests that what we require here is a causal explanation, and that all the explanation we have any right to expect has already been given.

The other kind of answer is found in Aristotle and Hare. In the course of answering the question 'How can weakness of will happen?' they both give some answer to the question 'What does happen in such cases?' Aristotle produces the man who is so drunk and befuddled with passion that although he can go on repeating 'I know I ought not to do this' he cannot fully realise what he is saying until he has sobered up again. Hare produces the case of the man who is up against psychological impossibility but who still feels remorse because he accepts the universal prescription (which seems to be a case of weakness of will only if the impossibility is not taken to be absolute), and also the case of self-deception or hypocrisy:

> We start off as if we were prepared to accept a certain moral principle as binding on everybody; and we start off by accepting it as prescriptive, and therefore as committing *us* in particular to acting in accordance with the principle. But when we consider how contrary to our own interests it is for us to act in accordance with the principle, we weaken. While continuing to prescribe that everyone *else* . . . should act in accordance with the principle, we do not so prescribe to ourselves (pp. 139–40 above).

The main objection to these accounts is not that they are wrong, that they do not fit any facts. It is that they do not fit all the facts. They are arrived at via a consideration of 'the problem', and the kind of relaxing-of-the-meaning solution offered in respect of a particular concept. The Aristotelian account could not (even if it were meant to) be plausibly applied to the man who says 'I know perfectly well that I ought to go to the dentist, but I keep putting it off, hopng the pain will go'. Hare's accounts do not seem to fit this case either. Very rarely would we seriously allow a plea of psychological impossibility here, and it seems odd to suggest that a man suffering from raging toothache does not really think that *he* ought to go to the dentist, or only thinks that he thinks he ought. Many cases of irresolution, overpersuasion, and easy discouragement are also left uncatered for. Moreover, can one, on the basis of an analysis of 'know' or of 'ought' which ties these concepts quasi-analytically to actual performance, rule out the possibility of someone doing what he knows to be wrong fully realising at the time that it is wrong, and not being psychologically compelled to do it? Was not Macbeth's such a case?

It is, in fact, the method that is mistaken. If what one wants is an account of what happens in cases of weakness of will, one would do better to take a variety of cases and consider what tends to happen in each kind, drawing material from poets, playwrights, and novelists, and from one's own plentiful experience. And if what one wants is a solution to 'the problem', it would seem best to consider first the meaning of the terms in question, and the variety of their meanings as applied to these different cases, in order to avoid an oversimplified posing of the problem, and an oversimplified solution which supports the favoured analysis of some other term.

PART THREE

Explaining Actions Against One's Better Judgement

XI Acting with reason

A. Phillips Griffiths

How can we ever know that someone did something because he thought it was the right thing to do? Failures to follow one's avowed moral principles are sufficiently attested by a discrepancy between what is demanded by the principles and what is freely done. But the coincidence of action and principle is no guarantee of conscientiousness; what, then, entitles us to say of a man that he did what he did because he knew he ought to do so?

A failure to do what the agent believes to be right will always, we expect, be capable of some explanation, though the correct explanation need not be an excuse. It would be extraordinary to say that someone failed to do what he believed to be right but that there was no reason for this, and equally extraordinary to say that someone did something knowingly, being fully conscious that it was wrong, and yet there was no reason, nor did he think there was any reason, why he should not have done what was right.

That is to say, if a man believes a certain course of action to be right, then in the absence of countervailing considerations he will follow it. If a man consistently fails to follow a course of action, where the explanation of each failure is radically different, so that to accept them as explanations of failure the man would have to have a character which changed completely from moment to moment, we conclude that he does not believe this course of action to be right. If someone says both that he believes that a course of action is one he ought to follow, and that he has no inclination, and does not in any circumstances try, to follow it, we do not believe him.

A preliminary answer to our question could be that *believing one ought to do something is, in the absence of countervailing factors, to do it*; hence, given that someone does something, and we know he thinks he ought to do it, in the absence of special circumstances we know why he did it. That is to say, the failures are detectable, and require explanation; the successes do not require explanation, and it is only this which makes the failure explicable; for if there were no norm to diverge from, the divergences would not constitute problems for us.

This answer is not, however, very helpful, because in a sense it does not tell us more than we already know. We want to know how we can say, in normal circumstances, that if a man does something he thinks right he did it because he thought it was right, or at least that he would not have done it if he had thought it was wrong. The principle (P) italicised above is no more than a bare licence to say this; and if we are doubtful about the possibility of our saying this on each particular occasion, then we are doubtful of the principle. The real problem is then how we can assert this principle, what sort of principle it is, and how we can justify it. What follows is a discussion of this problem.

The simplest answer to the question of what kind of principle (P) is, and how we justify it, is that it is analytic.

Professor Geach has discussed[1] the character of the principle *Normally, and other things being equal, a man who wants an A will choose an A he thinks good and will not choose an A that he thinks bad*, and argued that it is neither analytic nor a mere empirical generalisation. I think this is true, and that it is also true of the principle (P). Geach's reasons for saying this would show the same of (P), but I do not think they are correct.

Geach argues that if this principle shows the connection between thinking something good and choosing it, then that connection is not analytic because the qualification 'normally, and other things being equal', is necessary to it. Now I do not think that anyone would hold that the principle, simply without qualification, was true, let alone analytic. What could be claimed is that the whole principle as qualified was analytic. For there are principles so qualified which are obviously analytic; e.g. (S) *A brave man will not, normally and other things being equal, behave in a cowardly way*. The *ceteris paribus* qualification is here essential, for one can imagine exceptional circumstances in which a brave man would behave in a cowardly way; but they would have to be exceptional for us to go on calling him brave. But (S) tells us nothing about what actually goes on, and it is possible to gather nothing from it except perhaps something about the use of the word 'brave'; more important, 'Smith is a brave man, the situation is quite normal, with nothing exceptional about it, and Smith behaves in a cowardly way' is an obvious contradiction. (S) is therefore analytic. (Even if these two facts about the statement (S) are not sufficient conditions of analyticity, I should want to deny them of (P) and of the principle Geach is discussing; but noticing the *ceteris paribus* qualification is not sufficient to doing this, since the qualification is present in (S).)

Geach has succeeded in pointing out that in the case of the principle he is discussing it need not necessarily be either analytic or an empirical generalisation; but to show that it and the principle (P) are not analytic requires a longer investigation.

It will be illuminating to ask why (P) should be thought to be analytic. One reason is that it seems impossible to find a counter-example; this I shall discuss later. A further reason is that it seems to be demanded by the model of the practical syllogism. If the con-clusion of the practical syllogism is an action, or choice of an action, demanded by the conjunction of a moral principle and a statement of fact, then this demand must be a deductive one. Sincerely to state a moral principle is to say there is a reason for doing some-thing, and this is logically, deductively, connected with doing it. To fail to choose the action is, logically, also to fail to assert the pre-misses. To hold that there is a reason for doing something must logically involve doing it, at least in the absence of countervailing factors.

There are cases where what one holds to be a reason for doing something is analytically connected with what one in fact does, but I shall now try to show that these cases are special ones, and can only be understood in terms of cases where the connection is not analytic. The special cases are those in which thinking there is a reason depends on wanting something, where the criterion for wanting something is behavioural.

When we talk of *the* reason why somebody did something we may refer to many kinds of explanation, including causal ones. But when we talk of *his* reason for doing something we have to refer to a fact which the person concerned knew about, and which he re-garded as *a* reason for doing what he did. We may also talk of *a* reason for doing something which is never *his* or anybody's reason; for example, we may say there was *a* reason for doing something which we do not know was done, or which we know was done but when we do not know why it was done.

The concept of *a* reason is therefore prior and necessary to the concept of *his* reason. Doing something conscientiously, or with good reason, analytically involves holding something to be *a* reason. But only in some cases is holding something to be *a* reason analytic-ally connected with doing something; namely those in which *a* reason becomes *a* reason in virtue of someone's wants.

His reason can always be stated in terms of his wants; for example

'His reason for leaving was that he had promised; he wanted to keep his promise' or 'His reason for leaving was that it was cooler outside; he wanted to go where it was cooler'. In some cases, but not in all, *his* reason can in addition be explained by his wants; for example 'His reason was that he had promised; and he wanted to appear trustworthy' or 'His reason was that it was cooler outside; and he wanted to clear his head'. In these cases, what is by implication claimed to be *a* reason by him, and sometimes even what is *a* reason at all, is such in virtue of his wants.

In mentioning his wants in this way, we have given a sufficient explanation of *his* reason. We say his reason for leaving was that it was cooler outside, and further inquiry might be terminated with the reply that he wanted to clear his head. We do not, so long as going to a cooler place was indeed a means to the required end, ask 'Is the fact that he wanted to clear his head a reason for going where it was cooler?' because in every case the fact that someone wants something is *a* reason for his trying to get it.

We do not mean by 'want' here pleasure-seeking, desire, craving, or poverty, but something more general (of which craving, etc., are explanations rather than species). What we want is not so general to cover all that we do, for we make mistakes and cause accidents without wanting to. It does cover what we knowingly do. Within the limits of what we knowingly do, saying that we wanted to do what we did is vacuous, in this sense of 'want'. Hence it is possible to say truly 'He knew what he was doing, so he must have wanted to do it'; though it is only perhaps the possible equivocation between 'wanting to' and 'being glad to' which makes this trivially true thing worth saying. There are, it is true, other grounds than that an act was knowingly done on which we say 'He must have wanted to do it', including cases where we say he did not know what he wanted, or did not know what he did. But in such cases wanting something may be *the* reason why somebody did something, but it cannot be *a* reason for the agent, and therefore cannot be *his* reason, for it is a necessary condition of a fact's being regarded as a reason by someone that the person concerned should believe or know this fact. Where he did not know what he did, knowledge of what he wanted cannot be used as an explanation of what was unknowingly done. Hence, while what we want goes beyond the sphere of what we knowingly do, what is held to be a reason for doing something in virtue of what is wanted does not go beyond what is or might be knowingly done.

The best possible criterion for wanting something in this sense of 'wanting' is behavioural; so long as what is done is knowingly done, one does what one wants to do, necessarily, and that one does something is a sufficient reason for saying that one wants to do it. A reason which is a reason in virtue of the fact that I want to do something can only be held by me to be a reason if I am prepared to admit that I want to do the action concerned. It follows that my holding that there is such a reason is, other things being equal, sincerely saying I shall do the action concerned. It is contradictory to say that one has a reason for going out – namely that one wants to – that nothing at all is stopping one going out, that one has no reason at all for not going out, but that one has decided not to go out.

There is then a class of cases where believing that there is a reason for doing something is, in the absence of countervailing conditions, to do it, and where the connection is analytic. But this is not only a special class of cases, it is also one which is dependent for its possibility on a class of cases which are quite otherwise; as I shall now try to show.

Why should one say, when one just wants to go out, that one has a reason for going out? 'I am going out' would be an appropriate remark when one has simply to get up and go. 'I want to go out' is an appropriate remark when one is hindered. 'I have a reason for going out' is appropriate in neither of these circumstances. Such a remark seems rather on the defensive, and appropriate when going out would be regarded as somewhat untoward, either as something usually not done, or as something which it might be thought that there is a reason for not doing. Where it is unusual, then to say one has a reason for doing it removes the suspicion that the action is just an accident or erratic absent-mindedness; where it might be thought that there is a reason for not doing it, that the action is not unconsidered.

To say that one has a reason, when one merely wants, is not to say much more than that the action was knowingly done. It is appropriate when the status of the action as something done rationally (though not necessarily reasonably) is in question. It is the bare minimum of rational action that we should do what we want to do, and regard the fact that we want to do it as a reason for doing it; but this is only to say that if our actions are to qualify as rational behaviour, we should know what we are doing.

Besides the bare minimum of rational behaviour, there are the various degrees of rational behaviour within it. To act reasonably is not to act with any reason, but to act with good reason, or at least to avoid that which there is good reason to avoid. The whole structure of standards of reasonable behaviour, including moral standards, which is expressed in terms of what there are good reasons for doing or avoiding, is independent of what any given person may want. Were it not, it would be identical for each person with what each person in fact does. This is true even of a holy will, for whether a given will is holy is a contingent matter.[2] A standard may include reference to what people want, in the sense that it may require people to do what they or others want, if they are to be reasonable; indeed a 'thelemic' standard would require that nothing but the agent's wants be taken into account. But *qua* standard it would be distinct from what the agent wants, otherwise there would be no point in having it. Moreover, it is presupposed in, and therefore prior to, all talk about what is a reason in virtue of wants, because it is only by reference to such a standard, and what it requires, prohibits, and allows, that there is any necessity to have recourse to the mention of reasons in such cases. To subscribe to such a standard – to say that one holds something to be a reason or good reason for doing something – is not logically to imply anything about one's wants or anyone else's wants, or hence to imply anything logically about one's behaviour in the way that talking about reasons constituted by one's wants is to imply something about one's behaviour. And even the fact that the holding of these latter reasons is logically connected with what one in fact does is dependent on the possibility of talking about reasons which are logically independent of one's wants.

There is then bound to be a certain circularity in trying to understand what it is to hold that there is a reason in terms of behavioural criteria, of wanting. An example of this is to be found in Professor Hare's attempt to look on the principle (P) as analytic. In such behavioural criteria, he argues, not only a man's actions, but also his feelings should be taken into account, in order to account for weakness of will or other failures to practise a principle one holds (see Chapter V above). Hare says that when a moral principle is not obeyed, we can still say that a man holds it if he feels remorse. But remorse is more than just feeling sorry, or regret, and it can be distinguished from these as regret for having disobeyed a moral principle. In order to feel this, one must first hold the principle; and thus holding the principle is a prior condition of feeling remorse, and cannot be constituted by it. That is to say, holding that there is a reason for doing something cannot be constituted by the feelings one has when one does not do it, for unless the idea of a standard which one has failed to reach is present in addition to the feelings, the feelings constitute no more than accompaniments of action, like toothache or nausea.

A further difficulty in discussing the alleged analyticity of the principle (P), though one which will throw light on our problem, is the fact that it is impossible to find a crucial case whereby the principle may be tested, and in so far as we seem to be able to construct such a case, the analyticity of the principle seems to be confirmed. A man who consistently claimed to believe a moral principle to be correct which he has consistently failed to follow must, in the absence of explanation, and if (P) is analytic, be said simply not to believe the principle to be correct, but only to assert that he does. And this is not wildly implausible. However, the consideration of a detailed example may lead us in a different direction.

A man may say that he knows perfectly well that it is wrong to hurt others; and without watching how he behaved towards others in this respect, we could be forced to the conviction that he is sincere. We could find that he goes to very great trouble to defend his moral view when it is challenged, that it plays a crucial part in the determination of the advice he gives others, and that he expresses withering contempt for those who deny his view. The criteria might be roughly the same as those we use to decide whether the views of some academic theorist are sincerely held or not. In general, he has a fanatical love of truth, and in this particular case this love of truth is evident to the full. We then turn to see how far his moral attitude is borne out in practice. We may be dismayed and surprised to find that he is quite spiteful, vindictive, callous and cruel. This need not lead us to say he is insincere in his moral views, for he might be weak-willed, or hasty, and suffer for his derelictions tempests of remorse; though perhaps to remove all doubt from our minds he would have to hang himself. But let us now imagine we find no such explanation. He is often callous towards suffering when it would cost him nothing at all to be compassionate, and yet he does not enjoy suffering for its own sake. He is cruel for no reason, and airily admits, perhaps passionately asserts, that what he did was wrong; and claims also that this does not trouble him.

As it stands, this case does not allow us to rule out every kind of explanation which could be admitted under the *ceteris paribus* clause of the principle (P). While this man's use of moral language may seem like everyone else's, it may turn out not to be; we could discover it was for him a very elaborate game, where the rules were in part learned and in part formed by analogy with the learned rules. This man's moral principles would then be no more than rules for the production of judgements, judgements which are mere noises except that they are demanded by the ritual of the game. The object of the game is to produce the right noise in the right situation, and the rightness of the noise is determined by the rules of the game. It would be difficult to rule this out as a possible explanation, unless we assume something like the following of our imaginary case. The man produces a new moral judgement which can only be the product of new moral insight, which is of the order of a moral revelation to us. We can now say that it is impossible that this should be explained by the hypothesis that for this man making moral judgements is a game; for if it were only a game, the rules of his game would have to be picked up from other players, or extended from given rules by analogy, and startlingly new rules, new moral insights, could not be produced in this way. There are no higher-order rules for producing moral rules, and if there were we should not expect them to exclude reference to practical experience.

I think we might similarly dispose of any other way of explaining that the utterance of rules in this imaginary case is not anything like having moral knowledge (not even like having it and not having it, let alone having it and not using it).

We might also try to explain the case not as one of a failure to understand the nature of moral principles but as one of a failure to apply them in making moral judgements. I do not say 'making moral decisions' advisedly; in so far as moral decisions are decisions to act, this would be to beg the whole question. The failure could be of three kinds. First, he might simply fail to know the relevant facts. This is easily disposed of by more detailed specification of the case, as is the second sort of failure, the failure not to know but to marshal and pick out relevant facts. Thirdly, he may know the facts, and unerringly pick out the right facts, link these with his principles and make the right moral judgements: but this could be for him some sort of blind, mechanical function, an automatic, legalistic 'going by the book'. It would be cleverness rather than wisdom. But we could rule this out by saying that this man is sensitive in the extreme to the nuances of cases; that his description of a case in which he thinks some action is morally demanded is not only clear, but moving to us; that he talks like a man of sympathy, insight, and fellow-feeling, to the extent that he can make ordinary men feel ashamed of their own crudity in dealing with moral problems, as if they and not he were the legalistic blunderers. He talks like this, but does not act like it.

In short, by all the possible criteria, except those connected with action, this man is able to make and does make moral judgements, and not merely enunciate moral principles like an actor on the stage, or a sincere man blinded to the facts. In such a case, I do not think we could happily say that the man's moral views were sincere; but neither could we happily say that they were not sincere.

We might, at first, simply not believe him when he says that he does not care, and think he is concealing his remorse; perhaps his conscience pursues him in his dreams. Ruling such possibilities out, we should have to start looking for explanations of the man's behaviour in morbid psychology. We would be reluctant to do this, because we began with two views of a man's behaviour neither of which in itself leads us to ask for any kind of explanation not concerning the rational behaviour of ordinary men (good and bad ones). Looked at from either point of view alone, we have exhibitions of integrated rationality; in the one case, a man with strong moral beliefs and great moral insight; in the other, a man quite callous and wicked. One who was either of these things alone, we should not be tempted to call anything but quite sane. But when we put the two sides together we are faced with a human paradox, a man who is almost a moral genius and monstrously wicked. This is senseless, and we must consider such a man a morbid case.

This means we can make sense of the case only by treating it as a clinical one. We are no longer dealing with a rational agent, but with a pathological patient. This cannot be a crucial case in considering the status of principle (P) because it removes itself right out of the context in which it makes sense to try to apply the principle: the context of talk about rational beings.[3] It is therefore only an apparent point in favour of saying that (P) is analytic that no counter-case can be constructed to (P). It is not that one must say that the man in this case is insincere, but that one can no longer talk of him as sincere or insincere. To say 'He thinks he ought to, but he doesn't care whether he does or not' is to use language appropriate to rational behaviour, but in a case where this remark is without qualification true, such language cannot apply. There is no possible application for this statement, though not because it is self-contradictory.[4]

A further case may suggest that the principle (P) is not only not analytic, but that it is simply false. The case we have considered is that of a man who believes he ought to do something, but to whom it is a matter of indifference whether he does it or not; and such a case, worked out in detail so that all rational explanations are excluded, leaves us with a human enigma, a psychological problem, not a rational man. But the case could be strengthened by saying that this man is not indifferent to what he does; it is important to him to do what he thinks he ought *not* to do. The principle (Q) 'Given that he thinks he ought to do A, he will, other things being equal, do not-A' is one which could be used to predict his behaviour. The principle (Q) seems to be not merely contradictory, but the contrary, of (P). I have argued that (P) cannot be false; I admit (Q) might be true of someone. How can any statement be necessarily true if its contrary may sometimes be true?

In the case where what was done was a matter of indifference, it would not make sense to speak of *his* reason for doing what was done; recourse must be had to explanation in terms of *the* reason. But in the stronger case, when anything is done an explanation of *his* reason is possible, namely tbat it was wrong to do what was done. Is not this then a case within the sphere of rational behaviour?

The utter pointlessness of the moral ponderings of the man in the first case is removed in the second case. The man who does not care whether what he does is right is doing something pointless when he asks if something is right; but the man who wants to do what is wrong must ask such questions in order to act to his own satisfaction.

This case must, then, be accounted for.

When a man says he did an action because it was wrong, we may ask him why. He may say (i) 'Well, I just wanted to; and in general I want to do what is wrong' or he might say (ii) 'It wasn't that I wanted to; I thought I ought to; and in general I think I ought to do what is wrong'.

(i) This is like saying 'I knew x was wrong, but I wanted to do y, and that is why I did x', which does not contravene (P), since an explanation in terms of what was wanted is given. Where y is, for example, putting one's shirt on a horse, and x is failing to provide for one's children, the failure is explained in terms of love of gambling; but it may still be true that if it were not for one's love of gambling, one would provide for one's child. The formal character of this is not changed by making y 'doing whatever was wrong'; one might then put one's shirt on a horse, not because one loves gambling, but because one loves doing what was wrong; but it would still be true that were it not for this unusual bent, one would have done what was right. The further question of what makes somebody want to do what is wrong may be difficult to answer, like the question of why people like to gamble; but this does not mean that the case cannot be accommodated under the *ceteris paribus* clause of (P).

(ii) This might explain the answer (i); but in any case it involves a logical muddle, and acting on it can be explained, and hence accommodated under the *ceteris paribus* clause of the principle (P), as action arising from a muddle, like the action of a man who spent a fortune trying to discover by experiment what happened when an irresistible cannon-ball met an immovable post. For while saying 'I want to do what I ought not to do' is not a contradiction, 'In general I ought to do what I ought not to do' simply is a contradiction.

The counter-case involving the principle (Q), if in fact multiplied, would make the principle (P) generally not applicable as a principle of prediction, but it would not prove it false, any more than 'everyone is a lunatic' or 'drug-addiction is almost universal' would show it to be false. Moreover, the principle (Q) presupposes the principle (P), since the principle (P) is necessary to talking about what people think they ought to do.

If the principle (P) is not analytic, it is perhaps more obviously not an empirical generalisation . Certainly, it is possible to find out that someone more or less generally does what he ought to do; or that he does not, and perhaps that the principle (Q) applies to his behaviour. The old man, wandering round at the Games looking for a seat and finding nothing but callous derision, was eventually offered a place by the Spartans. 'All the Greeks *know* what is right,' he said, 'but only the Spartans *do* it.' He was voicing the fruits of his experience, no doubt. But he could have discovered by experience only that the Athenians were in general weak-willed, or selfish; not that there is no explanation for their lack of conscientiousness. To find out by observation that people without exception do what they think they ought to do is impossible, for people do not without exception do this; to find that people do not do what they think they ought to do, even where they have no reason to do otherwise, is also impossible, but not because it does not in fact happen, but because there is nothing which could count as such.

The principle (P) cannot then be falsified. This is not to say, however, that it is cut off entirely from what is empirically the case. Unless people did in fact think about what they ought to do, it would be useless, without application. It would be useless unless men were rational. Some people might seem to think, pointlessly, about what they ought to do, not caring about whether they did it; they would then be irrational, though if there were others who did care, we might still want to describe the unconscientious ones as if thinking about their duty. But if everyone were in this way irrational, how could we take their words? As words meaning what we mean, as words meaning something entirely different, or as words at all? How could we discover that this was the situation for all men, except by comparison with some men for whom it was not so? To diverge from the norm of rationality in this way is to presuppose the possibility of the application of this norm to other cases. Without this, the description can only be described in terms of the non-rational; in terms of 'people' acting and, oddly, making noises when they do. These noises become words when we presuppose the use of words, a rational activity.

Talk about what irrational people pointlessly say or think can only be by analogy with what rational people think, as we apply such talk usefully to animals; and the problems and complexities which arise when we press the analogy too far can be guarded against only by our bearing in mind that it is only an analogy.

Someone who said on more than a few occasions and in every way seemed to mean, that there were reasons for doing something, that he had no reason at all not to do it, but that he would not do it, would proclaim that he lacked one of the necessary conditions for regarding his behaviour (I mean not just his external actions, but his mode of life) as rational. This condition is not that he should act on the right reasons – rational people are often wicked or imprudent – but that at least, holding reasons to be reasons, he should act on them, other things being equal.

What then is the status of the principle (P)? It is not a principle necessary to the explicability of all behaviour, for it is not required for the understanding of the behaviour of electrons, machines, animals, or men so far as the behaviour of men is like the behaviour of these. But it is a principle necessary to the explicability of the rational behaviour of men; and it is justified by the fact that to question it is to move out of the sphere in which, if it could be false, it would be false.

The problem I have been discussing is not the problem of *akrasia*. There being such a principle as (P) is, rather, a necessary condition of the problem of *akrasia* arising. *Akrasia* leads to a problem about failures to follow one's moral principles, but it is only the principle (P) which allows us to talk about failure in this respect at all. It follows that we should expect a discussion of the principle (P) to be necessary to a proper discussion of the problem of *akrasia*. I should claim that the mistake of regarding the principle (P) as analytic has led some contemporary moral philosophers into saying some paradoxical things while dealing with such problems as weakness of will, the possibility of sincere self-criticism, etc. More important still, a consideration of (P) suggests that it not only makes the problem of *akrasia* possible, it also limits the sort of answer which may be given. It limits it to the extent that it would seem that no general account of failure to follow a principle one holds, or to act in accordance with judgements one sincerely makes, is possible. The elucidation of what constitutes an explanation of such failure such that one does not at the same time rule out that the moral beliefs are sincere would be the filling-out of possible kinds of *ceteris paribus* clauses in the principle (P). It need not be the case that there is any homogeneity between the various kinds of explanation, and such homogeneity could certainly not be established, since it is impossible to find a principle on which the kinds of explanation possible may be exhaustively enumerated. The *ceteris paribus* clause concerns an open class of classes of possible explanations. The progress of psychology could never affect the status of the principle (P), but it could certainly increase the range of types of explanations which could be used to give content to the *ceteris paribus* clause. No general account of failure to follow moral principles can, then, be given, since there need be nothing in common between the totality of explanations possible, and the idea of the totality of explanations possible must be regarded as a limit rather than an enumerable sum.

XII Oughts and wants

Neil Cooper

Moral weakness is a stumbling-block for philosophers as well as for ordinary men. It is a fact of our experience that we are sometimes tempted to depart from our moral principles, and that while at times we resist successfully, at other times we succumb. A man is said to be 'morally weak' if, while accepting a moral principle that he should or should not perform certain actions, he fails to conform to it, although it would be possible for him to do so. It is typical of the morally weak man that he is conscious that he is not behaving as he ought to behave and as he should behave, and consequently feels guilty or remorseful. It is sometimes thought that the existence of moral weakness poses an insoluble problem for prescriptivism, the view that it is the distinctive function of moral judgements to do such things as commend, recommend or enjoin. Prescriptivism, unlike descriptivism, makes sense of the fact that we are guided by and at least sometimes act upon our moral principles, but does not seem able to explain the other side of the coin, the fact that we sometimes fail to act on them. I shall try to show in this paper that while the existence of moral weakness is difficult to explain on an extreme prescriptivist position, yet if prescriptivism is suitably modified, it can accommodate moral weakness.

I

In the extreme form given it by Hare (in *The Language of Morals* and *Freedom and Reason*) and others, the prescriptivist thesis is that moral judgements, in particular, moral 'ought'-judgements, are (i) fully autonomous, of our own making, (ii) fully prescriptive, where this is interpreted as 'entailing an imperative' or expressing an injunction or decision, (iii) overriding, furnishing stronger reasons for action than any other reasons. Now the man who is in a state of temptation addresses moral 'ought'-judgements to himself in relation to his present and future action. They are of the form

'I ought to be doing A' or 'I ought to do A'. If these are properly prescriptive, then, on the extreme prescriptivist view, they entail first-person imperatives of the form 'Let me do A', and since moral 'ought'-judgements are overriding, these imperatives must express decisions to act. Hence, on this view, if the man is sincere in his 'ought'-judgement, he is logically committed to a decision to act. And if he has *really* decided to act in a certain way, provided he is mindful of his decision and does not change his mind, he must so act if it is physically and psychologically possible for him to do so. Thus the extreme prescriptivist does not allow that it logically possible that a man should fully believe that he ought to be behaving in a certain way, be conscious that he could so behave and yet not do as he ought. Let us take an example. Let us suppose that a man is questioned by the police for an alleged driving offence. He knows that he ought to tell the truth (or, to put it negatively, that he ought not to tell lies), he knows that he can tell the truth, but tells a lie, because he thinks that he will be charged if he tells the truth. In this case he is quite sincere in thinking that he ought to tell the truth and this is shown by the fact that he is conscious of condemning himself while he is telling the lie as well as afterwards. He is further conscious while he is telling the lie that he could have spoken the truth. He has no feeling while he is speaking that the lie is being forced from him by forces beyond his control; this would be to experience psychological necessity. It is because he is conscious that he could have done otherwise that he blames himself for lying, even though he gets off scot-free as a result.

It will not do to explain away *all* such examples as insincerity on the one hand or as a kind of psychological compulsion on the other, as Hare appears to do in his two books. It is of course true that many people pay lip-service to moral principles which they do not in fact hold. In such cases their insincerity is revealed by the general pattern of their behaviour. True, some people may show what they really believe only when the external sanctions which they fear are removed, but one's real beliefs are shown not only by one's actions but also by one's feelings. A man who is insincere not only makes no genuine attempt to live up to the moral principles he pretends to hold, but does not experience guilt or remorse at his failure to do so. It is not be denied that such people exist, but they are not properly called 'morally weak', since they do not depart from their real moral principles, only from their pretended ones.

The view that moral weakness is a kind of psychological impossibility has been recently maintained by Hare (Chapter VIII

above). He argues that in weakness a man is overpowered by desire and that thus we have here a case of psychological impossibility
which, by an application of the 'ought'-implies-'can' principle,
downgrades or reduces the moral 'ought' or makes it 'off-colour'.
This is for several reasons a difficult view to maintain. First, if I
prescribe the physically or psychologically impossible, unaware of
the impossibility, my 'ought' is none the less prescriptive, i.e. used to
recommend, even if it can be rebutted by someone who points out
the impossibility. The mere fact of impossibility is not sufficient
to cause every antecedently uttered 'ought' to be instantly down-
graded. In general, psychological impossibility does not down-
grade an 'ought' unless the speaker is aware of it. Moreover,
whether all weakness is really psychological impossibility 'in a
deeper sense' or not is irrelevant; the important fact is that we are
sometimes convinced that we are able to act otherwise and in such
cases there is no good reason for saying that our use of 'ought' is
'off-colour'.

Further, if the kind of psychological impossibility envisaged is
one which excuses, then it must be contrasted with a state of affairs
where no such excuse is admissible. But the kind of psychological
impossibility which Hare identifies with weakness is one which
applies to all human action. Thus what goes for the morally weak
man goes for the morally strong man too. If the weak man acts
as he does because the strength of his selfish desire makes it impossible for him to act otherwise, the morally strong man likewise
acts as he does of necessity because the strength of his virtuous
desire makes it impossible for him to act otherwise, and so any reinforcing 'ought' addressed to him must be likewise downgraded
or 'off-colour', if 'ought' indeed implies 'can do otherwise'. On this
view, then, all human action becomes psychologically necessary,
only action 'in the line of least resistance' is possible, and so every
'ought' becomes 'off-colour' and not genuinely prescriptive. But if
this is true of every 'ought', it will not show that an 'ought' addressed to a morally weak man is any different from any other
'ought'.

Again, while it is certainly true that some people at some times
are conscious of its being psychologically impossible for them to
act in accordance with their principles, this is not true of all cases
of moral weakness. There are indeed some people who are unable
to control themselves on some occasions, and these are the most
dramatic cases of moral weakness. But they are not the most
typical cases. Like Aristotle (*Nicomachean Ethics*, bk vii, 1150 b19),

we should make a distinction between *propeteia*, precipitate action, and *astheneia*, genuine moral weakness. There is a difference between the soldier who runs away in a moment of blind panic and the soldier who after deliberation yields to the temptation to desert. To suggest that all weakness is basically psychological impossibility is to confuse losing control of oneself with ordinary succumbing to temptation. We need to be reminded that we may 'succumb to temptation with calm and even with finesse'.[1]

We may appeal also to the phenomenology of temptation. When we are faced with temptation, we are not conscious, when we yield, of finding it psychologically impossible to do what we believe we ought to do, nor are we conscious, when we successfully resist temptation, of merely acting in accordance with psychological necessity. Rather we are conscious of finding difficulty in doing what we believe that we ought to do; sometimes we do what we ought to do despite the difficulty, while at other times we fail to do what we ought to do because of the difficulty. We praise those who overcome the difficulties and blame those who allow themselves to be overcome or deterred by them. Whether we ought to allot praise and blame in this way may indeed be questioned, but it is a fact that most of us do so. We think, whether rightly or wrongly, that we are responsible for the way we respond to temptation, and since our use of language is determined by the way we think rather than by the way things are, we employ a clearly on-colour 'ought' in addressing and talking about both morally weak and morally strong people, and this we shall no doubt continue doing until the dawn of 'Walden Two'.

II

If, then, there is a central kind of moral weakness, which is not reducible either to insincerity or to psychological impossibility, we need to show how it is possible for a consistent prescriptivist to recognise its existence.

To begin with, it should be noticed that the word 'prescriptive' has been used in two related senses in discussions of these problems. In the technical sense given it by Hare it means 'entailing an imperative', in its loose sense it means 'providing reasons for action, being used to commend, recommend, enjoin and so on'. I shall argue that, if we are going to characterise moral language as 'prescriptive' with any plausibility, we should for a number of reasons apply the word in its loose sense only.

In the first place, there is one class of moral judgements which are prescriptive in this loose sense but are not necessarily over-riding, and therefore first-person future-referring 'ought'-judgements of this class will not entail or involve decisions to act. I refer to the moral judgements made by the positive morality of a society. These moral judgements are generally neglected in prescriptivist treatments of moral weakness. When I say, 'I morally ought not to do A', I may either be merely voicing the morality of the group in which I live or making an autonomous moral judgement, a moral judgement of my own, which may or may not be identified with the moral judgement made by my group in general. If I am voicing the morality of my society I am not talking from an 'external point of view' (to use Professor Hart's terminology) but from an 'internal' point of view; I am not describing or talking about the rules and standards of my society, I am endorsing and applying them. When I speak from the internal point of view I regard the fact that an action is approved of or prescribed by my society as a reason for approving of the action or as a reason for doing it myself. However, I do not necessarily regard it as an over-riding reason for doing the action. Hence if we are making positive-moral judgements, it is no self-contradiction to say, 'I know that I ought to do A, but I am not going to'. There is no conceptual difficulty in accommodating moral weakness within a purely social theory of morality. We often do feel guilt of a kind when we deliberately violate the rules and conventions of the society in which we live, even when these rules and conventions do not embody the standards and values which we ourselves think to be most important and overriding. But these are not central cases of moral weakness. The central cases occur, not when we consciously fail to live up to social or positive morality in some respect, but when we consciously fail to live up to our own autonomous morality, when we fail to live up to the standards which we set ourselves.

III

However, even if we confine our attentions to autonomous moral 'ought'-judgements, as I shall do from this point onwards, first-person 'ought'-judgements do not necessarily involve decisions to act. As seen above, according to Hare's thesis one can derive from a first-person moral 'ought'-judgement, referring to the present or future, a singular imperative of the form 'Let me do X', where such an imperative expresses a decision to act. I shall argue, in the first place, that from the fact that somebody accepts a first-person moral 'ought'-judgement, referring to the present or future, one cannot infer that he has decided to act in accordance with it, but can merely infer that, in a minimal sense of 'want', he wants to act in accordance with it.

If I say to you, 'You ought to do A', one may infer from this that, if I am sincere, (i) I want A to be done, and (ii) I want A to be done by you. The word 'want' here is used in a minimal sense, in which it can be applied to anything one is in favour of for any reason whatsoever, as opposed to the Kantian sense, in which it is applied to anything one has a natural urge or inclination towards. (In this minimal sense I may be said to want something for which I have no inclination for the sake of some further desired end. For instance, I may be said to 'want' to have my appendix out, in order to get rid of the pain, however much I may dislike the operation itself.) Further, if I say to myself, 'I ought to do A', one may infer from this that, if I am sincere, I want A to be done by me, that is, I want to do A (in the minimal sense of 'want', though not necessarily in the Kantian sense). This is a pragmatic implication. The statement that I want to do A does not follow from the statement that I ought to do A; it only follows from the statement that I have sincerely asserted 'I ought to do A'.

Now it might be objected that to say, as I have, that a first-person 'ought' does not entail a decision, but rather pragmatically implies or involves a want or desire, does not get us very far, for, it might be said, the kind of wanting involved is not so very different from deciding. The criterion of somebody's wanting something, it might be said, is his trying to get it, and if he does not try to get it, he does not really want it; at most, it is only an idle wish which does not count as desiring or wanting. But trying to get is only, as Professor Anscombe points out, 'the primitive sign of wanting'.[2] It is not the only sign. Apart from the purely primitive sign of wanting, there are also the *post eventum* criteria, pleasure in the fulfilment of the desire or alternatively distress over the non-fulfilment. There are also other more sophisticated criteria for determining the existence of a want, word-association tests, for example, such as have been used by experimental psychologists for determining the strength of drives. The behavioural expression of wanting is complex. In some kinds of wanting the trying-to-get behaviour is dominant, in others the *post eventum* behaviour is primary, while the overt trying-to-get behaviour may be minimal. It is this latter sort of wanting, wanting not necessarily manifested in trying-to-get or in this case trying-to-conform behaviour, which, I suggest, we have when we sincerely assert a first-person 'ought'-judgement. Thus while we cannot simultaneously try to achieve two aims which we know to be incompatible or carry out two decisions which we know to be incompatible, we can have simultaneously two desires or wants whose simultaneous satisfaction we know to be impossible, and recognise that one of them will have to go unsatisfied, at least for the present. Since the wants are incompatible, unless a compromise is possible one of them will remain in existence without being manifested in trying-to-conform behaviour. First-person 'ought'-judgements are analogous to wants of this kind rather than to crude trying-to-get wants or to decisions.[3] For there are situations where two or more conflicting 'ought'-judgements apply, and one can only act upon one of them, at any rate at one time. For instance, I believe both that I ought to tell the truth and that I ought not to hurt other people's feelings, and it may sometimes be the case that I cannot reconcile the two, and so cannot conform to one of these principles without violating the other. 'Ought'-judgements stand in perpetual danger of such conflicts.

Since, then, moral 'ought'-judgements involve a certain kind of wanting, the criteria of which are more complex than trying-to-get or trying-to-conform behaviour, the criterion of somebody's accepting a moral 'ought'-judgement must be of the same order of complexity.

IV

Somebody might well object to what I have been arguing on the following line:

> What you have been maintaining is all very true of moral principles framed in terms of Rossian prima facie 'ought's, but not all 'ought's are of this potentially conflicting kind. Some of them surely are overriding in the sense that those who hold them do not allow any other moral 'ought'-principle to take precedence as a guide to action. (This is the sort of attitude which an

extreme Utilitarian has towards the Principle of Utility or a naïve pacifist has towards the principle that one ought never under any circumstances to take human life.) If such an over-riding 'ought' involves a want or desire, it is a want or desire to do something more (more strongly or intensely) than anything else, and this is surely tantamount to a decision. If somebody accepts a fundamental moral principle, that is, a principle which he does not allow to be overridden by any other principle, to the effect that he ought to do actions of a certain kind, then he must want to do actions of this kind more intensely than he wants to do anything else. It follows from this that, supposing that every-body must act 'in the line of least resistance', he cannot but act in accordance with his moral principle, whenever it is possible for him to do so.

But the presupposition of this argument does not hold. While it is true that if I think that I morally ought to do A, I think that I ought to-do-A-in-preference-to-anything-else and hence I must want, in the minimal sense of 'want', to-do-A-in-preference-to-anything-else, it does not follow from this that I must want to do A more intensely than I want to do anything else. For to say that I have a want or desire to-do-A-in-preference-to-anything-else is to say nothing about the intensity of that desire. There is no necessary one-one correlation between the order of priority of a man's moral principles and the order of strength of his desires. One's desires and inclinations may fluctuate from time to time, but one's moral beliefs are not necessarily affected by 'every momentary gust of passion'.

I suggest, indeed, that a man's moral principles are those of his principles of action which in a cool hour he is least prepared to abandon belief in, however much he may be tempted to deviate from them in the heat of the moment. In this respect they resemble 'functionally *a priori*' principles in a science, principles which in the exposition of a scientific theory we are prepared to stick to, come what may. It does not of course follow from this that our moral principles are always framed or formed 'in a cool hour'. Occasionally, as happened once to Russell, a lasting change in moral attitudes can take place in a moment of deep emotion. All that I am maintaining is that moral principles are 'settled principles of action' and that a man's moral principles are those which he regards 'in a cool hour' as the most important. It is because of this cool-hour quality that moral principles can be appealed to when I am no longer able to see things steadily, when I am biased by particular passions and emotions, and a level-headed judgement is difficult to arrive at. Hence a moral principle cannot be identical with a *hexis proairetike*, a disposition to make choices of certain kinds. Moral principles are dispositions to approve or disapprove, to recommend or disrecommend (a useful word even if obsolete). We show what our moral principles are not only to the extent that our own conduct conforms to them, but also in situations where we are required to give advice to or pass judgement on others. Of course, it may well be the case that in giving advice I do not notice the difficulty or odium of the course I am recommending or do not imagine how I should feel in the heat of the moment, if it were I to whom the advice were addressed. ' 'Tis one thing to know virtue, and another to conform the will to it' (Hume, *Treatise of Human Nature*, iii(i)1). It may be the case that I should be disinclined above all other things for my moral principle to be applied to me, but I cannot infer from this by some rule of universalisability that it is my moral principle which should be revised or abandoned. There is certainly a conflict here, a conflict between my moral principle and my desire that it should not be applied to me. I cannot act in accordance with both and so I must choose between them as guides to action. However, the one of them cannot 'knock out' or give the logical *coup de grâce* to the other. In this respect they are quite unlike two conflicting beliefs about matters of fact. Both the moral principle and the opposing desire logically can co-exist in a clear-thinking person. Clarity of thought is no anodyne against the torments of being tempted.

    We are not, then, logically compelled to reject a moral 'ought'-principle just because we have an opposing desire which is temporarily stronger. For since 'ought'-principles are prescriptive towards actions, they are also prescriptive (although only weakly prescriptive) towards the desires to perform these actions. If I believe that I morally ought not to perform certain actions, then I logically must have an unfavourable attitude towards the desire to perform such actions. I must believe that it is not a good thing to want to perform them and that therefore I ought not to foster such desires. Moral beliefs are as much concerned with the regulation of our passions as with the regulation of our actions. Somebody who believes that he morally ought to do something and that this 'ought' is overriding, must believe that he ought to foster the desire to do it. While our having or not having certain desires is not within our control, it *is* within our power to foster or discourage the desires that we have. The morally weak man is the man who accepts a moral principle, believes that he ought to foster the desire to live up to it (or discourage the desire not to live up to it), but because he is unsuccessful in sufficiently fostering the one desire (or discouraging the other) sometimes fails to live up to his principle. If he is to be regarded as sincere in professing a moral principle, he must not only feel guilt and remorse when he fails to live up to it, but he must also try to foster the desire to act in conformity with his principle or try to discourage the desire not to act in conformity. He will only be open to the suspicion of insincerity if he fails even to try to foster the 'right' desires. Unless he really and fully believed that he ought morally to perform an action, he would not think that he ought to foster his desire to do it. On the other hand, unless he was liable to yield to temptation, he would not need to try to foster some desires at the expense of others. In the eyes of the morally weak man his moral principle has 'authority'. But because it has authority, this does not make it completely efficacious. This is where extreme prescriptivism went wrong. On the other hand it was right in stressing that in order to have authority moral principles must have *some* 'power' or efficacy. If a man professes a moral principle without its making any difference at all to his behaviour on any occasion, then we may rightly doubt his sincerity. If a man genuinely holds a moral principle, he will make some effort to conform his behaviour to it, where the term 'behaviour' includes desires as well as actions. In the end it may be held that the man did not try hard enough, but this is a defect in his conduct rather than evidence of insincerity.

I have tried to show that the fact of moral weakness can be accommodated by a modified prescriptivism. If, as I have argued, moral 'ought'-judgements are only prescriptive in a loose sense, involving wants rather than decisions or injunctions, and the criteria for the existence of these wants are not to be crudely or over-behaviouristically interpreted, the possibility of a man's failing to live up to sincerely held moral principles can be recognised and explained.

XIII Wants, desires and deliberation[1]

John Benson

QUEEN. Oh, this is weakness! Subdue it!
CELIA. We know it's weakness, but the weakness is so strong!

Iolanthe.

Since it is Mr Cooper's wants rather than his oughts that I find puzzling, and since also what he says about the latter depends on what he says about the former, I propose to devote my reply to wants.

The structure of Cooper's arguments is very clear. It is this: (i) The central case of moral weakness is that of avoidable failure to act in accordance with a sincerely held moral principle (I shall refer to this as 'the central case', or alternatively as 'Pauline weakness'). (ii) The central case cannot be accounted for on a strict prescriptivist analysis of moral 'ought'-judgements. But (iii) a modified prescriptivism can be proposed to the effect that assenting to a moral principle involves wanting to conform to it. (iv) On the modified view the central case is consistent with the analysis of assenting to a moral 'ought'-judgement; since (v) in the relevant sense of 'want' the following can be jointly true: (*a*) P wants to do A; (*b*) P could do A; (*c*) P fails to do A.

I am not going to consider what intrinsic merits the modified prescriptivist analysis may have. So far as I can see it is recommended solely on the grounds that it would accommodate the central case, and I shall confine myself to considering whether it would. I shall argue that (v) is prima facie a paradox which Cooper fails to resolve. And plainly if (v) is not acceptable neither is (iv), and if (iv) is not acceptable then either (i) or (ii) has to be abandoned. I shall not try to decide which it ought to be.

I consider first how the problem of moral weakness is related to that of weakness of will (section I). Then (section II) I indicate the nature of the objection I want to make to Cooper's account of Pauline weakness, developing this (sections III and IV) through the examination of an example. Next I sketch a positive account of wanting (section V) and in the light of it criticise Cooper's analysis of this concept (section VI). Finally (section VII) I try to show that, this analysis being defective, Cooper has not shown that his characterisation of the central case is coherent.

I

Moral weakness is just one variety of weakness of will. We speak of a person's will being weak in some cases of his failing to do what he has promised, decided, intended, resolved to do, or what he wanted, longed, desired, was inclined to do, or thought he ought or that it would be a good thing to do. Only in some cases. Not where the failure is due to extreme recalcitrance of things or physical incapacity of the agent. Not where the agent perversely, or at least deliberately, does not do what he promised, etc. And perhaps not where there are certain kinds of psychological obstacle, such as irresistible impulses or uncontrollable desires. One must say 'perhaps not' in this last case because in a sense it is a defect of the will that there should be impulses that it cannot resist and desires that it cannot control. Still we often speak as though there were a type of case which is to be contrasted with these, in which the will does not capitulate in the face of overwhelming odds, but voluntarily surrenders or even connives at its own defeat. What is this distinction? What are the criteria for deciding that someone could not resist a desire? Any account of weakness must give an answer to this question and to a number of other questions that are related to it: e.g. is it possible in some sense voluntarily to give way to a desire that leads me to do what I do not really want to do?

The conceptual difficulties involved in these questions make it misleading to pose the problem of moral weakness in the way that Cooper does: 'It is typical of the morally weak man that he is conscious that he is not behaving as he ought to behave and as he could behave, and consequently feels guilty or remorseful'. It is implied that the occurrence of weakness in this sense is a pretty plain sort of fact and that what is problematical is how a prescriptivist analysis is to avoid the paradoxical implication that there is no situation of which this could be the correct description. But the notions of being conscious of not behaving as one ought and of being able to behave otherwise are so obscure that the most we can sensibly claim is that we may be able to find interpretations of them such that the favoured description of moral weakness would be true in some substantial sense. The puzzles about moral weakness are not solely created by nor can be solved solely by analysis of moral judgements.

This is borne out by Cooper's treatment of the topic. He gives an analysis of moral judgements which in effect reduces the specific problem of moral weakness to the general problem of weakness of will. Sincerely asserting that I ought to do A is said to entail wanting, in some sense, to do A. This requirement is proposed in place of the more stringent one proposed by Professor Hare because it would show that a man may do what he ought not when he both believes that he ought not to do it and could refrain from doing it. But the consequence does not obviously follow. It does so only if a man may want to do A and fail to do it even though he could do it. That this is possible needs to be shown. After all philosophers were puzzled to understand how a man can willingly do what he does not want to do long before prescriptivism was heard of. It is interesting to notice that Hare seems to think it is obvious that if making up my mind what I ought to do were merely a matter of deciding what I most want to do, then I would simply do it. (Hence Socrates' denial of weakness, which in Hare's opinion would be justified if the premiss were true.) Cooper, however, rejects this inference on the grounds that what I want in-preference-to-anything-else is not necessarily what I want most intensely, and so I do not necessarily do what I want in the first sense. This distinction is simply pointed out. But is it so obvious? I confess that when I attentively consider within myself whether there are two objects before my mind I cannot tell, and when I think of examples and try to sort them I do not find that the distinction provides an intuitively clear sorting-guide.

In order to decide whether Cooper's account does enable us to explain moral weakness, we should need a satisfactory analysis of the concept of wanting, of the relation of wanting to action and of both to deliberation and choice. This would obviously be an impossible task for a single paper even if I were competent to carry it out. But in the course of my comments on Cooper's paper I shall hazard views on these topics and hope that a more detailed analysis would show them to be not too wide of the mark.

II

I shall begin by explaining what I find the main difficulty in Cooper's account of wanting and failing to act. He rejects Hare's suggestion that the central cases of moral weakness are those in which the agent is overcome by desire. One of his reasons for rejecting it is that this type of explanation would be applicable to all human acts and so would not serve to explain the distinction between those who succeed and those who fail in living up to their moral beliefs. Another is that the explanation fails to distinguish between loss of control and 'ordinary succumbing to temptation', which is compatible with acting after deliberation. Yet when (section IV) he distinguishes between wanting to-do-A-in-preference-to-anything-else and wanting to do A more intensely than anything else, he appears to be suggesting that when someone fails to conform to a moral principle which he holds, this is because, although he wants to do the action prescribed in-preference-to-anything-else, he acts on (or even *chooses* to act on) a contrary desire which is stronger or more intense. But now it seems that Cooper is permitting himself the very explanation of weakness that he objected to in Hare. If it is a different explanation, we do not seem to be told how it is different. Is giving an explanation of this kind compatible with saying that the agent could have acted otherwise? If not, then one of the supposed features of weakness must be abandoned. But if it is compatible, then we seem still to need an explanation of why he didn't if he could. Again, what is the bearing of this account on the distinction between loss of control and ordinary succumbing to temptation? In criticising Hare, Cooper seemed to be implying that an explanation in terms of the strength of an opposing desire was incompatible with succumbing after deliberation, but in his own account he seems to assume that it is compatible, as it must be if we are to say that a weak agent succumbs without ceasing to want to conform to his principle. But now what *is* the difference between loss of control and ordinary succumbing to temptation?

Cooper either accepts or considers it unnecessary for his purposes to dispute the principle that action is always 'in the line of least resistance'. I think he must accept it, since only on this assumption is he justified in saying that 'the kind of psychological impossibility which Hare identifies with weakness is one which applies to all human action'. That is, he is saying that whatever a man does results from his strongest desire, and so we cannot distinguish on this basis between the man who *could not* act other-wise and the man who could but didn't. What does the principle mean? It might mean (1) that the strongest desire is by definition the desire on which the agent acts, in which case one could not non-vacuously explain any action by reference to the strength of desire. Or it might mean (2) that it is a well-established empirical general-isation with no significant exceptions that the strongest desire determines action. Whichever view Cooper takes, there are diffi-culties for his account. If he accepts (1) I think it follows that he has offered *no* account of weakness at all, for on this interpretation to say that a man did not-A although he wanted to-do-A-in-preference-to-anything-else because his desire to do not-A was the stronger is to say no more than although he wanted to-do-A-in-preference-to-anything-else he in fact did not-A. The puzzle remains untouched of why he did not do A. If on the other hand he accepts (2) then his account of weakness must remain incomplete unless he can give some criterion of the strength of a desire which is indepen-dent of the resulting action. Moreover it must be possible to say that although desire was stronger, it could have been overcome. If it is (2) that Cooper holds, then what he is saying comes to this: a man may genuinely want to-do-A-in-preference-to-anything-else, but because he has a desire to do not-A which is stronger than his de-sire to do A he does not-A, although he *could* have done A and indeed may have considered the matter and *chosen* to do not-A. This is surely prima facie paradoxical? If one objects to it it is not because one feels that it is impossible genuinely to want incom-patible things. It is because one feels that it is implausible to sup-pose this independence of the agent's ranking of the objects of desire from the strength of his desires.

III

It will bring this difficulty into sharper focus to look at an example that Cooper uses to point up the distinction which, following Aristotle, he makes between precipitancy and weakness proper: 'There is a difference between the soldier who runs away in a moment of blind panic and the soldier who after deliberation yields to the temptation to desert' (p. 193 above). Can we say of the second soldier that what he wanted to-do-in-preference-to-anything-else was to remain at his post? To answer this we need to notice an ambiguity in the phrase 'after deliberation': this may or may not imply 'in accordance with deliberation'. These two meanings give us two possibilities to consider.

Suppose, first, that the description of the soldier as yielding after deliberation is to be taken as implying that he acted according to the result of his deliberation. To say that someone has, in this sense, acted after deliberation is to say that he has reflected upon the outcomes of the alternative courses of action, has made up his mind which of these outcomes is the more desirable (the one he prefers), and has then decided on that course of action which is most likely to realise the preferred outcome. If we remember that we are to suppose that the soldier genuinely wants to stay at his post, then his reasoning may be represented somewhat as follows:

The soldier prefers death in battle to dishonourable safety.
He knows that by deserting he will avoid death and gain safety at the cost of honour.
He decides to desert.

But the conclusion is inconsistent with the joint truth of the premisses. If we suppose that the soldier is genuinely of the opinion that he will avoid death by deserting but at the cost of honour, then we cannot also think that he genuinely prefers death in battle to loss of honour and safety. It may be that this is not the preference he would avow to himself or to others between campaigns, and I am not saying that the choice he makes on the eve of battle shows that the between-campaigns avowal must be insincere or mistaken. I am only saying that on this occasion, in so far as his desertion not only follows but is in accordance with the result of his deliberation, it shows that for this time he wants to-save-his-life-in-preference-to-anything-else. I cannot see what other account can be given of those cases in which we suppose that the agent deliberates and acts upon the conclusion of his deliberations. For a man who deliberates must ask himself 'Which of these two actions shall I do?' If A is likely to realise one situation (S_1) and B is likely to realise a different situation (S_2), the question will then be 'Which do I want more?' If the answer is S_1, then, in so far as he is rational, he will decide to do A. Since action is not necessarily rational, one cannot of course say that he *will* do A, or even decide to do A. But if he does not at least decide to do A then it will not be true that he acted on deliberate choice. It is clear, too, that when the agent asks himself 'Which do I want?' he is not trying to discover which is the stronger of his desires in any sense that can be distinguished from asking which of the two states he would prefer to be realised. It must then be most misleading to say of someone who succumbs to the temptation to desert in this way, i.e. who chooses to desert in order to save his own life, conscious that that is his reason, that he follows the stronger desire although what he wants-in-preference-to-anything-else is to conduct himself as befits a soldier. That may be what he generally or in a cool hour wants. But it is not what he wants on this occasion. His weakness will have to be accounted for, not by saying that although his preference remained firm for honour his desire for life was stronger, but by saying that in the face of danger his preference did not remain firm, he could not hang on to his conviction that honourable death is preferable to ignoble safety. Cooper wants to use his distinction between strength of desire and preference-ranking to show that there is a kind of wanting that is constant through the fluctuations of desire (or wanting in another sense). This account is, however, inapplicable to the kind of case which Cooper takes to be the central kind of weakness, that in which, after deliberation, a man succumbs to temptation, if 'after – ' means 'after and in accordance with – '

IV

There is, however, a second possibility to be considered: that when the soldier is said to desert after deliberation what is meant is merely that his action follows a period spent in deliberating. It might be that he reasons in the way set out in the last section, concluding with the decision not to desert, but then deserts. This is the possibility that Cooper may have in mind if he is following Aristotle faithfully, for Aristotle says that the weak (those afflicted by *astheneia*) 'deliberate, but then are prevented by passion from keeping to their resolution'; whereas the precipitate (those afflicted by *propeteia*) 'are led by passion because they do not stop to deliberate'. But if this is the distinction that Cooper is making, it is not at all obvious that he is right in suggesting that the view that Pauline weakness is basically psychological impossibility rests upon a confusion between loss of control (precipitancy) and ordinary succumbing to temptation (weakness proper). The apparent force of this point seems to derive from the failure to distinguish between the two possible meanings of 'acting after deliberation'. People who suffer from depression often form definite desires, e.g. to attend to their work as usual, may deliberate and decide what to do, all to no effect; they may persist in thinking that if only they pulled themselves together they could do it, long past the point when resolutions and efforts of will have become useless. Why should we suppose that only a passion that prevents me from thinking about my actions at all can put it out of my power to act on my principles or according to my real wishes? That absence of tumultuous emotion is no sure sign that one's actions are under control is not a recondite piece of psychological lore, and not even philosophers can be excused for being ignorant of it.

Perhaps part of what Cooper has in mind in quoting Austin's remark about succumbing to temptation 'with calm and even with finesse' is that the manner in which one prosecutes the course of action that results from one's having succumbed need not be uncontrolled. (In fact I wonder if he isn't borrowing the phrase but forgetting the example – a simple case of unscrupulous greed). But it is surely quite wrong to think that the fact that one carries out a series of actions in a calm and heedful manner shows that one had it in one's power to choose to act otherwise and to carry that choice into effect. The deserter who manages his defection with calm and finesse may have a hard job persuading a court-martial that he could not help deserting. One does not look to courts-martial however, for an appreciation of such moral and psychological niceties, and from the fact that he could deliberate about *how* to get away and could act on the outcome of that deliberation it does not follow that he could also act upon the outcome of his deliberation about *whether* he should get away. Calculated behaviour may still be compulsive.

V

It might be suggested that in raising these difficulties about Cooper's account of Pauline weakness I am overlooking or misunderstanding the distinction he makes between different senses of 'want', of which the most important seems to be the distinction between wanting-in-preference-to- and wanting-more-intensely-than-. If the distinctions are accepted, need there be any inconsistency in saying that one may be led by desire to do A while conscious that one could do otherwise and while still wanting, in some real sense, to do otherwise?

I do not think that his distinctions are groundless, but they will not do as they stand. I believe that when their defects are remedied they prove to be ineffective in resolving the paradox involved in his characterisation of the central case of weakness. Before examining them I shall venture some positive observations (not, in their main lines, original).

The expression 'conflict of desire' can refer to two different types of situation. One is the type of situation in which, say, a rat which has been deprived of both food and sexual satisfaction is presented with suitable and attractive food and a suitable and attractive mate. We should expect the rat to exhibit bodily symptoms (e.g. glandular secretions) appropriate to both appetites and to display both food-approaching and mate-approaching behaviour, and the conflict would presumably be terminated by the rat's finally going for one or the other. We should not be inclined to describe the rat's behaviour in terms of 'considering the alternatives' and 'deciding which to take first'. The other type of situation is exemplified by a man who wants to go to the football match and also to stay and watch the film on telly. He resolves this conflict by deciding which he wants more, and this means considering various aspects of the rival objects, rather than looking within his breast in an effort to find out which he wants more. His decision to go to the match rather than watch the film will follow from his decision that he wants to do the former more than the latter, and in turn deciding that that is what he wants is the upshot of a process of thought. The wants that enter into a conflict of the second kind are not raw psychic data. The man who, after considering the matter, says that he wants to go to the match is expressing a valuation rather than reporting a fact, and the conflict is analogous to a conflict of beliefs in that settling the conflict is more like looking for evidence than trying to predict which of two contestants will prove the stronger.

Human beings can of course experience both kinds of conflict, but it is a bad mistake to interpret the second on the model of the first. There is a strong temptation to do so which is encouraged by the currency of meteorological and military metaphors, applied with equal readiness to both kinds of conflict. Where it is conflicts of the second kind that we are talking about, differences of strength *are* differences of preference. The question whether what I want is something I can control does not arise in the context of this kind of conflict. Rather what determines whether I am in control of myself is how effectively I can bring my actions into conformity with what (in this sense) I want. But there is the kind of want – which I shall distinguish by calling it 'desire' – which enters into the first kind of conflict. It does not depend upon deliberation and is not the evaluative upshot of any process of thought. Nor consequently can it be given a ranking on a scale of preference, and so cannot conflict with what I want in the way that two of my wants can conflict. It does make sense to speak of controlling desires, whereas it makes no sense to speak of controlling wants; I may want to control my desire but be unsuccessful because it is too strong. When this happens I have been prevented from doing what I wanted to do by my desire. My will has been frustrated. A desire is something that happens to me, like a toothache, and just for that reason it is something I can wish to be without, or be glad I no longer have (as Sophocles according to Cephalus in the *Republic* was glad to have reached the age when he no longer had sexual desires to distract him). It makes good sense to avoid situations in which one's desires might be satisfied, but it makes no sense to avoid the opportunity of doing what one wants to do. The force of this last distinction can be brought out more sharply in the following way: if someone is to be correctly described as wanting to do A, it must be the case that, other things being equal, he would do A if he had the opportunity and physical capacity. The other-things-being-equal proviso covers, primarily, possible conflicting wants. It could still be true that he wants to do A even though it should happen that he never does so. But contrast with this the case of a man who makes a resolution, or takes a vow, to remain celibate. And let us assume that this is not just a matter of accepting celibacy as a necessary consequence of assuming a particular calling, but that he embraces it as part of the good life. He still has sexual desires, but we cannot interpret this as meaning that he *wants* to gratify them, thus implying that he would, other things being equal, gratify the desire if he had the opportunity and the physical capacity. For here the proviso will have to be read in part: if he did not want to remain celibate, which comes to the same as: if he wanted to gratify his sexual desire. If desire is interpreted as want, then the he-would-if implication becomes vacuous.

Wants can but desires cannot be expressed as the major premisses of pieces of practical reasoning. But though this means that it is a kind of category mistake to speak of conflicts between wants and desires, there is all the same a loose sense in which they conflict: they can be competing determinants of actions. A desire can prevent me from doing what I want to do because it puts it out of my power to act upon the results of my deliberations, or it can put it out of my power to deliberate. Besides being a possible obstacle to my doing what I want to do, however, desire can obviously be one of the factors that I take into account in deciding what I want to do. The relationships between my wants and my desires are complex and various. In the first place I may have a general want to satisfy my desires, subject to conditions of various kinds. Secondly my awareness of certain specific desires may influence my choice in the sense of being one of the things I take into account in making up my mind what I want to do. For instance, in deciding which of two girls I want to marry I may ask myself which of them prompts my sexual desires more strongly. Desires do not automatically have but they may be accorded the status of wants. Not even the most insistent of my desires have to be accorded that status, and I may decide that what I want is a life that frustrates a great many of my desires. Such a choice may be perverse, or even ridiculous, and lead only to the discovery that 'The life of solitary men will be certainly miserable, but not certainly devout'. I may come to the conclusion that I am not capable of controlling my desires but still refuse to accommodate them by adjusting the system of my wants; I may come to the conclusion that I was misguided or self-deceived in thinking that the satisfaction of my desires was not very important to me, and consequently went wrong in making up my mind what I wanted; I may not clearly formulate what I want in such a way that I can distinguish it from what I desire, so that it is not clear to me whether my backslidings ought to tell me that I do not after all really want to do what I somehow find myself failing to do.

This last possibility is an important one, both because it shows that so far I have been assuming an over-rigid separation of desire and want, and because it indicates what seems to me a very central kind of weakness of will. One is very often unwilling to acknowledge that the satisfaction of a desire is incompatible with what one wants, and one may avoid having to do so either by not formulating one's wants clearly, or by not deciding on an order of priority among them, or by not considering whether they are compatible with one another and with one's desires. One's wants do form a system of a kind, but one that is very incompletely articulated. The situation in which I am quite clear what I really want to do but knowingly give way to the temptation to do something inconsistent with it is, I should have thought, comparatively uncommon in the lives of most people.

VI

Cooper distinguishes between two senses of wanting: a minimal sense in which what one wants can be 'anything one is in favour of for any reason whatsoever', and the Kantian sense, in which what one wants is something towards which one has 'a natural urge or inclination'. This distinction has a family resemblance to the one I have made between wanting and desiring, but whether he would acknowledge an actual kinship between them I do not know. If he is intending his distinction to be understood in this way, then one thing that is strange is that he regards his non-Kantian wanting as wanting in a *minimal* sense. Part of the difficulty lies in his use of the label 'Kantian'; for Kant seems to hover between thinking of inclination as something which involves acting on a maxim and thinking of it as an impulse which causes but in no sense provides a reason for action. So I cannot decide whether Cooper regards a natural urge or inclination as something that could feature in practical reasoning – as something that the agent could mention as his reason for acting in a certain way – or whether, as I should say, it is something that, if it moves to action, does so unmediated by deliberation. The phrase 'natural impulse or inclination' does seem to suggest something that comes unbidden, that is not a result of reflection. If this is what Cooper intends it to suggest, he is characterising as 'minimal' the sense of wanting in which we explain a man's deliberate actions by saying that his reason for doing what he did was that he wanted such-and-such. And this is surely the primary sense of 'want' in speaking human behaviour?

Another doubt about what Cooper's minimal sense of wanting amounts to arises from the fact that the only illustration he gives is of wanting as a means something for which one has no inclination. This does not help us to see how his distinction applies to things that are wanted for their own sake, as it must if it is to do the job it is required to do in the analysis of assenting to a moral principle.

Nor do I think that Cooper has successfully made out a distinction between wants for those whose existence trying to get is the primary criterion and wants for whose existence other criteria are primary. For, first, there are certainly situations in which it is consistent with a man's wanting something that he makes no attempt to get it, for instance when there is something else which he wants more; but this does not show that the want which is not satisfied is a different *kind* of want from the want which is satisfied. And, secondly, to speak of a 'sort of wanting' which is 'not necessarily manifested in trying-to-get' suggests that there is some other sort of wanting which is necessarily thus manifested. But what sort of wanting is that? Nothing of the sort holds good of – for example – natural urges. That a man never makes advances to women will only count against his having sexual urges in the absence of evidence that he has other wants whose satisfaction he regards as more important and incompatible with sexual satisfaction. Cooper is, I think, failing to distinguish between a logically necessary condition of wanting: that one would, given the opportunity and capacity, other things being equal, attempt to satisfy the want; and the claim that trying-to-get is indispensable as evidence of a want. The word 'criterion' often obscures this distinction. He has perhaps been misled here by his concern to rebut the suggestion that in his minimal sense wanting is little different from deciding. But to this the correct answer is not that there is a special kind of wanting which is exempt from the need to prove itself in performance, but that in no case does wanting involve more than being committed to deciding to act *given certain conditions*.

The final objection to his account that Cooper tries to meet is that if an overriding moral principle involves a want, this want must be tantamount to a decision, and it is this point that the distinction between the relative strength and the order of preference of wants is introduced to deal with. I have three comments to make on this distinction:

(1) The objection has a more general application than he envisages. It can be raised even if there is no principle which is admitted to be overriding on all occasions. In a particular situation to which two or more principles apply and give rise to a conflict of obligations, one of them will normally be held to take precedence, i.e. to be *overriding on that occasion*. It will follow on Cooper's account that the agent must here and now want to act on that principle in preference to anything else.

(2) The distinction is presented in what is, at least in appearance, a question-begging way. Immediately after saying that to want to-do-A-in-preference-to-anything-else does not imply anything about

the intensity of the desire, Cooper observes that 'There is no necessary one-one correlation between the order of priority of a man's moral principles and the order of strength of his desires' (p. 197 above). Taking this to be an obvious truth, we might be led to think that it supports the validity of the distinction between wanting-in-preference-to- and wanting-more-intensely-than-. But in fact the distinction derives no support from this truth. Indeed unless the distinction is made out independently, the invariance of moral conviction relative to the strength of desire will count against the view that it is a necessary condition of assenting to a moral principle that one should want to conform to it.

(3) As I have already urged, the distinction between strength and preference is not a distinction between two different aspects or dimensions of the same thing, namely wanting-or-desiring. Rather we need a distinction between wanting and desiring. It is wants that enter into deliberation, are themselves decided upon after reflection, and can be ordered on a preference scale. Whereas desires are brute impulses, or dispositions thereto, which we just have, and which can be ordered according to strength. I would contend that, understood in this way, the distinction lends no support to Cooper's account of the central case of weakness.

VII

Cooper's account is faced with a dilemma. If we assume that the question concerns what a man wants to do and what he could do at the time of action, then what are we to say about cases of failure to do what one wants to do because of the promptings of desire? First there is the possibility that although in general one wants to-do-A-in-preference-to-anything-else, on this occasion, having a desire to do B (which is incompatible with A), one deliberates and decides to do B. In this case, as I have argued in section 3, one's *preference at the time* is to do B. That one could have done A is at least not ruled out here; perhaps if one had decided to do A one would have succeeded in carrying out the decision.

Second there is the possibility that one decides to do A but is prevented from carrying out the decision by an opposing desire. In this case one may want to-do-A-in-preference-to-anything-else not only dispositionally but occurrently, and if there is no reasonable doubt that this is so, then it can only be concluded that the failure to carry out the decision shows that one lacked the power to do so. It may be true that in general one has the power to do A when there is nothing one wants more, but it cannot be true that one has the power on this occasion. As Stuart Hampshire points out in *Freedom of the Individual*, we discover our powers by finding what we can do when we have the will, and we discover their limits when we fail to do what we have the will to do.

Cooper's central case of moral weakness seems to be a crossbreed of these two cases, which requires that the backslider (occurrently) wants to-do-A-in-preference-to-anything-else, *and* (occurrently) can do A, and yet fails to do it. This is impossible, and so his characterisation of the central case is incoherent. I think that he supposes it to be possible because he treats a want/desire as something that can function simultaneously as an element in deliberation, and as such is chosen as a guide to action, and yet as a kind of force which determines action not because it carries the agent's preference but because of its strength. I have tried, in section V, to show that this view of wanting is itself incoherent.

Much of my criticism of Cooper misses the mark if he is not supposing that both the 'want' and the 'can' are occurrent in the central case. There are several points in his account at which the disposition/occurrence distinction cries out to be made. But I think it must be his real view that both are used in an occurrent sense, for, first, there would not otherwise be much point in his refusing to accept an explanation in terms of psychological impossibility; and, secondly, he does want it to be true that the backslider can be fully accepting his moral principles at the very moment when he is failing to conform to it.

Yet at the end he seems to retreat from this position: 'We are not logically compelled to reject a moral "ought"-principle just because we have an opposing desire which is temporarily stronger. For since "ought"-principles are prescriptive towards actions, they are also prescriptive (though only weakly prescriptive) towards the desires to perform those actions. . . . While our having or not having certain desires is not within our control, it *is* within our power to foster or discourage the desires that we have' (pp. 198–9 above). The question is: Have I the power, given the desires that I have here and now, to act on them or not as I choose? The possibility of my working on my desires so that on a future occasion my moral muscles will be in better shape is quite consistent with my present failure being due to a desire which I *now cannot* resist. We are back with psychological impossibility.

I conclude with two general comments on weakness.

First, the two types of case described at the beginning of this section are not the only types. These are, I suppose, ideal types which presuppose that the elements in the situation are sharply distinguished. I suggested at the end of section V that the central cases – certainly the most common cases – of weakness are those in which either the agent or the spectator or both are quite unclear about what the agent wants and what he desires and hence about what his powers are. I am not at all persuaded of the importance of the alleged central case, as defined by philosophers of an anti-socratic persuasion, nor consequently am I dismayed by the sup-posed paradoxicality of explanations of weakness that exclude it.

Secondly, although I agree in a general sense with Cooper's re-marks about the possibility of cultivating and discouraging desires, I am not very sure just what these exercises consist in and think that this would be a topic worth exploring. A good part of it, I imagine, is a matter of trying to get clear in one's mind just what it is that one does want. Also, I should welcome the recognition that the suppression of desires is sometimes just not worth the sweat and one would do better to adopt a principle which is easier to live with. Writers on ethics still tend to speak as though the task of the will is to beat the passions into submission in the interests of morality. There is also the task of exploring one's powers in order to discover what principles one can realistically commit oneself to. Weakness of will is sometimes what, in our zeal for self-castigation, we call the inevitable result of moral *hubris*.

XIV Further thoughts on oughts and wants

Neil Cooper

In the present situation in moral philosophy we appear to be confronted with a choice between so-called descriptivism on the one hand and a radical prescriptivism on the other. If you hold that moral judgements are descriptive of moral facts, that they are static, theoretical and contemplative, then you have to face the problem of how it is that people can *act* on their moral judgements, how a moral judgement can be a reason for *action*. On the other hand, if you hold that moral judgements are dynamic, practical and prescriptive, you have to face the problem of how it is that people can sometimes fail to act on a moral judgement which they genuinely accept. What we need here is some middle way which will account for both conformity and non-conformity to moral principles. This is the point of the modified prescriptivism I have suggested in Chapter XII.

I have tried to show that moral principles are not mere dispositions to choose, but also dispositions to judge and advise and regret, that they are principles of appraisal as well as of conduct. We use them as such when we judge ourselves and others to be 'morally weak'. This is why I have taken what I have called '*a* central' (not 'the central', as Benson repeatedly says) kind of moral weakness or failure as a test case which sheds light on the role of moral judgements and principles in general. There are, of course, other kinds of non-conformity to professed principles, cases of insincerity, of unrealised knowledge, of being unclear about what one really wants, cases of change of moral viewpoint and of psychological compulsion. The type of conscious moral weakness which I have tried to study, a kind wrongly called Pauline by Benson, poses an insoluble problem for prescriptivism unless this is suitably modified, and I have tried to produce a modification which will do justice to both the theoretical and the practical aspects of moral judgements.

This central kind of moral weakness is not the morbid or pathological condition of those who literally cannot control themselves, but rather the condition of ordinary people who generally live up to their moral principles but occasionally lapse, though they are mindful at the time of their moral principles and are conscious that they could live up to them on the particular occasion of their failure. If prescriptivism is held in its radical and uncompromising form, if 'ought'-judgements are mistakenly held to imply imperatives or decisions, if deciding what you ought to do is misidentified with deciding *to* do, then no place is left in our analysis for this central kind of moral weakness. I accordingly tried to modify prescriptivism by arguing that 'ought' pragmatically implies 'want', that is, that if anyone asserts that he ought to do something, he thereby implies that – in a wide and inclusive sense of 'want' – he wants to do it. I rather misleadingly called this sense of 'want' minimal to distinguish it from the Kantian sense, so that in this sense of the word it is applicable to anything one is in favour of for any reason whatsoever. In this wide sense, a man may equally be said to want to do something, whether he wants to do it for its own sake or wants to do it as a means to something else which he wants, and a man may be said to want to do something, whether his want 'comes unbidden' (in Benson's language) or is the result of reflection. Further, 'want' is not here used in the sense of what a man wants, all things considered – the summary sense of the word. Rather it is used in its non-summary sense in which one may simultaneously want incompatible things. In this latter sense a man who wants something is only 'committed to deciding given certain conditions' (I quote from Benson). Because of this escape-clause, ordinary wants can conflict with one another (unlike summary wants and decisions), and since oughts involve wants, ordinary oughts are liable to the same sort of conflicts. Oughts, then, can co-exist both with opposing oughts and with opposing desires, and so a person, however clear-thinking, may both hold a moral principle and be unwilling to apply it to himself. As I said in Chapter XII, 'clarity of thought is no anodyne against the torments of being tempted'.

A man who is tempted, then, both wants and does not want to perform an action. Whatever he does in the end, he does what in some sense he does not want to do. Thus whether he resists temptation or succumbs to it, his situation will be correctly described as a failure to do what he can do and what in some sense of 'want' he wants to do. While this will be a correct description it will be a truncated one, and this is why Benson's proposition (v) on p. 200

misrepresents my position. When the man who has been tempted resists successfully, he does what he believes he ought to do but does it reluctantly. When on the other hand he succumbs, he does what he is naturally inclined to do, despite wanting to live up to his moral principles. If it were impossible, as Benson implies, for a man to fail to do a possible action which he wants to do, then it would be impossible for the tempted man to act either way, either to withstand temptation or to succumb to it. But this is plainly false. It follows that it must be possible for a man to fail to do a possible action which he wants to do. However, I not only wish to say that it is possible for a man to fail to do what he can do and wants to do, but also that it is possible for him to fail to do what he most wants to do even when he *can* do it, thus denying the thesis, which Benson mistakenly ascribes to me, that it is psychologically necessary to act in accordance with one's strongest desires or 'in the line of least resistance'. If I did accept this thesis, we should indeed be back with psychological impossibility.

If our sole criterion of what was our strongest desire were the sequel of the desire, what one subsequently did, then it would seem to follow that it was necessary to act in the line of least resistance. But in conformity with my argument in Chapter XII, our criteria for what somebody wants most are complex and include not only what he subsequently does, but also his introspective reports and the *post eventum* phenomena of satisfaction and disappointment. If we take these complex criteria, it would be a mistake to suppose that we are all under a compulsion to act in the line of least resistance, although this is no doubt true of, for instance, the kleptomaniac. What must be true of all of us, since the sequel of one's strongest desire is a part-criterion of it, is that we have at the very least a *tendency* to act in accordance with our strongest desire; that is, if my strongest desire is to do a possible action A, then it is probable that I shall do A. The man who tries to resist temptation is in a predicament, that of struggling against a desire which is as strong as or stronger than his desire to conform to his principle. If his conduct were psychologically necessitated, he could achieve nothing by struggling, but since we only have a tendency to act in accordance with our stronger desires, it is possible for him to resist his strongest desire. The man who resists temptation is the man who successfully struggles against this tendency. The man who is episodically morally weak and succumbs to temptation either does not struggle against this tendency on this occasion or does not struggle hard enough. The view that in general we have a tendency, not a compulsion, to act in accordance with our strongest desire makes sense of the fact that in temptation we are faced with a *problem*. The man who is tempted knows what he ought to do but is still undecided what to do.

Moreover, the coolly weak man who yields to temptation, unlike the man who loses control of himself, acts for reasons. As I say in a part of Chapter XII which Benson ignores, he finds difficulty in doing what he believes he ought to do and this difficulty is his reason for not doing it on this occasion. He knows that it is difficult for him to do what he believes he ought to do, because on other occasions he has had to try long and hard to succeed in doing it, and in knowing that it is only difficult he knows that it is not impossible. On the other hand, the difficulty of a task can be *my* reason for not undertaking it. But because it is my reason on this occasion, I am not committed to thinking that it is a good reason, a reason which I and others ought to give weight to on similar occasions. If I universalised this reason, there might be a case for saying that the reason was a moral reason, that because I allowed it in effect to override my moral views, my erstwhile moral views were my moral views no longer. But if I do not universalise this reason, the case for saying this falls to the ground. Thus, in the case of the deliberate deserter my soldier has a reason for running away which he does not universalise. He runs away to save his life, but it does not follow from this that he thinks that running away should be preferred or is *preferable* to an honourable death.

I have argued that the man who is episodically morally weak is not submitting to necessity, but just failing to struggle or failing to struggle hard enough against his tendency to act in accordance with his strongest desire. Perhaps 'at a deeper level' (to use Hare's expression) it all depends on whether you have it in you to struggle or not to struggle against temptation, and so whatever you did would in the last analysis be psychologically determined. But the general thesis of determinism is not here at issue. For in denying the necessity of acting in the line of least resistance, I have not been denying ordinary psychological determinism. What I have been denying is what might be called 'epithumetic determinism', the theory that human action is determined by the strongest desire. This theory is absurdly simple-minded, since it supposes (i) that desires are the only determinants of human behaviour, and (ii) that the strength or intensity of these desires is the only relevant determining factor. Both these suppositions are false.

Further, whatever the truth-value of determinism, we can show that there is a sense in which the weak man *could* have withstood temptation. My account of moral weakness requires, as Benson points out, that I hold that the man who lapses not only can in general or dispositionally act in accordance with his moral principles, but can on the particular occasion of his weakness. But how can one show that any person can do something on a particular occasion when he does not in fact do it? A knock-down *ab esse ad posse* argument is excluded here from the very start. Moreover, a sceptic might allege that one cannot show that someone can do something on a particular occasion by examining other occasions. Yet this is exactly what we have to do. We show inductively (or whatever you like to call it) that on a particular occasion we can do something which we do not in fact do by pointing to other occasions when we actually do it. *Ab esse* on other occasions, *ad posse* on this. And this is where our moral lapser differs from the compulsively weak man. The lapser does sometimes act on his moral principles. By doing so he justifies us in saying that he can live up to his moral principles, even when he doesn't.

But even if the psychological-impossibility account of moral weakness were in fact true, it would not affect my argument. For this concerns the use of the word 'ought', and I have been concerned to maintain (i) that 'ought' implies 'want' and (ii) that 'ought' is often used to and by people who believe that it is possible for them to do or not to do what they believe they ought to do. The use of words depends not so much on the way things are as on the way people think they are. How people use the word 'ought' is dependent not on its actually being possible for moral agents to act otherwise but on 'ought'-users believing that it is. It is a fact that people have this belief that certain kinds of moral failure are avoidable. And it is because they have this belief that it will not do to say that an 'ought' addressed to a morally weak man of this kind is off-colour while other 'oughts' have an impeccable logical respectability.

I now want to turn to criticisms of Benson's paper, and first, Benson's treatment of my distinction (pp. 197–8) between wanting-in-preference-to and wanting-more-intensely-than. The considerations which led me to make this distinction are as follows. If we accept

   (1) that 'ought' implies 'want'; and
   (2) that a fundamental 'morally ought' means 'ought in preference to anything else';

then it would seem to follow that

(3) a fundamental 'morally ought' implies 'want in preference to anything else'.

Such a wanting is a wanting of reflection and comparison. That there is such a preference has no consequence for the strength of the individual wants or desires considered *apart*. I may prefer A to B in so far as I think A preferable to B, but my unreflective desire for B may be in fact stronger than my unreflective desire for A. Take the case of the moderationist, the man who thinks that moderation is a good thing. He thinks that while desires may be counted as prima facie good reasons for doing an action, strong or intense desires are a bad thing, and hence the stronger desire does not provide the better reason. It is possible, then, to think that there are better reasons for doing A than for doing B (to prefer A to B in one sense of the word 'prefer') and yet at the same time to desire B more intensely than one desires A (in another sense of 'prefer' to prefer B to A). Benson's failure to distinguish these two senses of 'prefer' vitiates his treatment of the deliberate deserter in section III of Chapter XIII. He is right in interpreting me as holding that the deserter acts 'according to the result of his deliberation'. The deserter's conviction is that (as Benson correctly states on p. 206) 'honourable death is preferable to ignoble safety', and in so far as 'prefers' follows from 'thinks preferable' he prefers honourable death to ignoble safety. Yet at the time of action he unreflectively prefers (in the sense of 'likes better') ignoble safety. Our deliberate deserter deliberates in that he asks himself the question 'What shall I do?' He knows what he ought to do, he knows what is really preferable or desirable, but knowing this does not make the decision for him. Even though he thinks that an honourable death is preferable or should be preferred, he may nevertheless at the time of action prefer safety to death (in the 'desire more' or 'like better' sense) and yield to this latter preference.

Provided, then, that one recognises the ambiguities in the word 'prefer', my distinction between strength of desire and preference-ranking stands. Indeed this distinction has some affinities to Benson's own distinction between desires and wants. For, like his wants, my preference-rankings, as he calls them, are deliberate and reflective, while the strength of desires is something which 'comes unbidden', even if it can be influenced by deliberate policy. Now one's preference-rankings and moral beliefs are relatively stable, in this respect like ordinary non-moral beliefs. The order of strength of one's desires on the other hand is not at all permanent, being non-reflective and non-belief-dependent. That preference-ranking and order of strength of desires differ is indeed conceded by my opponents. For they maintain that, weakness being psychological impossibility, the morally weak man desires to do something else more than he desires to do what is highest in his order of preference, and that this stronger desire is what prevents him from choosing what is highest in his order of preference.

My whole position may be alternatively expressed as an attack on the argument which leads people to suppose that moral weakness is nothing but psychological impossibility. This argument may be reconstructed in the following sorites (where '—→' means 'entails'):

1. X believes he ought to do A—→X wants to do A (Weak Prescriptivism).
2. X believes he ought morally to do A—→X believes he ought to do A in preference to anything else (Paramountcy Thesis).
3. X believes he ought to do A in preference to anything else—→ X wants to do A in preference to anything else. (From (1) and (2) apparently.)
4. X wants to do A in preference to anything else—→X wants to do A more strongly than anything else (Reduction Thesis).
5. X want to do A more strongly than anything else—→X tries as hard as he can to do A (Energeticist Thesis).
6. X tries as hard as he can to do A—→X does A if he can (necessary truth linking trying, possibility and action).
7. X believes he ought morally to do A—→X does A if he can. (From (3), (4), (5), (6) by Hypothetical Syllogism).
8. X believes he ought morally to do A and does not do A—→X cannot do A.

It has been one purpose of this paper to argue that (7) and (8) are false, and if this is so, it would follow that at least one of the premisses of the above argument must be false. In the first place, we can eliminate (6) from suspicion, as it would be universally accepted as necessarily true. Second, premisses (1) and (2) together furnish a modified form of prescriptivism which is, I have argued, acceptable. The suspect premisses are therefore (4) and (5), and one or both of these must be false. What I have called the 'Energeticist Thesis' seems to me to be the specious offspring of analytical behaviourism illicitly mated with a puritanical moral athleticism. The thesis may, however, be rendered analytic if we regard it as tantamount to a part-definition of 'strongest desire'. This is in effect what is being provided by those who maintain that it is logically necessary to act 'in the line of least resistance'. If the thesis is made analytic in this way, it is plain that the Reduction Thesis – (4) – must be false, and this is what I argued in Chapter XII.

Let us now examine Benson's distinction between desire and want. While I cannot agree that Benson's distinction is justified by the ordinary use of these words, there is certainly a difference between raw-material desires, natural inclinations which are given, and those wants which are the result of deliberation. The former are passive; in the latter we are active. Hence the traditional contrast between the desires and the will. It is, however, easy to exaggerate the difference and Benson has, I think, gone astray here. First, not all preference 'depends on deliberation' as Benson implies. Some preferences involve desiring something more than something else and, like Benson's 'desires', arise 'unbidden'. Second, desires are surely susceptible to a similar anaysis to that which Benson gives of wants. Benson says of the celibate (p. 209 above) 'he still has sexual desires, but we cannot interpret this as meaning that he *wants* to gratify them, thus implying that he would, other things being equal, gratify his desire if he had the opportunity and the physical capacity. For here the proviso will have to be read in part: if he did not want to remain celibate, which comes to the same as: if he wanted to gratify his sexual desire. If desire is interpreted as want, the he-would-if implication becomes vacuous.' The argument, however, does not work. Of course he wants to satisfy his sexual desire, i.e. he would gratify his desire if he had the opportunity and physical capacity and *did not regard celibacy as 'part of the good life'*. This last condition does not come to the same thing as 'if he wanted to gratify his sexual desire'. Third, Benson seems to confuse two different things. On p. 209 he says that desires do not 'depend upon deliberation' in the sense of not being the result of deliberation; while on p. 211 he says that they cannot be used as reasons for action. But these are entirely different things. I can certainly agree that desires in his sense are not reached by deliberation, but it does not follow from this that they cannot be reasons for action.

Benson might, I think, have revised his account of desires and wants had he considered the relationship between moral beliefs on the one hand and wants and desires on the other. If I accept a moral 'ought'-judgement to the effect that I ought to do A, does it follow that I want to do A or that I 'desire' to do A? Benson gives no explicit answer to this question, although he appears to take it for granted that the answer is that I want to do A. But this answer is untenable if he sticks by his own explanation of the distinction between wants and desires. For he says on p. 209: 'A desire is something I can wish to be without or be glad I no longer have. It makes good sense to avoid situations in which one's desires might be satisfied, but it makes no sense to avoid the opportunity of doing what one wants to do.' But it sometimes happens that one finds one's moral principles irksome and wishes that one were without them. Moreover, one might try to dodge the opportunity of doing what one believes to be one's duty. So it would seem that moral beliefs are on these counts more akin to Bensonian desires than they are to Bensonian wants.

These considerations suggest that the distinction between desires and wants is not as clear-cut as Benson seems to imply. Nevertheless some such distinction needs to be made. Consider what I shall call the Paradox of the Lenten Abstainer. A man has been in the habit of giving up for Lent what he most wants to do. On reflection he realises that what he most wants to do *is* to give up what he most wants to do for Lent. What is he to do? For if he gives up what he most wants to do, then he gives up giving up what he most wants to do and so he doesn't give up what he most wants to do. If, on the other hand, he doesn't give up what he most wants to do, then he doesn't give up giving up what he most wants to do and so gives up what he most wants to do. The paradox has a formal resemblance to the Class of Classes Paradox and the possible solutions are also similar. One solution is to say, using the sequel criterion of 'most wanting', that it is impossible to give up what one most wants to do for, if one gave it up, it would necessarily not be what one most wanted to do.

Alternatively, we could try to distinguish between different orders of desires and say that the desire to give up a desire must be of a higher order than the desire one desires to give up, and our Lenten Abstainer can therefore only desire to give up a *lower-order* desire. On these lines one might try to use Benson's distinction between want and desire to take the sting out of the paradox. The Lenten Abstainer *wants* to give up his strongest desire, but that want cannot itself be considered as a desire *pari passu* with other desires. The trouble with this solution is that the Lenten Abstainer, unlike the class of all classes that are not members of themselves, is not a mere abstraction of dubious significance but a genuine possibility. There could well be a man who had such a 'passion' for self-denial that he realised that this passion was just as much in need of restraint as the more common-or-garden passions to which he normally denies satisfaction during Lent. So what started life as a Bensonian want can end up as something nearer a Bensonian desire.

Finally, I want to say a few words about Benson's tailpiece remarks about desires and principles. He says (p. 215 above) that he would 'welcome the recognition that the suppression of desires is sometimes just not worth the sweat and one would do better to adopt a principle which is easier to live with. . . . There is also the task of exploring one's powers in order to discover what principles one can realistically commit oneself to.' Between principles and practice, ideal and fulfilment, there will in any normal morality be a gap – this gappiness is an essential feature of the moral life and is made manifest in the tension which may exist prior to action between principle and desire. Tension of this kind requires resolution. There are three possible resolution-policies. The first is to strain every moral muscle to make our desires conform to our principles. It might be thought that because of 'the direction of fit' of moral principles, this was the only logical possibility, but this would be an over-simplification which ignored the possibility of assessing moral principles themselves in the light of the rigour of their demands. In the extreme case it might be impossible for anybody to conform to the ostensibly adopted moral principles, to bridge the gap between morality and practice, so that the morality was impracticable. On the other hand, it might be held that the effort required to adhere to principles in the teeth of opposing desires was more than could reasonably be required of ordinary men. So a second resolution-policy would be to accommodate moral principles to desires. This policy, if consistently carried out, would make morality superfluous. If we are to rig our principles to suit our admittedly fluctuating desires in any case, there is hardly any point in having moral principles at all. Plainly, then, it is the third policy or family of policies which is to be accepted. This consists in a mutual accommodation of principles and desires so that on the one hand an unreasonably great strain is not put on members of the community and on the other hand attainable ideals are not needlessly sacrificed to human frailty. This third resolution-policy allows for the possibility of moral weakness or failure by at any rate some individuals on some occasions. It is a necessary feature of any rational morality that it should leave some room for moral weakness. The same applies to a conceptual analysis, and it has been my aim to suggest a conceptual analysis which would provide moral weakness with a logical niche.

XV Further thoughts on oughts and wants[1]

John Benson

My main objection in Chapter XIII to Cooper's thesis was to his contention that a man may, after full deliberation, choose to do something other than what he wants to do most. His clarifications do not remove the grounds of the objection to his thesis as I then understood it, but they draw attention to an interpretation of it to which the objection would not so clearly apply. The alternative interpretation would, however, raise doubts about whether Cooper is entitled to call himself even a modified prescriptivist.

It is common ground that a man can have incompatible wants and that in choosing to satisfy one of them he will be failing to satisfy the other(s) and thus, in a sense, failing to do what he wants to do. Cooper says that I imply that it is impossible for a man to fail to do what he wants to do, but he does not say where in Chapter XIII I imply this, and what I *say*, in sections V and VI, is that it *is* possible (e.g. – in a paragraph from which Cooper quotes – 'there are certainly situations in which it is consistent with a man's wanting something that he makes no attempt to get it, for instance when there is something else which he wants more' (p. 212 above)).

I confess to having not only implied but said that it is inconsistent with a man's wanting A more than B that he chooses to try to get B rather than A, and *a fortiori* inconsistent with his wanting A more than anything else that he should fail to choose to try and get it. Cooper was contending that such failure is possible after full and lucid deliberation and may express the choice in which the deliberation issues. My argument against this has nothing to do with its being psychologically impossible not to act on such a want. (Hence I do not recognise my own reasoning in the sorites on p. 222.) It depends upon what I take to be a logical feature of wanting (in an inclusive sense that embraces both reflective wants and 'natural inclinations'): to say that a man wants A entails that he will, if he has the opportunity and capacity, and unless there is something else he wants more, attempt to get it. A consequence of this is that practical reasoning is reversible, so that if a man who deliberates about what to do decides to do A rather than B, when he has the opportunity and capacity to do either, it follows that he does not want to do B rather than A.

Cooper avoids saying, even in his further thoughts, whether he is using 'want' to refer to a concept with this feature or not. He persists in using the notion of a criterion as though it were unambiguous and in consequence his thesis is ambiguous. To have a criterion for X may be to know what features are necessary and/or sufficient for something to *be* an X, or it may be to know what has to be the case for one to have reasonable/conclusive grounds for saying 'Here is an X' – and these are only the most obvious possibilities, as the literature on Wittgenstein's use of the word 'criterion' amply demonstrates. If a man wants *p* he will, *ceteris paribus*, try to bring it about that *p*. This gives a criterion in the first sense. Of course if a man says that he wants that *p* and we observe that he tries to bring it about, this will provide us with evidence that he *did* want it, and in this way the two senses are connected. On the other hand failure on his part so to act is not conclusive evidence that he did not want it, but this does not show that preparedness to act is not a logical requirement. A man may have long wanted to do a certain thing without having done it because the cost to his other wants would have been too great. We may still be able to tell that he did want to do it, so that here his action can be dispensed with as evidence. But in so far as we have evidence that he wanted to do it, we have evidence that, *ceteris paribus*, he would have done it.

What a man does may be evidence of his being in a certain state of mind even when preparedness to act in some specific way is not part of what it is to be in that state of mind. Thus a man who admires a picture may manifest this by trying to possess it, but neither this nor any other determinate action is a necessary condition of his admiring it, and for this reason admiration is not a volitional concept.

I was assuming in Chapter XIII that Cooper's weak or inclusive sense of wanting was still intended to be volitional, and I tried to follow out the consequences of its being so. But if I now understand him correctly, his inclusive sense includes states of mind which are non-volitional or problematical in this respect. First, there is the fact that he uses the phrase 'to be in favour of' in elucidating the weak sense of 'want'. This phrase covers a wide range of states of mind, not all of which have to do with the will. It is surely strained to use 'want' to cover the whole range, and moreover to do so makes the connection between wanting and action too indeterminate for Cooper's purpose. A second, more important, indication is the distinction – which I am reproved for overlooking – between two senses of 'prefer'. This seems to be the distinction, in natural terms, between wanting more and thinking better. Now to include thinking good or desirable (Cooper uses only the latter word) as a species of wanting is to beg an important question. It is a move that yields a plausible interpretation of the thesis that 'ought' pragmatically implies 'want', for it is indeed plausible that thinking that one ought to do A involves thinking that it is the best thing to do. But how is thinking that an action is the best thing to do related to the will to do it?

If Cooper meant that thinking that one ought to do A implies thinking that A is the most desirable (best) thing to do, he should have said so. What is extraordinary, supposing that he did mean this, is that he should think that he has taken the high road to a solution of his problem. If his analysis is correct he has succeeded only in showing that moral weakness is a special case of weakness of will (since there are many kinds of good). This is a useful result, no doubt, but should not be taken to be a solution. It still needs to be asked what is the connection between thinking something desirable and acting so as to realise it. Thus, for instance, one must ask whether for Cooper there is any necessary connection (that is, any connection of a conceptual kind, even if looser than entailment) between thinking it desirable to do a certain action and having an inclination to do it, or, as we would naturally say, wanting to do it. If not, then just how is the thought of an action, or of something to be realised by an action, as good or desirable related to the doing of the action? On some views of what it is to think something to be good, it is just a contingent fact that one has or has not an inclination of the will towards what one thinks good. On others what one thinks good is simply what one wants. Cooper has, in response to my earlier criticism, drawn a sharp distinction between thinking desirable and liking better (what I call wanting more) without considering how they are related. I am inclined to put this omission down to the fact that he thinks of these as two senses of 'want', and so assumes that they must have something in common. His original attempt to distinguish the two senses in terms of the relative importance of the trying-to-get criterion gets nowhere in the absence of an account of the relation between a concept and its criteria. Why should trying-to-get be even a part-criterion of thinking good? It is no good just saying that our criteria are complex. It is necessary to say how they are interrelated, and in what sense they are criteria.

I take it that an essential feature of a prescriptivist analysis is that it makes the connection between assenting to a moral principle and acting on it an internal one. Cooper wants the connection to permit of exceptions, but unless it remains an internal one his theory will be open to the challenge levelled by prescriptivists against descriptivists: how can a moral judgement provide a reason for action? To meet this challenge Cooper needs to show how thinking something to be good provides a reason for action. And surely the history of the problem of *akrasia* (which is emphatically not merely *moral* weakness) shows that this is where the real difficulties start.

One necessary move in filling out Cooper's theory would be to specify what sort of description is to be given of the object of the want which is implied by assent to a moral judgement. If I think that I ought to prevent a drunken friend from driving home from my party, I shall not think the action desirable just under that description, but as preventing danger to other road-users or something of that sort. It is commonly the case (whether necessarily is, of course, disputable and disputed) that what is desired under such a description can, by virtue of so doing, be seen to fall under some recognised desirability-characterisation. It needs to be emphasised, however, that not all desirability-characterisations characterise an action as morally desirable; it is not only the wants involved in moral judgements that involve reference to a good to be realised.

In the light of this it can be seen that what I wanted to say about the by now overworked example of the deliberate deserter is not readily disposed of by Cooper's distinction between two senses of 'prefer'. I represented him as torn between two *goods*, honour and security, in securing either of which he stands to lose the other. Cooper says that he reflectively prefers (thinks preferable, i.e. thinks the greater good) honour, but unreflectively prefers (likes better) security. And likings (the order of strength of desires), he says, are not reflective or belief-dependent. But it is clearly wrong to imply that the strength of one's desires is entirely unrelated to one's judgements of the relative value of their objects. The deserter's desire to run away will be related both to his particular beliefs about the dangers he would be likely to meet and to his judgement of how much his life means to him. It may be that the desire is related to beliefs which are exaggerated or distorted by emotion, and is thus not coolly reflective. But whether *distorted* by emotion or not (for sometimes, as with the Baron de Stogumber at the execution of Joan of Arc in Shaw's play, moments of intense emotion show a man what he really values), judgement is involved, and it is often appropriate to explain such a case by saying: at that moment nothing seemed so desirable as just to go on living.

It might be conceded that there is a tendency for the strength of a desire to be positively correlated with the agent's estimates of desirability, and indeed that there is a connection between them. But it might still be urged that the former cannot be analysed in terms of the latter, that the correlation is by no means perfect, and that a desire may have a degree of strength which exceeds what could be accounted for by the desirability estimate. Two comments may be made about this. First, the exponent of this view would need to give a clear sense to the concept of strength and to specify the criteria of its measurement. Secondly, he would need to produce convincing examples of weakness which showed quite clearly the need for the distinction, and these would need to be more than the usual schematic examples. I suspect that this condition would be difficult to meet, not only because the phenomena (inner thoughts and feelings) are elusive, but more seriously because there is no conceptually neutral terminology in which they can be described, and so no hard facts against which theories can be tested.

Cooper does not attempt to meet the second condition. His examples (a glasshouse dweller's criticism, this) are few and thin. His remarks about the strongest desire suggest how he would try to meet the first condition, but they are not sufficient. One has, he says, a tendency to act on the strongest desire, that is, it is probable that one will do so. This is necessarily so since the sequel is at least a part-criterion of the strongest desire. Since, however, it is only a part-criterion, it is not necessary that one should act on the strongest desire. Now, first, it is of course true that if the sequel is not a necessary condition of the strongest desire, it follows that it is not necessary that one should act on the strongest desire. But Cooper is putting the cart before the horse if he is offering the antecedent here as an explanation of the consequent. It is surely because we can say that there is only a tendency to act on the strongest desire that we can also say that the sequel is not a necessary criterion. If so it must be possible to explain what is meant by 'strength' without reference to the sequel. Secondly, it is unclear what is meant by 'tendency' and consequently what is meant by 'strength'. Suppose that one's having a tendency to do A consists in its

usually being the case that one does A (in appropriate circumstances). The trouble with this is that so interpreted the tendency
provides no explanation of one's doing A on any particular occasion,
whereas it is natural to suppose that reference to the strength of a
desire does provide such an explanation. Let us improve on this by
saying that the tendency consists in its always being the case that
one does A unless certain specified circumstances, e.g. one's putting
up a struggle, obtain. But now there is the difficulty that a tendency,
so defined, is not the sort of thing that can be struggled against.
Thirdly, there may even be circularity in Cooper's position, since
he appears to say both that the possibility of not acting on the
strongest desire shows that we have only a tendency to do so, *and*
that because we have only a tendency to do so it is possible not to act
on the strongest desire.

The difficulty I find in understanding what Cooper means by
the strength of a desire is intensified when he says that his account
makes sense of the idea that in temptation we are faced with a
problem, i.e. that of making a decision between conflicting reasons.
It isn't a difficulty of deciding which are better reasons, it seems,
for the weak man is supposed to know what course of action is
supported by the best reasons, since he is presented as acting
against this knowledge; rather it is a matter of deciding whether
to act in accordance with these reasons or not. Now is this a
problem of deliberation, of considering reasons? What reasons
remain to be considered? If it is a different sort of problem, what
exactly does struggling consist in? Repeating injunctions to oneself in a stern inward whisper, trying to stop thinking about the
alluring object, reproaching oneself, and so on? There *is* this kind
of thing. But if it fails is it entirely appropriate to say that in
succumbing to temptation despite one's (inadequate) efforts one is
acting for a reason?

There is one type of desire for which a sense of relative strength
can be readily, if roughly, specified. It includes, or perhaps is confined to, bodily inclinations such as hunger and thirst. Here there
are differences of intensity, introspectively discernible, and roughly
correlated with measurable factors such as time of deprivation.
The degree of intensity of a desire in turn is correlated with its
causal strength, for which a rough measure can perhaps be given
by reference to the felt difficulty of restraining movements (e.g. of
drinking). Now here we do, I would agree, want to leave room for
degrees of difficulty short of impossibility; not every case of succumbing to such a desire, where there is a better reason for

abstinence, will justify speaking of compulsion. In cases of compulsion (psychological impossibility) one's own agency is nullified. In the less extreme cases it is impaired in such a way that it would be incorrect to attribute the action to one's own agency in the fullest sense, i.e. as a result of deliberation.

Faced with a conflict of (at least contingently) irreconcileable desires, I have chosen to leave to the justice or mercy of the reader the verdict on whether anything of the constructive part of my Chapter XIII survives Cooper's criticisms, and to take a second look at some of his central points in the light of his further thoughts. My aim has not been the purely negative one of making life difficult for a brave new theory. It has been to draw attention to the great difficulties in the cluster of concepts involved in the discussion of *akrasia*, because it seems to me that Cooper takes altogether too short a way with them in order to get on with the job of saving prescriptivism in some form. I do not share his view of the importance of this job, and taking the problem of *akrasia* in this limited context distracts attention from the basic work that needs to be done in moral psychology. Cooper shows what his priorities are when he states that even if his opponents were right about what moral weakness is, it would not affect his argument, since the use of words (moral words in this case) 'depends not so much on the way things are as on the way people think they are' (p. 220 above). Those who are interested in the way things are may grant him victory on these terms, but will hardly join him in celebrating it.

XVI Acting against one's better judgement

Irving Thalberg

A generalised form of the question I will raise has been pivotal in controversies about thought and action. This general question is somewhat long-winded: 'If a person has reasons to do something, and none against it; if he has no competing reason to do something else instead; and if he is not prevented from acting; then does it follow logically that he will act when he believes the occasion is suitable?' More briefly but abstractly: 'Given propitious circumstances, is there a conceptual connection between motives and deeds?'

I am going to investigate a less sweeping version of this problem. Only the relation between behaviour and value judgements which are reasons for action will concern me. That is, I will ask whether there is an entailment between a man's belief that a particular action would be enjoyable, profitable, right, courageous, loyal, or whatnot, and his undertaking the action. Naturally I assume that other types of occurrences or states than our value judgements can figure as reasons why we act. Our emotions and cravings might be reasons. Also, what concerns me here is only one logical consequence of the value judgement–action entailment, namely the doctrine that if a man does *not* act when he takes the occasion to be suitable, it follows that he did *not* make the value judgement with full conviction at the time he failed to act.

This doctrine is part of what we mean by the Socratic Paradox. In such Platonic dialogues as *Meno* (77, 88–9, 96–9), *Protagoras* (351–8), *Phaedo* (67–70), *Gorgias* (467–8, 509) and *Republic* (436–444), Socrates defends the paradoxical theory that when people act wickedly, or to their own disadvantage, it is only because they are ignorant. Deliberate wrongdoing and imprudence appear to be logically impossible. Aristotle's reaction in the *Nicomachean Ethics* is that the Socratic thesis 'plainly contradicts the observed facts'. Yet Aristotle's attempt to clarify the observed facts also seems to head for a Socratic conclusion.

Post-Kantian philosophers tend to transmute Socrates' Paradox into a problem about the comparative strength of moral reasons, as opposed to considerations of personal advantage, sensuous gratification, glory, and other selfish goals. Historically and theoretically, this approach is a mistake. For Greek thinking, there is no antithesis between morality and enjoyment. Furthermore, our theoretical problem loses half its sting if you suppose that whenever a man elects to do something he has moral reasons not to do, he always expects some gain or gratification to overbalance his moral turpitude.

My treatment of the Socratic Paradox begins with a case that will not drag us into this side-issue. A person has compelling grounds of *all* sorts against some line of endeavour, but decides to go ahead anyway. Against Socrates, I contend that such behaviour may be irrational, but it need not spring from ignorance, overpowering temptation, or any similar excusing condition of the agent's mind. But I side with Socrates to the extent of agreeing that such conduct baffles us, and we are inclined to suspect that the agent is unaware of his folly, or somehow unable to control himself. Finally, I maintain that nevertheless any theory of what it is to have and give reasons for acting must provide for counter-instances to the Socratic view.

Now for some detailed contributions to the analysis of this wrangle. I hope that the following story depicts the kind of situation philosophers have been trying to elucidate:

My landlady is curious about the letter that arrived for me today from Hong Kong. I have received one like it every week. She is too inhibited to ask me what is in these intriguing epistles, and she has a variety of reasons not to remove one from my mailbox and break the cachet. For one thing, I am certain to notice her tampering, and a nasty row will ensue. I will surely pack up and leave, after having denounced her to the other tenants. Snooping would result in financial loss to her, and it would impair her reputation. Furthermore, it's not as if she were desperate for something – anything – to do. She is halfway through a gripping detective novel; and if she tires of reading, neighbours are on hand for gossip. Even if it would be more entertaining to read the letter which arrived today, this gratification of her curiosity could not possibly make up for the disagreeable consequences. Besides, she has moral scruples. She has made it a policy, and a habit, to respect her tenants' privacy. Can she justify the deed by bringing it under some other moral principle? For instance, perhaps I am an espionage agent; if so, she could claim that it is her patriotic duty to see if today's message contains nefarious instructions. No, she realises the whole idea is absurd. Besides, if she really suspected me of subversive activity, the proper thing would be to call the FBI.

She reviews all these considerations, estimates that she has compelling reasons to leave the letter in the mailbox, and calmly decides to have a peek at it just the same. So she warms a steam-iron to the right temperature, carefully unseals the letter and reads it through.

I believe that this fiction represents a prima facie exception to Socrates' claim that rational people never deliberately undertake a course of action which they judge to be more disadvantageous or wrong than alternatives. My suggestion is not that it is rational to behave as the landlady did, i.e. that she acted rationally. To act rationally is, perhaps by definition, to undertake the course of action which is supported by the most cogent reasons. Nevertheless, our heroine seems to qualify as a rational person in many respects. She acts for an end. She correctly calculates how to attain her goal. She is informed about her current situation. She has made a systematic survey of the consequences of her deed. And she has taken account of her obligations, duties and moral principles. Let us allay the suspicion of compulsive behaviour by supposing this is her only delinquency to date, and that she never repeats it.

If we ask *why* she decides to open the letter, we get two different answers:

(1) She just thinks (decides) she will; she has no reason to do it.

(2) She has a reason. It might be any or all of the following: (*a*) she wants to open this particular letter; (*b*) she wants to open the correspondence of other people, and opening my letter is doing the kind of thing she wants to do; (*c*) she wants to acquaint herself with the contents of this particular letter, or to discover secrets about other people; therefore opening this letter is a means of doing something else she wants to do. Despite these grounds she has for opening the letter, she realises that she has better grounds to refrain. Which is to say: she believes that, in the circumstances, what she wants to do is not the best thing to do.

Reply (1) is colloquial enough, but misleading. She wonders what is in the envelope. If she had no reasons *against* the deed, wouldn't her curiosity be a reason for her to open the letter? If so, then answer (2) is a more perspicuous account. It makes the obvious but important point that she believes her curiosity is an inadequate reason for her to open the letter, because of the grounds she has to leave it alone.

I will not try to articulate the landlady's, or anyone else's, criterion for rating some reasons as more cogent or better than others. I find no warrant to follow Nowell-Smith and other contemporary moral philosophers in assuming that moral grounds are superior to non-moral ones. Nowell-Smith appears to equate superiority with psychological impact upon the agent; he says that a person's moral principles are his 'relatively dominant' dispositions to choose, which 'he would not allow to be overridden by any pro-attitude other than moral principle'. Nowell-Smith's explanation is as follows:

> [a person] cannot [logically] wonder what he ought to do if there is a moral principle on one side and not on the other. If I regard something as immoral, then however trivial it may be and however great may be the non-moral advantages of it, I cannot debate with myself whether I ought to do it; and we discover what our own moral principles are very often by putting just this sort of question to ourselves.
>
> (*Ethics*, (Harmondsworth, 1954) p. 308)

This assumption sounds either question-begging or vacuous: question-begging if it settles by stipulation the empirical issue whether people's moral attitudes in fact prevail; and vacuous if the superiority turns out to be nothing but moral superiority. In any case, I do not take our protagonist to be in the predicament of a Christian or a Kantian moral agent, who believes he *should* do one thing, although he should *like* to do something else. The landlady is not torn between duty and pleasure, between self-interest and the moral law. She recognises that it would be wrong *and* unprofitable, all in all, to steam open my letter.

This approach to our problem is faithful to the Socratic tradition. Plato's fullest statement of the Socratic thesis in *Protagoras* (Chapter I above) takes a hedonistic moral outlook for granted. Recall how Socrates gets his argument going: first he convinces Protagoras that one cannot have any other standard in mind but pleasure and pain, when one judges something to be good or evil. Socrates then demolishes the popular opinion that men often voluntarily and knowingly fail to do what they believe is best, under the impression that some other course of action would be more pleasant. If your criterion of superiority is pleasure, he argues, then you would be inconsistent to think one action best and think another more pleasant. So if you elect to do something less pleasant, when you could do something more pleasant, you must be suffering 'not only from defect of knowledge in general, but of that particular knowledge which is called measuring' enjoyment and suffering. The hedonistic background reappears in Socrates' summation:

> Then if the pleasant is the good, no one who either knows or believes that there is another possible course of action, better than the one he is following, will ever continue on his present course when he might choose the better. To 'act beneath yourself' is the result of pure ignorance; to 'be your own master' is wisdom. . . .
>
> Then it must follow that no one willingly goes to meet evil or what he thinks to be evil. To make for what one believes to be evil, instead of making for the good, is not, it seems, in human nature . . . (p. 36 above).

For our purposes, this conclusion, aside from its narrow hedonistic premises, will represent the Socratic Paradox. It is, to be sure, a special case of the more sweeping doctrine that Virtue is Wisdom, which I shall not examine.

A striking feature of the Socratic thesis is that few writers, including Plato, have made it true by definitional fiat. Instead they portray the man who fails to do what he judges best as a person who is not quite master of himself, or who is partially unaware of his actions and their consequences. They conclude, and I tend to agree, that a man in *that* sort of condition should not be charged with deliberately failing to do what he had reason to do. However – and this will be my first argument – these accounts cannot explain away other, less dramatic types of failure. For convenience, the landlady will serve as a model to test the adequacy of four prominent analyses of 'failing to do what one has reasons to do' and 'doing what one has reasons not to do'. Then, after explaining what makes the Socratic thesis appear so plausible a doctrine about choice and action in these analyses, I shall outline some general arguments to show the legitimacy of counter-examples to the Socratic view. Consequently this examination should reveal why Socrates' claim is paradoxical – difficult to maintain yet nearly impossible to reject.

We should begin with Socrates' contention that a person who fails to do what he judges best is bound to be labouring under some form of ignorance. A literal interpretation of this theory will hardly account for the landlady's behaviour. She has not overlooked or

miscalculated the amount of pleasure and suffering that will accrue
to her as a result of her deed. In fairness to Socrates, however, we
should recall his discussion of another cognitive disorder, similar
to, but not exactly like error. Call it 'hedonic illusion', a term I
borrow from J. J. Walsh (*Aristotle's Conception of Moral Weakness* (New York, 1963)). This state resembles the following kind
of perceptual illusion: A duck-hunter goes out during sub-zero
weather and waits in ambush for his prey. He carries a ther-
mometer, and he can see that the air-temperature remains constant.
As time goes by, nevertheless, he not only feels chillier, but it feels
to him as if the air is growing colder. He is tempted to believe,
contrary to his better judgement, that the temperature is dropping.
Now for a hedonic parallel, in which *feeling pleasure* has the same
disturbing effect upon one's judgement as *feeling chilly* did in the
perceptual example: George is having a whale of a time with some
old cronies, guzzling beer, playing billiards, singing and exchanging
smoke-room stories. He had planned to leave for a lively dance at
this time. He is quite sure that he would have more fun there, and it
is only a few blocks away. But why should he go? It seems so much
jollier here! Although he doesn't really believe it, he is inclined to
believe that the dance will be less amusing.

Returning to my example against the Socratic thesis, we have to
ask: Is the landlady in circumstances that tempt her to disregard
her hedonic appraisals of the various courses of action? It seems to
me that the 'proximity', or foretaste, of opening the letter need not
disturb her judgement any more than the proximity of the alternatives – continuing to read her novel, taking coffee with her neighbours, and so forth. At the time of her decision, she is not sufficiently
absorbed in the illicit joy of perusing the letter for us to attribute
her misdeed to the deceitful influence of this pleasure. So her failure
is not ascribable to the cognitive defect of hedonic illusion.

Does our case represent any of the additonal types of failure that
Aristotle lists in bk vii of *Nicomachean Ethics*? Has the landlady
forgotten her moral principles? Does she throw prudence to the
winds? Does she follow the wicked policy of doing wrong, or the
perverse rule of courting disaster? There is no evidence for any of
these conjectures. Is she self-indulgent, claiming the right to violate
her moral principles whenever she feels like it, or making an exception to her prudential policies 'just this once'? Apparently not: she
simply decides to do something which is wrong and foolish, but
claims no excuse or justification for it. Is she irresolute? No, because an irresolute person would first decide to leave the letter

where it is, and then decide to read it. Perhaps she is weak-willed. That is impossible too: a weak-willed person begins by deciding to do the right thing; then he fails to stick by his decision. Our heroine never toys with the idea of respecting my letter.

How about incontinence? Aristotle says an incontinent man is one 'whom passion masters so that he does not act according to the right rule, but does not master to the extent of making him believe that he ought to pursue such pleasures without reserve' (*Nicomachean Ethics*, bk vii, 1151a). An incontinent person may or may not have resolved to act as he judged best. I fear this talk of overpowering passions will suggest the following fallacious argument:

'We said earlier that the landlady opened the letter because she wanted to. Then she must have wanted to do that more than she wanted to do anything else at the time. In other words, her strongest desire was to open the letter. But how could she resist her strongest desire? Plainly it overwhelmed her, and she did not act voluntarily.'

This 'demonstration' that our protagonist was a victim of incontinence blurs a crucial distinction between two senses of 'desire'. To speak of desires is sometimes only to speak of preferences. In this sense, I most strongly desire what I prefer to do. But we also speak of cravings as desires. A person's cravings may be at variance with his preferences. George may long for tobacco but prefer to do without it. In this latter sense of 'desire', George can struggle with his desire to smoke; he may conquer it or succumb to it. In case he combats his desire, but takes to smoking again despite the fact that he prefers not to smoke, we can say his desire, i.e. his craving, is irresistible. But what would it mean to say that a man cannot resist his top preference? Suppose he 'yields' to it: he would have to prefer and *prefer not* to do the same thing! And similarly if he vanquishes it. It appears self-contradictory to refer to the landlady's top preference for opening the letter as an 'irresistible desire'.

Maybe the dispute thus far has only whetted the appetite of the incontinence-theorist. He might retort that the landlady is enslaved by an uncontrollable craving, which just happens to accord with her top preference. This objection would read: 'She cannot help doing what she does, because even if she preferred not to open the letter, her passion would overwhelm her.' My reply is that there is no independent evidence for this hypothesis. In fact, her calm manner, as she forms and executes her plan, counts decisively against the claim that she is in the grips of temptation, fury, overarching ambition, or any similar condition that would prevent her from doing what she judges best. She simply prefers not to.

So much for attempts to explain away the landlady's deliberate failure to do what she judged best as a case of Aristotelian incontinence. Now I want to look briefly at a less notorious theory which is found in John Stuart Mill's *Utilitarianism*. While discussing 'higher' and 'lower' pleasures, Mill asks whether people ever choose a lower pleasure when another gratification is available to them which, from their own experience, they know to be superior. Mill thinks so:

> Men often, from infirmity of character, make their election for the nearer good, though they know it to be the less valuable; and this no less when the choice is between two bodily pleasures than when it is between bodily and mental. . . . Many who begin with youthful enthusiasm for everything noble, as they advance in years sink into indolence and selfishness.
>
> (*Utilitarianism*, Everyman ed. (1957) p. 9)

How can they fail to do what they have excellent reasons to do? Mill adopts a Socratic outlook:

> I do not believe that those who undergo this very common change, *voluntarily choose* the lower description of pleasure in preference to the higher. I believe that . . . they have already become *incapable* of the other. . . . It may be questioned whether anyone who has remained equally susceptible to both classes of pleasures ever *knowingly and calmly* preferred the lower. . . . (Ibid., pp. 9–10; my italics.)

As I described the landlady, she had a number of alternative ways of enjoying herself, many of them as pleasant and far more respectable than opening the letter. What grounds are there for attributing her choice to insensitivity vis-à-vis these other pastimes? Let us observe her. Has she been attending to her novels? Did she turn up her nose at conversation with the ladies next door? Was she bored with her usual recreations after she finished reading the letter? I think it is possible that she had to tear herself away from her novel, that she manifested the greatest reluctance in declining the invitation to coffee, when she decided to read the letter from Hong Kong; and that she returned eagerly to her usual distractions after she had perused the letter. In these circumstances, we have no grounds for agreeing with Mill that she did not really, or freely, choose the lower pleasure of opening my letter, because the alternatives had lost their charm for her. And it would trivialise Mill's reasoning to insist that the very fact of her choice to do something else proves that her customary pleasures had lost their appeal. Incidentally, it would be nonsense to propose the *ad hoc* explanation that the landlady might have been suddenly overwhelmed with indifference towards everything else at precisely the moment when she decided to open my letter. We need independent evidence for this state of mind. Why assume that it will be forthcoming, except to preserve the Socratic thesis at all costs?

Now I propose to conclude this survey of doctrines by appraising the views of Professor Hare in his book, *Freedom and Reason* (see Chapter VIII above). His exclusive concern is with moral weakness, which is failing to act upon one's moral convictions. Hare assumes, by the way, that 'moral principles are, in a way that needs elucidation, superior to or more authoritative than any other kind of principle' or reason we can have for acting. As I objected already when I mentioned Nowell-Smith's statement of the same assumption, I have no idea what this superiority or authority could be. Are moral considerations supposed to be motivationally more potent than any other? That is the very problem here: moral principles do not always win out. And it would be completely uninformative to be told only that moral reasons have greater *moral* authority. At any rate, Hare's assumption is easy to accommodate. We specify that my landlady believes the most *important* reason she has not read my letter is that this would be wrong, for her and for anyone else in similar circumstances. Since she goes ahead and does it anyway, she is guilty of moral weakness. The question for Hare is whether we are ever entitled to claim that she acted knowingly and voluntarily.

Hare's doctrine is that 'the typical case of moral weakness, as opposed to hypocrisy, is a case of "ought but can't"' (p. 142 above). The peculiarity of a morally weak person is that he 'is *physically* in a position, and strong, knowledgeable and skilful enough, etc., to do what he thinks he ought'. In what sense is he unable to act? Hare suggests that 'the impossibility is psychological'.

Socrates' explanation of how men fail to choose the best course was psychological too. But Hare diverges from the Socratic view that a morally weak individual fails because of forgetfulness, inattention to or misinformation about his circumstances, or any other cognitive derangement. Then why is it psychologically im-

possible for Hare's morally weak person to do what he believes he
ought to do? As illustrations, Hare cites Medea's inability to resist
her love for Jason, although she believes she ought to; and St
Paul's failure to overcome 'the law of sin' that is lodged in his unspiritual nature. As I understand them, these instances of 'overpowering desire' have no tendency to show that our *patronne*
cannot (psychologically) do what she judges best. We have no
evidence for ascribing vehement lusts and cravings of these kinds to
her.

Let us examine Hare's general characterisation of psychological
impossibility, to see what bearing it might have on the landlady's
conduct. Hare distinguishes two species of this infirmity, both non-
cognitive:

(I) We adopt some universal moral rule, with the intention of
acting on it. When we find it difficult or disadvantageous to continue
regulating our conduct by our principle, we undergo an involuntary
change of attitude. In Hare's terminology:

> While continuing to prescribe that everyone *else* (or at any rate
> everyone whose interests do not especially concern us) should act
> in accordance with the principle, we do not so prescribe to our-
> selves (for to do this fully and in earnest would commit us to
> acting) (pp. 139–40 above).

(II) The other type of morally weak man prescribes to himself,
but in a peculiar way. Hare likens him to a 'divided personality':
one half of him transmits moral injunctions to a disobedient or
flabby partner. Hare thinks we may also compare the weak man to
a 'single personality' who has stopped prescribing to himself, 'although there may be a part of him that goes on prescribing' (p.
144 above).

Description (I) hardly fits our landlady's case. Her change of
attitude is deliberate: she decides to stop acting on her moral
principles. Furthermore, Hare's explanation for her lapse is unacceptable: she does not cease 'prescribing' to herself because she
sees a 'non-moral' advantage in violating her commitment. She
believes it would be contrary to her interest to open the letter. Her
egoism is neither a road-block nor a stumbling-block on the path
of righteousness.

The second diagnosis cannot possibly illustrate how our heroine's
– or anyone's – moral failure is involuntary. And this is not because
Hare's metaphors are vague, unscientific or otherwise objectionable.

The imagery of 'two souls within one breast' and 'the unheeded conscience' is apt and suggestive. However, these pictures of the weak man count against Hare's thesis, viz. that it is psychologically impossible for such a man to do what he believes he ought to do. For consider the relationship of prescribing and executive halves in a divided personality. Why doesn't the executive partner do what the other half said it ought to do? Does it have opposed moral principles, or is it unconvinced by the speaker's reasoning? On either view, we would have quite a different situation from the one Hare envisages: we would have disagreement or uncertainty within the agent, not full-fledged moral conviction. Then could the executive moiety be *physically* unable to do what it has been persuaded it ought to do? The complaint, 'Half my personality lacks the physical power or skill to do what it believes best', makes no sense. Perhaps we should say, when a morally weak man does not act on his principles, 'The executive half of his personality is suffering from a *psychological* disability'. Then, in consistency, we must postulate a further split within the rebel faction, in order to explain *its* weakness, and so on *ad infinitum*. One more possibility remains: the executive half of a weak man's personality just refuses or omits to act as it believes it ought to act. If we accept the idea that some halves of some people act this way, how can Hare use this fantasy to persuade us that undivided people cannot (psychologically) elect to behave the same way? A similar argument will show that Hare's 'lonely advocate' metaphor is equally self-defeating. I conclude that Hare has given us no grounds for saying that the case we have considered is an instance of 'ought but can't'.

Does my argument thus far rest upon one far-fetched (and by now overworked) anecdote? Here is an easy recipe for producing any number of counter-examples to the Socratic thesis. Suppose the agent believes he has better reasons, as he understands this term, to do X rather than Y. Suppose that he is not the victim of any physical or psychological misfortune (duress, coercion; lack of strength, skill or opportunity; ignorance, absence of mind, vehement passion, overpowering temptation, inebriation, drug-addiction, insanity) which prevents him from doing X or forces him to do Y. Then suppose he coolly resolves to do Y rather than X, and goes ahead, with full knowledge of the nature and consequences of his deed. He cannot justify his decision or his behaviour, at the time he acts, by citing his reasons. And neither he, nor his judges, can excuse his choice or deed, because our formula precludes all the standard pleas. Plato, Aristotle and Hare give a specious plausibility

to the Socratic conclusion because they confine their attention to excusable failures – the failures of uninformed or disturbed people.
Mill, for his part, concentrates on people who have grown callous.
But these philosophers cannot say, in defence of a person who met
the above specifications: 'He couldn't help doing it, because he just
thought he would'; 'He's not responsible for what he did, because
he wanted to do it'; 'He's not at fault, because he decided to do it'.

Perhaps this explains why a Socratic view of choice and intentional conduct is so hard to avoid. Our primary concern, as agents,
advisers, critics and sympathetic bystanders, is to find reasons for
choosing and doing. When something wicked, imprudent, disastrous,
pointless or inept is done, we can always raise the question whether
the deed was an accident, or due to constraint, mistake, oversight,
aberration or some other mitigating circumstance – including at
times 'bad luck'. Now since we find no justification or excuses for
a man's voluntary and knowing failure to do what he believes best,
we are at a loss to explain his action in our usual terms. It has no
place within our scheme for assessing conduct. In exasperation we
wonder, 'How could he?' The correct answer is not, however, 'He
couldn't possibly have done Y voluntarily and knowingly, when he
had better reasons to do X'. The correct answer is 'He shouldn't
have' or 'He has no excuse for doing Y'.

The moral-sounding reaction, 'He shouldn't have done Y', deserves a brief comment. You cannot always say this of a person who
had better reasons to do X instead. Otherwise you would be endorsing the dubious principle that everyone including Nero,
Genghis Khan, Torquemada and Hitler, ought to do what he
judges best. In fact, however, aren't we inclined to feel relief, rather
than disapproval, if such people fail to carry out atrocities they
believe they ought to commit? The point is that we often hold that
some action, which another person believes he ought to perform, is
wrong or inadvisable in some way. If he fails to perform it, then we
would be inconsistent if we maintained our disapproval of the
action he was contemplating, but condemned him for failing to
carry it out. Only when we share the agent's belief that he ought to
do X is it logically possible for us to decry his failure. This
reasoning proves, incidentally, that you cannot interpret the
Socratic Paradox, 'Men never do act willingly and knowingly
against their better judgement', as a high-level moral injunction,
'Men never *ought* to act willingly and knowingly against their
better judgement'. In some cases only is it plausible to give a moral
interpretation of our acceptance of the Socratic Paradox.

The most adequate general explanation I can suggest for our Socratic disinclination to admit that people ever deliberately fail to do what they judge best is that people's behaviour is one of our most prominent criteria of evidence regarding their practical judgements. On this account, it is a rule of evidence, rather than logical truth, that actions speak louder than words. Since a man's failure to do what he says he believes he ought to do is never conclusive, it is possible for us on occasion to give more weight to his words. Naturally we should look for additional evidence that confirms his professions of belief. For example, if it is a case where he claims that he believed the action X would have been more to his interest than Y, and we come to the same conclusion, that would back up his profession. Another species of confirmatory evidence consists in feelings of remorse and self-condemnation that the agent has about his failure. If on previous occasions he had acted on the beliefs he claims to have held this time, that would also buttress his present claim.

Many such items of confirmatory evidence appear in the story of my landlady. But instead of spinning out that counter-example any further, I want to say something about the significance of such counter-examples to the Socratic Paradox. In closing, then, I will sketch two arguments which suggest that these odd cases have a legitimate place in any philosophical explication of what it is to have reasons for acting. Each argument takes some unanalysed thesis for granted, and shows how it leads to the conclusion, 'Although you have reasons to do something, you might knowingly and voluntarily fail to do it' or – more trenchantly – 'Ought implies might not'.

(1) Assume that only free agents need to consider, or to be given, grounds for doing and choosing. Assume, furthermore, that a free agent is one who is entitled to assess reasons for their cogency and germaneness to his interests. A man acts rationally, let us say, when he elects to do what he finds cogent reasons, in the circumstances, to do. If all this is, logically and psychologically, within his power, then it must be within his power (to decide) *not* to do what he has good grounds for doing.

(2) Think of the ideals people may have as reasons for acting: economic, scholarly, athletic, artistic, social, political, religious, moral and so on. When we say that it is our ideal to sculpt and 'live' with the intensity of Benvenuto Cellini, or to be completely original in some domain of endeavour, part of what we mean is that we have, and expect to have, difficulty in conforming to our

ideal. Not only do we expect occasional lack of success in our endeavours, but we foresee that, at times, we will be disinclined to try. For example: Sugar Ray Robinson is my ideal in pugilism, precisely because I lack his technique, endurance and sang-froid; and because I am inclined to throw in the sponge, or to launch desperate haymakers, instead of attempting to box as skilfully and courageously as he did. My hope is that by asking myself, 'What would he do now?', I will find a reason to exert myself. However, if we assume that my immediate ideal is to make the attempt to box like Sugar Ray, then we must admit that I might decide not to make this effort. 'I ought (ideally) to try' implies 'I might not'. And my failure need not be due to rage, terror or any other passion, but simply to lack of zeal.

It seems, therefore, that any analysis of having and giving reasons which allows these doctrines concerning free agents and their aspirations must do without the Socratic Paradox. Unfortunately the account which remains will provide no explanation, in terms of the agent's reason or excuse, for the agent's intentional failures to do what he believed best. Psychological explanation, which generally provides neither vindication nor extenuation, will have to suffice. Interestingly enough, the psychologist's first inquiries, 'Is the agent suffering from a compulsion to do what he believes is wrong, to express rebellion, to attract attention or chastisement?', hint at an excuse, and reinforce the old Socratic claim. However, as I have objected against the reasoning of Plato, Aristotle, Mill and Hare, there is no guarantee that we will find the independent evidence which is necessary to show that this one failure is a strand in some unconscious twine that holds the agent fast to his obsessions. And a single misdeed is not by itself proof that an excusable cognitive or emotional disequilibrium produced it.

Notes

Chapter II

Editor's note: Some of the footnotes to the original paper have been omitted, and others incorporated in the text in brackets.

1. In some recent discussions of explanations of weakness (see Chapters VIII and IX below), philosophers have not gone much further than discussing phrases that suggest explanations, whereas what is needed most is an elucidation of the models of explanation that can be offered.

2. Editor's note: The references are those normally employed in Platonic scholarship: the numbers and letters refer respectively to the pages and page subdivisions of the Stephanus edition of 1597 at Paris. These references appear in the margins of most modern editions of Plato's text.

3. Cf., e.g., J. P. Sullivan, 'The Hedonism in Plato's *Protagoras*', *Phronesis*, VI (1961) pp. 18–20; A. Sesonske, 'Hedonism in the *Protagoras*', *Journal of the History of Philosophy*, I (1963); D. Gallop, 'The Socratic Paradox in the *Protagoras*', *Phronesis*, IX (1964); and G. Vlastos's introduction to *Protagoras* (New York, 1956).

4. At 352e and again at 354e (pp. 31, 33 above) Socrates says explicitly that the argument is about (*b*).

5. Cf. 352b for the explanations, and 352d, 353c, 355b for the descriptions.

6. The pleasures of food, drink, and sex are the proper objects of weakness according to Aristotle (*Nicomachean Ethics*, bk iii, ch. 10, and bk vii, ch. 4).

7. See Sullivan, op. cit.

8. Gallop, op. cit., pp. 119–21.

9. *Lambanein* can also mean 'to receive', 'to accept', and possibly even 'to prefer'.

10. For a recent discussion of attempts to reduce teleological explanations (I), to those of type II, cf. I Scheffler, *The Anatomy of Inquiry* (New York, 1963) pp. 88–110. Several variants of teleological explanations are implicit in the patterns of practical inference that G. H. von Wright discusses in 'Practical Inference', *Philosophical Review*, LXXII (1963) pp. 159–79.

11. This premiss could be inferred from the fact that the pleasure of eating is near and the pain far, if it could be established that, in general, strength of desire varies (in some consistent way) with distance (space and/or time) of the object of the desire from the agent.

12. With minor modifications this kind of explanation can satisfy the Hempel–Oppenheim requirements of a scientific explanation provided that condition A is satisfied. The similar type of explanation that I cite below, employed by Neal Miller, does satisfy these requirements.

13. Neal E. Miller, 'Comments on Theoretical Models Illustrated by the Development of a Theory of Conflict', *Journal of Personality*, xx (1951–2) pp. 82–100. This is a careful and philosophically sophisticated account of experiments in verification of a theory that could be used to explain behaviour in cases of conflicting 'tendencies', 'responses', or 'drives', or 'motives'. One of the hypotheses verified by the experiments is: 'When two incompatible responses are in conflict, the stronger one will occur.' This article, and the related literature cited below, is worth reading by all those who talk of human beings being 'overcome', 'seduced', etc., by their passions, feelings, etc.

14. Jesse E. Gordon, *Personality and Behavior* (New York, 1963) pp. 389–426. Gordon applies the Miller models to human behaviour, but Miller's care and clarity are nowhere to be found, and Gordon leaves us in the dark as to how strength is to be measured in the case of humans. Gordon does not display the caution and safeguards that are necessary when models, successful in the case of lower animals, are applied to humans. General applications of the Miller models are summarised in B. Berelson and G. A. Steiner, *Human Behavior: An Inventory of Scientific Findings* (New York, 1964) pp. 271–6. Cf. especially C6 and C6.1.

15. *Social Psychology*, 23rd ed. (New York, 1960) ch. ix. McDougall quotes with approval William James's conception of the problem in cases of 'moral conflicts': 'I (ideal impulse) in itself weaker than P (the native propensity). I+E (effort of the will) stronger than P.' McDougall thinks that the occurrence of weakness exemplifies the first proposition, which he treats as a law of psychology, and thus can easily be accounted for; it is the occurrence of the opposite of weakness that is difficult to account for, and here the problem is the analysis of E. He uses the language of strength constantly but he does not seem to see that there is a problem about giving a sense to the notion of 'stronger than'.

16. *An Examination of Sir William Hamilton's Philosophy* (London, 1867) ch. xxvi.

17. Berelson and Steiner, *Human Behaviour*, p. 271, C5.

18. '. . . harried along and driven out of his senses' (W. Wayte, *The Protagoras of Plato* (Cambridge, 1871) p. 147).

19. It is worth noticing that what I have said here does not necessarily hold of explanations in terms of strength where condition A is satisfied in the first way (I). Socrates' remark at 357c, when he reverts to the language of strength, is no objection to what I am saying here.

20. I am indebted to Professor Rosalind Ekman Ladd and to Mr Jonathan Malino for many helpful comments.

Chapter III: Translator's Notes

1. *Iliad*, bk xxiv, lines 258 f.
2. *Nicomachean Ethics* (EN), bk vii, ch. 5.
3. EN, bks ii–v.
4. EN, bk vi, ch. 5, 1140 b4–6. (Editor's note: In this and the next chapter, detailed references to the text are those normally employed in

Aristotelian scholarship and are to the Bekker edition of 1831–70. In this system of reference the first number refers to a page, the letter to one of two page columns and the last numbers to lines.)

5. EN, bk vi, ch. 7, 1141 b16; ch. 8, 1142 a24.

6. EN, bk vi, ch. 13, 1144 b30–1145 a2.

7. i.e. if I am to be able to deduce from (*a*) 'dry food is good for all men' that 'this food is good for me', I must have (*b*) the premiss 'I am a man' and (*c*) the premisses (i) *x* food is dry', (ii) 'this food is *x*'. I cannot fail to know (*b*), and I may know (*c*)(i); but if I do not know (*c*)(ii), or know it only 'at the back of my mind', I shall not draw the conclusion.

8. i.e. in scientific reasoning.

9. i.e. determines action (cf. b10).

10. Even before the minor premiss of the practical syllogism has been obscured by passion, the incontinent man has not scientific knowledge in the strict sense, since his minor premiss is not universal but has for its subject a sensible particular, e.g. 'this glass of wine'.

Chapter IV

1. Editor's note: The references are again to the Bekker edition (see note 4 to Chapter III). Where a reference is to part of the extract in Chapter III, it is usually accompanied by the appropriate page reference, as here. The three headed sections of Chapter III are referred to as chapters 1, 2 and 3 of bk vii.

2. *On the Structure of the Seventh Book of the Nicomachean Ethics* (1879) chs i–x; reissued in 1912 with a postscript on the parallel versions.

3. EN, 1102 b14–25, 1166 b6–10; *De Anima*, 433 a1–3, 433 b5–8, 434 a12–15.

4. 'Tithenai ta phainomena', in *Aristote et les Problèmes de Méthode* (1961).

5. *Aristotle's Conception of Moral Weakness* (New York, 1963).

6. *De Anima*, iii, 427 b24–5.

7. *Revue Philosophique*, CXLV (1955). An English translation is to be found in R. Robinson, *Essays in Greek Philosophy* (Oxford, 1969).

8. The practical syllogism is discussed in chs xi (pp. 228 ff) and xii of *Aristotle's Ethical Theory*. The most important texts in Aristotle are *De Anima*, Γii, 434 a16–21; *De Motu Animalium*, 7, 701 a7; EN vi. 7, 1141 b14–21; 8, 1142 a20–3; vii. 3 a29–63.

9. 'Rationalism and Intellectualism in the Ethics of Aristotle', *Mind*, LI (1942) p. 355.

10. 'Unreasonable Action', in *Practical Ethics* (London, 1898) p. 254.

11. *Physics*, 204 b4–10, and *De Generatione et Corruptione*, 316 a10; cf. *Topics*, 105 b21.

12. H. H. Joachim, *Aristotle: the Nicomachean Ethics, a Commentary*, edited by D. A. Rees (Oxford, 1966).

13. *Aristotle's Theory of Practical Cognition* (Kyoto, 1958) p. 278.

14. A fuller account of the reasons for the views expressed in this paragraph is given in chs xi and xii of *Aristotle's Ethical Theory*.

Chapter V

1. Strictly, 'always, if physically and psychologically able'.

Chapter VI

1. I am not considering cases of 'apparent' conversion, although these are interesting: thus a man may sometimes, under pressure of extraordinary physical conditions or even in the face of certain types of persuasive argument, be brought to conclude that he has been fundamentally mistaken all along, and he may refer to the situation as being one in which *at the time* he genuinely experienced a changed outlook: such situations are described in the scenes of inquisition and interrogation portrayed in novels like *1984* and *Darkness at Noon*. But the question of how far the conversion was a genuine one is decided by what happens afterwards.

2. Douglas Hyde, *I Believed* (London, 1931) p. 221.

Chapter VIII

1. *A Treatise of Human Nature*, bk III, I, i. For a recent development of this objection, see A. C. Ewing, *Second Thoughts in Moral Philisophy* (London, 1959) ch. 1.

2. G. E. M. Anscombe, *Intention* (Oxford, 1958) p. 67.

3. Cf. *Freedom and Reason* (FR), 9.1.

4. FR. 8.4 f.

5. Cf. Ewing, *Second Thoughts in Moral Philosophy*, p. 13.

6. For a somewhat more detailed account, with which I largely agree, see Mr P. L. Gardiner's very helpful article 'On Assenting to a Moral Principle' (Chapter VI above).

7. See J. L. Austin, *Philosophical Papers* (Oxford, 1961) p. 130 (also in *Aristotelian Society Proceedings*, LVI) (1956–7) p. 8.

8. See P. H. Nowell-Smith, *Ethics* (Harmondsworth, 1954) Index s.v.

9. Ovid, *Metamorphoses*, vii, line 20.

10. Translated from the *New English Bible*. The new translators, by writing 'The good which I want to do, I fail to do' (the Greek has merely 'I do not do'), show that they agree with my interpretation of the passage.

11. See Chapter V above. For the use of 'command', see *The Language of Morals*, 1.2.

12. FR, 4.1.

13. I owe this useful way of putting the matter to Gardiner, op. cit.

Chapter IX

1. See on this issue a very illuminating paper: J. R. Bambrough, 'Socratic Paradox', *Philosophical Quarterly*, x (1960).

2. See *Meno*, 98b.

3. For an actual example of moral weakness in Plato, see *Republic*, 439e.

4. *Second Thoughts in Moral Philosophy* (London, 1959) pp. 9–18.

5. All subsequent unprefaced page references are to Chapter VIII in this anthology.

6. P. H. Nowell-Smith, *Ethics* (Harmondsworth, 1954) pp. 263–7.

7. *L'Être et le Néant*, pt I, ch. 2, section 2.

8. Cardinal Newman wrote that 'assent, however strong, and accorded to images however vivid, is not, therefore, necessarily practical. Strictly speaking, it is not imagination that causes action; but hope and fear, likes and dislikes, appetite, affection, the stirrings of selfishness and self-love' (*The Grammar of Assent*, p. 82, quoted in Sorel's 'Letter to Daniel Halévy').

9. See, e.g. p. 140 above where feelings or guilt replace 'real pre-scriptiveness' in cases of self-deception. Note the slide from logic to psychology.

Chapter X

1. Chapter III above. Cf. *Magna Moralia*, ii. 4–6.

2. He omits two lines which suggest the more Aristotelian interpretation that things seem different under the influence of desire. 'For why do the commands of my father seem too harsh? . . .' (Ovid, *Metamorphoses*, vii, lines 14–15).

Chapter XI

1. 'Good and Evil', *Analysis*, xvii, 2 (1956).

2. This may be disputed in the case of God. I rely here on the term 'given'. A will defined as necessarily holy is not a will given as necessarily holy, just as a being defined as necessarily existent is not a being given as necessarily existent. A proper discussion of this point would lead us into traditional problems about the relation of God's will to God's knowledge of good; such a discussion would not be irrelevant to the present topic, and it is significant that the traditional voluntarist–intellectualist controversy is similar in many ways to contemporary controversies about choice and reason in morals.

3. I am not suggesting that explanation in terms of morbid psychology of any particular failure to act in accordance with practical reason implies that the agent is no longer being considered as a rational being. Such explanations are accommodated under the *ceteris paribus* clause of the principle (P). The case I am considering here is one in which in *general* there is such a failure, throughout a man's conduct.

4. I now (June 1969) think that my solution of the problem presented by this supposedly possible case was mistaken. I said that to treat the case as a clinical one removes it out of the context in which it makes sense to

try to apply the principle (P): the context of talk about rational beings. But our grounds for treating the case as a clinical one are that the man does genuinely believe that he ought to do things he is not for a moment inclined to do. It is only because we do use language of him which is appropriate to rational behaviour that we can say we are dealing with a pathological patient.

It is possible to characterise the man as believing that he ought to do what he is not inclined to do only because in general people cannot be like this. It is possible to know what someone means by saying he ought to do something only because he is speaking in a public language in which in general the use of such expressions is connected with practice. This, however, is not sufficient to the truth of the principle (P) which would be falsified if the supposedly possible case existed. It would suggest a weaker principle to the effect that the fact that someone believes he ought to do something is, in general, a good ground for expecting either that he will do it or that there are countervailing factors; though it is possible that there are cases where this expectation would not be satisfied.

However, there is good reason to doubt that the description of this supposedly possible case is coherent. In order to rule out possible explanations, I had to suppose that this man could produce impressive new moral insights. Now we could not regard him as producing impressive new moral insights if his general moral attitudes were themselves quite extraordinary (so much so that we hesitated to call them moral). For example, if he were constantly preaching the importance of making things as red as possible, could we ever say that some particular judgement of his – such as that we should encourage photography because people use red lights in dark-rooms, or that where we can't make things red we ought to make them green because we would then have more red after-images – showed insight and sensitivity? Any particular judgement would seem as dotty as the general principle. So to count him as having moral insights he would surely have, to some extent, to share our common moral attitudes: and that means he would have to be capable of human understanding and sympathy. And that surely means, *pace* Kant, a spontaneity of consideration, of love, and of charity, in human situations where the meaning of these attitudes can be grasped. I question whether Kant's 'honest fellow', who is 'cold in temperament and indifferent to the sufferings of others' but who nevertheless carries out his duties of benevolence from his reverence for the moral law, could exist; I doubt whether he would have any real understanding of what sympathy and charity were, let alone a belief in their desirability.

Chapter XII

1. J. L. Austin, *Philosophical Papers* (Oxford, 1961) p. 146.
2. G. E. M. Anscombe, *Intention* (Oxford, 1958) p. 67.
3. B. A. O. Williams, 'Ethical Consistency', *Proceedings of the Aristotelian Society*, supp. vol. XLII (1965).

Chapter XIII

1. Editor's note: This paper is a reply to the paper which appears as Chapter XII. Both were contributions to a symposium at the 1968 Joint Session of the Aristotelian Society and the Mind Association.

Chapter XV

1. I am grateful to my colleague N. J. H. Dent for a number of helpful suggestions.

Select Bibliography

(*a*) *Plato and Aristotle*

J. R. Bambrough, 'Socratic Paradox', *Philosophical Quarterly*, x (1960) pp. 289–300.

David Gallop, 'The Socratic Paradox in the *Protagoras*', *Phronesis*, ix (1964) pp. 117–29.

Norman Gulley, 'The Interpretation of "No One Does Wrong Willingly" in Plato's Dialogues', *Phronesis*, x (1965) pp. 82–96.

Richard Robinson, *Essays in Greek Philosophy* (Oxford, 1969) ch. 7.

J. J. Walsh, *Aristotle's Conception of Moral Weakness* (New York, 1963).

(*b*) *Late nineteenth-century discussion*

F. H. Bradley, 'Can a Man Sin against Knowledge?', *Mind*, ix (1884); and in *Collected Essays* (Oxford, 1935) i.

Henry Sidgwick, 'Unreasonable Action', *Mind*, xi n.s. (1893); and in *Practical Ethics* (London, 1898) pp. 235–60.

(*c*) *Recent discussions of the paradox and weakness of will*

C. A. Campbell, 'The Psychology of Effort of Will', *Proceedings of the Aristotelian Society*, xl (1939–40) pp. 49–74; and in *Free Will and Determinism*, ed. Bernard Berofsky (New York, 1966) pp. 345–64.

P. H. Nowell-Smith, *Ethics* (Harmondsworth, 1954) pp. 265–9, 284–6, 303–306.

Irving Thalberg, 'Remorse', *Mind*, lxxii (1963) pp. 545–55.

(*d*) *Wants and the explanation of action*

D. Davidson, 'Actions, Reasons and Causes', *Journal of Philosophy*, lx (1963) pp. 685–700; and in *The Philosophy of Action*, ed. A. R. White (London, 1968) pp. 79–94.

Rem B. Edwards, 'Is Choice Determined by the "Strongest Motive"?', *American Philosophical Quarterly*, iv (1967) pp. 72–8.

Richard Brandt and Jaegwon Kim, 'Wants as Explanations of Action', *Journal of Philosophy*, lx (1963) pp. 425–35.

(*e*) *Decision and choice*

T. F. Daveny, 'Choosing', *Mind*, lxxiii (1964) pp. 515–26.

M. C. McGuire, 'Decisions, Resolutions and Moral Conduct', *Philosophical Quarterly*, xi (1961) pp. 61–7.

(*f*) '*Could have done otherwise*'

M. R. Ayers, *The Refutation of Determinism* (London, 1968).
A. M. Honoré, 'Can and Can't', *Mind*, LXXIII (1964) pp. 463–79.

(*g*) *Self-deceit*

Herbert Fingarette, *Self-Deceit* (London, 1969).